ECO-FRIENDLY PRODUCTION OF BABY CORN AND MOONGBEAN

ECO-FRIENDLY PRODUCTION OF BABY CORN AND MOONGBEAN

By
Dr. Ekta Kumari
Assistant Plant Protection Officer (Weed Science)
Govt. of India
Ministry of Agriculture & Farmers Welfare
Department of Agriculture, Cooperation & Farmers Welfare
Central Insecticides Board and Registration Committee
Directorate of Plant Protection, Quarantine & Storage
NH-IV, Faridabad (Haryana)
(India)

D P H
DISCOVERY PUBLISHING HOUSE PVT. LTD.
INDIA

Published by:
Namit Wasan
DISCOVERY PUBLISHING HOUSE PVT. LTD.
4383/4B, Ansari Road, Darya Ganj
New Delhi-110 002 (India)
Phone : +91-11-23279245; 23253475; 43596065
E-mail : discoverybooksindia@gmail.com
discoverypublishinghouse@gmail.com
namitwasan9@gmail.com
web : www.discoverypublishinggroup.com

First Edition: **2021**

ISBN: 978-93-88854-54-2

Eco-friendly Production of Baby Corn and Moongbean

Printed at:
Infinity Imaging Systems
Delhi

Preface

This book is written on the basis of study conducted on a field experiment in Rabi seasons at agricultural research farm of B.H.U. Varanasi, U.P., India to study the effect of different microbial strain of bacteria and fungi in combination with various fertility levels on the performance of baby corn and their corresponding impact on soil health. The three major aspects have been covered in this book i.e. *(i) role of KSB and Trichoderma asperellum on baby corn on yield, quality parameter, nutrient content and removal, microbial population and biomass carbon of soil, soil health after harvest and economics of baby corn etc., (ii) status of potassium in soil; and (iii) residual effects of Potassium on moongbean.* I hope its results will be of interest to agronomists and soil scientist for improving K status in soil and profitability of baby corn. The Potassium Solubilizing Bacteria (KSB) and *Trichoderma* are microbial inoculant/bio-fertilizers that makes the unavailable form of K to available form in soil which was easily uptake by the plant. It was found equally effective in enhancing dry weight, quality attributes, higher economical yield of baby corn besides improving soil health. The recommendation is expected to reach the farming communities directly or indirectly for whom the book has been dedicated.

Pulse is an important source of dietary protein, energy, minerals and vitamins for mankind. These are the cheapest and alternate sources of animal protein, improves and sustains soil productivity through biological nitrogen fixation and addition of huge amount of organic matter to soil. Among the pulses in India, moongbean (*Vigna radiata* L.) is one of the popular short duration grain legumes which occupies third place after chickpea and pigeonpea and provides the best solution to protein-calorie malnutrition. It is a rich source of protein (24%), carbohydrates (60%), fat (1.5%), amino acids, vitamins and minerals and with wide adaptability that can be grown in all the three seasons in India.

In this book, all experiments are consisting of *Agrobacterium, Flavobacterium, Rhizobium* and fungal strain of *Trichoderma* and four fertility levels was laid out in a split plot design with 4 replication by keeping fertility levels in the main plot and strains in the subplot. Significantly higher growth attributes (plant height, LAI, dry matter), yield and yield attributing character, quality parameter, nutrient content and removal, microbial population and biomass carbon of soil, soil health after harvest and economics of baby corn (gross return, net return and B:C ratio) was recorded with F3 fertility level (100% NP + 75% K) remaining at par with 100% NPK (F4) along with *Agrobacterium sp.* followed by *Trichoderma sp.* The residual effect of 100% NP+75% K (F3) and 100% NPK (F4) also showed the same trend and showed higher values on yield attributing characters of moong, its grain and stover yields, nutrients content (N, P and K) and their removal by moong and residual available nutrients (N, P and K) in soil. Even though F4 (100% NPK) exhibited a little better result in respect of the performance of both baby corn and moong than F3 (100% NP+75% K) but it could not reach the level of significance in any of the years. F3 was therefore considered to be better option because of 25% saving in potassic fertilizer of the recommended dose.

So, this book gives us great pleasure to present before our readers, researchers on *"Eco-friendly Production of Baby Corn and Moongbean"* especially for baby corn and residual effect of potassium in moongbean because it cover detailed method of evaluation of potassium solubilizing bacteria and availability of potassium in soil. This book also provides comprehensive knowledge especially fundamental principles, experimental field application and estimation of residue and other experimental protocol. It is also extremely important to develop skill for the correct scientific farming of baby corn. This book will be highly useful for extension agencies, farmers, researchers including students and other stakeholders.

A particular thanks to the contributors and publishers for their contribution and assistance. I hope this book will provide a multidisciplinary forum to explore emerging areas in the field *"Eco-friendly Production of Baby Corn and Moongbean"*.

–Ekta Kumari

Acknowledgements

Today as I look back. I firstly, bow my head before omnipresent and omnipotent, Almighty Baba Vishwanath. I take this opportunity to acknowledge my reverence to Maa Gayatri that showered her grace and helped me to write this book smoothly.

From the innermost core of my heart I express my obligation, respect and honour to Dr. Avijit Sen, Professor and Ex-Head, Department of Agronomy, for his inspiration, timely criticism and benevolent help during investigation and preparation of this book. I feel extremely privileged to express my veneration for the eminent teaching faculty of Banaras Hindu University. Dr. Y. Singh, Professor, Department of Agronomy, Dr. Ram K. Singh, Professor, Department of Agronomy, Dr. B.R. Maurya, Professor, Department of Soil Science and Agricultural Chemistry, Dr. (Mrs.) Vijai P., Assistant Professor, Department of Plant Physiology and Dr. J.S. Bohra (Professor and Head), Dr. Ramesh K Singh (Professor), Dr. R.S. Meena, Assistant Professor for their authentic guidance, keen interest and valuable criticism during the preparation of this book.

The word would be insufficient if I would not thanked to my colleague Dr. Virendra Kumar, Assistant Director (Plant Pathology), Directorate of Plant Protection, Quarantine and Storage, NH-IV, Faridabad, (Haryana) for his constant support during completion of this book. He has provided constant guidance to me during writing of this book. A special thanks to him for his discerning comments, valuable suggestion, co-operation and helpful attitude towards me during the completion of this book.

"Mother is God on earth"

Emotions cannot be verbalized. I will always be indebted for the love, affection, care and blessings of my mother. I owe everything to her and it was only because of her that I got opportunity to complete this book. Indeed, words fail to express my thanks to my very caring sister (Shilpa) and very responsible brother (Tushar Kant) for always supporting me in my adverse. Last but not least, I record my sincere thanks from the core of my heart to all the well-wishers whose blessings propelled me to achieve my dreams and I ever remain thankful to all those who could not find separate names but had directly or indirectly helped me.

–Ekta Kumari

Contents

Introduction and Role

Maize (*Zea mays* L.) - the world's 3rd leading cereal crop is cultivated in an area of 150.05 m ha with a production and productivity of 1099.91 mt and 7.33 t ha^{-1} respectively. It merits a reputable place in Indian agriculture, where it occupies an area of 8.51 m ha with a production of 27.82 mt and average productivity of 3.27 t ha^{-1} (Crop statics maize, 2019) Maize is a crop with multifarious uses and its use as "baby corn" is gaining popularity all over the world. In India although cultivation of baby corn is of recent development, it is being practiced all over the country (Ramachandrappa *et al.*, 2009). Baby corn is a young finger like unfertilized cob of maize, preferably harvested at immediate silk emergence or within 2-3 cm long silk stage depending upon the growing season (Pandey *et al.*, 2002). The desirable size of baby corn is 6-11 cm in length and 1-1.5 cm in diameter and is used in various continental dishes. It has high nutritional value having 86-89% moisture, 8.2 g carbohydrates, 2 g protein, 0.2 g fat, 0.28 mg Ca, 0.86 mg P, 0.11 mg Fe, 0.05 mg thiamin, 0.08 mg riboflavin, 11 mg ascorbic acid per 100 g of fresh baby corn. It is a good sources of fibrous protein and easy to digest (Kawtra and Sahagal, 2007). Besides nutritive advantage, it is also free from residual effect of pesticides as it is harvested within a week of tassel emergence and the young cob is wrapped up tightly with husk and well protected from insects and pests (Kumar *et al.*, 2015).

The cultivation of baby corn is becoming popular among the growers in rural areas in recent years due to its diverse utility and high net returns (Verma *et al.*, 2012). Adopting such crops, farmers are able to get higher economic return in short period as compared to traditional crops because of which cost effective production and processing of baby corn can occupy an important place in the area of agri-business. India is emerging as one of the potential baby corn producing countries because of its low cost production technology.

Pulse is an important source of dietary protein, energy, minerals and vitamins for mankind. These are the cheapest and alternate sources of animal protein, improves and sustains soil productivity through biological nitrogen fixation and addition of huge amount of organic matter to soil. Among the pulses in India, moongbean (*Vigna radiata* L.) is one of the popular short duration grain legumes which occupies third place after chickpea and pigeonpea and provides the best solution to protein-calorie malnutrition. It is a rich source of protein (24%), carbohydrates (60%), fat (1.5%), amino acids, vitamins and minerals and with wide adaptability it can be grown around the year in India (Anwar *et al.*, 2007).

The excessive use of inorganic fertilizers leads to a decrease in the quality of soil and environmental stability (Lynn *et al.*, 2013). Biofertilizers are organic products containing living cells of different types of micro-organism, which have the ability to convert nutritionally important elements from unavailable to available form through biological process (Vessey, 2003). Biofertilizers play a major role in maize crop production and convert insoluble nutrient into available form for plant. Biological fertilizer application restricts inorganic fertilizers usage, thereby reducing environmental pollution, reducing farming costs, and maximizing yields (Srinivasrao, *et al.*, 2010).

Soil microbes have been reported to play a key role in the natural K cycle and therefore, potassium solubilizing microorganisms present in the soil could provide an alternative technology to make potassium available to the plant (Dadarwal *et al.*, 2009). Thus, microbial strains capable of solubilizing potassium minerals can conserve our existing resources and avoid environmental pollution hazards caused by heavy application of chemical fertilizers (Maurya *et al.*, 2014).

With the introduction of high yielding crop varieties/hybrids and the progressive intensification of agriculture, the soils are getting depleted in potassium reserve at a faster rate. Moreover, due to imbalanced fertilizer application, potassium deficiency is becoming one of the major constraints in crop production. This necessitates the search for an alternative indigenous source of K which can meet the need of the plant besides maintaining K status in soils (Srinivasrao, 2010). Otherwise addressing this nutrient imbalance and shortages in developing countries, it would be required to enhance the world production of potassium fertiliser (Meena *et al.*, 2013).

These fertilisers assume a great significance and constitute one of the key inputs for achieving high productivity. The cracks between removal and application of K fertilisers to crops are widening. Therefore it is imperative to understand the dynamics of potassium in soil in order to provide and maintain balance nutrition and potassium status in Indian soils (Bai *et al.*, 2015).

K is an essential macronutrient for plant growth and plays significant roles in activation of several metabolic processes including protein synthesis, photosynthesis, enzymes and provides resistance to diseases and insects (Anna and Francisco, 2012).

It activates a number of enzymes, including those involved in the synthesis of carbohydrates, provides resistance to disease and adverse environmental conditions and enhances utilization of N and P. It is the most abundantly available cation found in cytoplasm that regulates osmotic potential of cells and tissues of glycophytic plant species. Potassium nutrition in maize positively affects its growth and development (Srinivasarao *et al.*, 2010).

Moreover, K not only participates in nutrient transportation and uptake, but also confers resistance to abiotic and biotic stresses leading to enhanced production of quality crops (Maqsood *et al.*, 2013). In soil, K exists mainly in four different pools: mineral, non-exchangeable, exchangeable and labile K (Romheld and Kirkby, 2010). The concentration of soluble K in soils is meagre and its major portion (98%) exists as insoluble minerals. Though present in an abundant amount in soil, only 1 to 2% of potassium is available to plants, the rest being bound with other minerals and therefore unavailable to plants. Moreover, fixation of added nutrients/ fertilizers in soil reduces the efficiency of applied K fertilizers and thus, a large quantity of added fertilizers become unavailable to plants (Basak and Biswas, 2009).

Importantly, India is not self-sufficient in producing potassic fertiliser and almost the entire quantity is imported which is about 47.36 lakh tons (FAI, 2018-19) in India. Therefore efficient management of soil fertility becomes prime concern to the scientists in view of the increasing gap between production and consumption of fertiliser.

Under these circumstances, it becomes worthwhile to work on the bio-inoculants like KSB as a substitutive source of potassic fertilizer. The present experiment therefore, extends an opportunity to the scientific community to explore the possibility of using KSB as a substitute of costly remunerative fertilisers. Potassium solubilising bacteria (KSB) is preferable and feasible microorganism to solubilise unavailable form of K minerals into available pool for plant which will maintain the ecological balance and sustain agricultural production and environmental quality.

KSB (*Agrobacterium tumefaciens, Flavobacterium anhuense, Rhizobium pusence*) (identified and isolated by S.S.A.C, B.H.U.) help in enhancing the availability of potassium playing an essential role in dynamic soil environment by releasing the key nutrient from primary minerals and ores (Meena *et al.*, 2014a). The potassium solubilizing bacteria is a rhizospheric bacteria which solubilises the insoluble potassium (K) to soluble forms of K for plant growth and yield. The use of potassium solubilizing bacteria as a biological fertilizer is suggested to improve plant growth and uptake (Meena *et al.*, 2014b).

Identified microbes have beneficial effects on efficient plant growth either through nitrogen fixation, phosphate and potassium solubilization or mineralization. In addition, release of plant growth regulating substances, production of antibiotics, biodegradation of organic matter and nutrients cycling in the soil by KSB can also benefit the crop productivity and ecological sustainability (Pathak *et al.*, 2009).

Therefore, the inoculation with KSB and other useful microbial inoculants is expected to restore and maintain effective microbial populations in soil for solubilization of chemically fixed potassium and other macro and micronutrients to make it available to the plants for sustainable yield.

Another fungal biocontrol agent namely *Trichoderma* sp. is an endophytic plant opportunistic symbionts which is ubiquitous in nature. They have potential to control various plant diseases and improve crop production. *Trichoderma* sp. show symbiotic association with apoplastic part of plant roots and has direct effect on plants (Shoresh and Harman, 2008). It has positive effects on seed germination, plant nutrient uptake and fertilizer use efficiency, thereby improving plant growth and yield (Bal and Altintas, 2006). Therefore, it can be helpful in minimizing the use of chemicals in crop management practices for improving sustainability of agriculture.

Trichoderma asperellum (isolated and identified by M.P.P., B.H.U.) is a fungal genus found in many regions of the world. These fungi are ubiquitous in a wide variety of environments, showing up in soil, forests, wood, and paper, among other locations (Harman *et al.*, 2004). These fungi grow on symbiotic relationships with plants and promote abundant root growth so that they have plenty of roots to grow. *Trichoderma* sp. is applied as bio stimulants for seedling establishment, plant growth and plant defense. However, it is becoming increasingly clear that certain strains also have substantial direct influence on plant development and crop productivity (Sarma *et al.*, 2002). Also some species of *Trichoderma* have the ability to promote plant growth through different mechanisms, such as solubilization of phosphates, potassium and minerals such as Fe, Mn and Mg that have important role in plant growth (Mastouri *et al.*, 2010).

Trichoderma increases the rate of germination and seedling growth of maize. A number of mechanisms for plant growth promotion by *Trichoderma* have been proposed (Harman, 2006). *Trichoderma* promotes primary root length and root branching in maize by inducing lateral root growth. Combination of *Trichoderma* inoculum and fertilizers performs better than single application of either fertilizer or inoculum (Yedidia *et al.*, 2001).

Inoculation with potassium solubilizing bacteria is used as a source of potassium in crop production, which help reduce dependence on costly chemical fertilizers (Nishanth and Biswas, 2008). Thus, application of K solubilizing bacteria as biofertilizer can reduce the use of agrochemicals and support eco-friendly crop production.

Thus, management of nutrients through microbial inoculants or bio-fertilizer can play an important role in baby corn production for realizing higher yield and monetary returns so that it could be popularized among the farmers. Keeping all the above facts in view, the book entitled *"Eco-friendly Production of Baby Corn and Moongbean"* was carried out during the rabi seasons of 2017-18 and 2018-19 at the Agricultural Research Farm, Institute of Agricultural Sciences, Banaras Hindu University, Varanasi, (U.P.).

Present Scenario of KSB and *Trichoderma* on Baby Corn and its Residual Effect on Moongbean

A brief review of literature pertaining to the present book was done and presented below.

Impact of Fertilizer on Growth Parameters

Lin *et al.* (2002) demonstrated significant increase in K and P uptake in tomato plants inoculated with silicate dissolving bacterium (*B. mucilaginosus*) in comparison to the non-inoculated plants. Han and Lee, 2005 reported a synergistic effect of soil fertilization with rock P and K along with PSB and KSB on the improvement of P and K uptake and growth of eggplants grown under limited P and K soil in greenhouse.

Park *et al.* (2003) reported that bacterial inoculation could improve phosphorus and potassium availability in the soil by producing organic acid and other chemicals and stimulated growth and mineral uptake by plants.

Wu *et al.* (2005) conducted a greenhouse trial to evaluate the effect of three biofertilizers with K solubilizer (*Bacillus mucilaginous*) on growth of *Zea mays*. The application of biofertilizer containing mycorrhizal fungus and three species of bacteria significantly increased the growth of maize. This greenhouse study also indicated that half the amount of biofertilizer application had similar effects when compared with organic fertilizer or chemical fertilizer treatments. Microbial inoculum not only increased the nutritional assimilation of plant (total N, P and K), but also improved soil properties.

Sheng (2006) worked on potassium releasing bacterial strain *B. edaphicus* for plant-growth promoting effect and nutrient uptake by cotton and rape seed in K-deficient soil. Increased root and shoot growth was observed. K content also increased by 30 and 26 per cent respectively increased biomass and K uptake by the inoculation of potash solubilizer was also observed in chilli by Ramarethinam and Chandra (2005).

Experiments conducted to evaluate the potential of potassium solubilizing bacteria (KSB) in soils planted with eggplant revealed that KSB enhanced significantly the plant growth and soil nutrient level (Han and Lee, 2005). Significantly higher uptake of K by wheat grown in a K-deficient yellow-brown soil in Nanjing, China by a wild type bacterial strain *Bacillus edaphicus* NBT and their mutants MPs (+) and MPs(+)1 were also reported by Sheng and Huang (2002).

Supanjani *et al.* (2006) reported that integration of P and K rocks with inoculation of phosphorus and potassium solubilizing bacteria increased P availability from 12 to 21 per cent and K availability from 13 to 15 per cent in the soil over control and subsequently improved N, P and K uptake by *Capsicum annuum*.

Han *et al.* (2006) also reported the beneficial effect of *Bacillus mucilaginosus* on mobilization K from potassium mineral, and nutrient uptake and growth of pepper and cucumber on an Inceptisols in Korea. They found that the dry weight of cucumber plants inoculated with bacteria potassium dissolving bacteria alone increased by 23%, over non-inoculated treatment. Inoculation of pepper and cucumber plants with *Bacillus mucilaginosus, Azotobacter chroococcum* and *Rhizobium* resulted in significantly higher mobilization of potassium from waste mica which in turn acted as a source of potassium for plant growth.

Experiment conducted by Abou-el-Seoud *et al.* (2009) with potato revealed that bio-fertilization with silicate dissolving bacteria increased yield (tubers and shoots), tuber size, starch content, leaf area, and total chlorophyll content of potato.

Basak and Biswas (2009) studied the dynamics of K release from waste mica inoculated with potassium solubilizing microorganism (*Bacillus mucilaginosus*) and its effectiveness as potassic-fertilizer using sudan grass (*Sorghum vulgare* Pers.) var *Sudanensis* as test crop grown under two Alfisols. Results revealed that application of mica significantly enhanced biomass yield and K recoveries by sudan grass over control (no-K). Biomass yield, uptake and per cent K recoveries increased further when mica was inoculated with bacterial strain in both the soils than un-inoculated mica. Release kinetics of K showed significant release of K from mica treated with bacterial strain.

Bagyalakshmi *et al.* (2012) conducted a field trial to study the efficacy of indigenous potassium solubilizing bacteria (KSB) in combination with various doses of potash fertilizers along with recommended doses of nitrogen and phosphorus in tea plants. The flush shoots of tea comprising of three leaves and a bud were subjected to manufacture black tea, and it was found that almost all the tea quality parameters such as the aflavin, the arubigin, highly polymerized substances, total liquor colour, caffeine, briskness, colour and flavour indexes were greatly improved in KSB treated plants. Their findings confirm that the influence of indigenous potassium solubilizing bacteria on potassium nutrient exhibited improvement in the productivity and nutrient uptake by plants and quality parameters in tea plantations.

Parmar and Sindhu (2013) isolated potassium solubilizing bacteria for amelioration of K-deficient soils. They reported that KSB might lead to an alternative source for improvement of K nutrition in sustainable agriculture. Findings also showed that *B. megaterium* had a higher potential in K solubilization than *Arthrobacter sp.*

Prajapati and Modi (2013) conducted an experiment under hydroponics using micronutrient containing solution to evaluate the effect of potassium solubilizing bacteria KSB-8 (*Enterobacter hormaechei*) on cucumber. The results indicated remarkable increase in root length, flowering fruit setting, fruit maturing, K Content and Chlorophyll content. They concluded that KSB-8 (*Enterobacter hormoechei*) could be used as crop-enhancer and bio-fertilizer for cucumber (*Cucumis sativus*) and other K rich crops under hydroponic conditions.

Padma and Sukumar (2015) reported significant increase in growth, leaf yield, root volume and K uptake of mulberry in treatments receiving combined inoculation as compared to uninoculated and individually inoculated treatments. Increased leaf yield was also recorded in treatment with combined inoculation in presence of reduced dose of NPK (75%) indicating beneficial effects of bio-inoculants.

Prajapati (2016) concluded that the use of KSB having multifaceted beneficial traits would be highly effective for improving growth and yield of crops. In response to inoculation with these selected potassium solubilizing bacteria (KSB), significant increase in seed germination, root and shoot length, number of leaves and grain yield was recorded in comparison to un-inoculated control.

In an experiment, tomato (super chief cv.) seedlings were planted with single and combined application of potassium releasing (KSB: *Pseudomonas* sp. S19-1, *Pseudomonas* sp. S14-3), phosphate solubilizing (PSB: *P. putida* Tabriz, *P. fluorescens* Tabriz) and nitrogen fixing (NFB: *Azospirillum* sp. Acu9, *Azotobacter* sp.) bacteria in the nursery cultivation (Sheikhalipour *et al.*, 2016). The results showed that inoculation with bacteria had significant effect on average fruit weight, fruit length, number of fruits, percentage of marketable fruit, per centage of BER incidence and potassium content of fruit. The highest average fruit weight, potassium content of fruit, the percentage of marketable fruit, fruit length were observed with KSB treatment.

Saha *et al.* (2016) conducted a laboratory experiment and found that survival of KSB strains under stress towards high salt, pH and temperature may play an important role in *oryza sativa, musa paradisiaca, zea mays, sorghum bicolor* and *Triticum aestivum*. At 14 DAI 66% higher zone of solubilization was seen as compared to 7 DAI and significantly higher indole-3-acetic acid production by *Bacillus licheniformis* BHU18. They also found that K-solubilization rate increased with incubation periods and decreased with pH. The results suggested that the KSB strains isolated from the rhizosphere of subtropical crops were able to solubilize potassium in high salt, pH and temperature conditions. The diversity of KSB as bio-inoculants to release potassium provides a win-win situation. Therefore, it is crucial to adopt efficient KSB strain interventions for the judicious use of chemical and biological resources for maximizing food production and reducing pollution and rejuvenating degraded land for agricultural benefit.

Pramanik *et al.* (2019) isolated KSB strain (O–5) from tea growing soil and identified as *Bacillus pseudomycoides*. Strain solubilized 33·32 ± 2·40 µg K ml^{-1} in mica waste (MW; muscovite type mineral) amended broth after 7 days incubation at 30 ± 1°C. In a soil microcosm study under laboratory condition, *B. pseudomycoides* strain O–5 increased K availability by 47·0 ± 7·1 mg kg^{-1} after 105 days incubation, while the strain released 104·9 ± 15·3 mg K kg^{-1} in MW treated soil. In this study, application of isolated *B. pseudomycoides* with MW significantly increased K availability in soil, and that in turn facilitated K uptake by tea plants.

Impact of Fertilizer on yield and yield Attributes

Potash mobilizer on brinjal recorded an increased potash uptake and plant biomass in treated plots as compared to the control (Nayak, 2001).

Sheng *et al.* (2002) reported a significant increase in shoot and root dry wt and greater uptake of K by cotton and rape by the application of K-bearing mineral (illite) inoculated with potassium releasing bacteria *Bacillus edaphicus* NBT.

Sheng *et al.* (2003) studied the effect of inoculation of KSB *Bacillus edaphicus* on chilli and cotton and found an increase in P and K content in plant biomass.

Mikhailouskaya and Tchernysh (2005) studied the effect of inoculation of K mobilizing bacteria on severelly eroded soil and found an increase in wheat yield upto 1.04 t ha^{-1} over moderately eroded soil without bacterial inoculation.

Ramarethinam and Chandra (2006) recorded an increase in brinjal yield, plant height and K uptake over control by the inoculation of potash solubilizing bacteria (*Frateuria aurantia*). They also reported that bacteria belonging to the family *Pseudomonaceae* obtained from the agricultural soils of Coimbatore region of Tamil Nadu, India solubilized K considerably which promoted crop yield.

Sugumaran and Janarthanam (2007) found an increase in the dry matter production by 25 percent and oil content by 35.4 percent of groundnut. Available P and K also increased from 6.24 to 9.28 mg/kg and 86.57 to 99.60 mg/kg respectively in soil due to inoculation with *B. mucilaginosus* (KSB) over uninoculated control.

Archana *et al.* (2008) conducted an experiment to study the effect of potassium solubilizing bacteria on growth and yield of maize. Efficient K solubilizing bacteria *Bacillus* sp. was used and the result showed that there was an increase in growth, nutrition and yield of maize. The results indicated that all the inoculated bacterial isolates significantly increased plant growth, nutrient uptake and yield component of maize plant over absolute fertilizer control.

A field experiment was conducted at Rajasthan to evaluate the effect of integrated nutrient management in baby corn (*Zea mays* L.) and the results showed that higher plant height and dry matter accumulation were obtained under 75% of RDF + 2.25 tonnes vermicompost/ha and biofertilizers than rest of the treatments (Dadarwal *et al.*, 2009).

Impact of Fertilizer on Soil Health

Khudsen *et al.* (1992) isolated potassium solubilizing bacteria from rock and it showed higher activity in potassium release from acid leached soil which improved moongbean seedling growth. Phosphorus solubilizing bacteria and silicate bacteria play an important role in plant nutrition by increasing P and K uptake by plant.

Sheng *et al.* (2003) reported that solubilization of illite and feldspar by microorganisms is due to the production of organic acids such as oxalic and tartaric acids and capsular polysaccharides, which help in dissolution of minerals to release K.

Sheng and Huang (2002) reported that potassic bacteria of sorghum, increased biomass and P and K contents. The effect of KSB (*Bacillus sp.*) on grain yield and plant silica content of rice and available silica in soil were also found to be positive (Raj, 2004).

Styriakova *et al.* (2003) reported that the activity of potassium dissolving bacteria played a pronounced role in the release of K from feldspar that increased CEC, organic carbon and other soil health parameters.

Clarson (2004) found an increase in K uptake with increased yield in yam and tapioca while treating the plants with potassium mobilizer in conjunction with biofertilizers and chemical fertilizers.

Mikhailouskaya and Tcherhysh (2005) reported that inoculation of K mobilizing bacteria on several eroded soils increased wheat yield by 1.04 t/ha which were comparable with yields on moderately eroded soil without bacterial inoculation.

Badr *et al.* (2006) found that potassium uptake improved markedly with inoculation of bacteria in the tested soils compared to control. A detailed understanding of how bacteria affect mineral dissolution rates is essential to quantify mineral weathering on global element cycling. The extent of potassium solubilization by *B. edaphicus* in the liquid media was more and better growth was observed on illite than feldspar.

Sheng and He (2006) recorded an increase in root and shoot growth and significantly higher N, P, and K content in wheat by the inoculation of *B. edaphicus* grown in a yellow brown soil with low available K. The field experiment recorded increased yield in tomato crop due to inoculation of silicate dissolving bacteria *B. cereus* as bioinoculant along with feldspar and rice straw on K releasing capacity (Badr, 2006).

Hu *et al.* (2006) collected K solubilizing strains from the soil and characterized them phenotypically and phylogenetically. They were found to effectively dissolve mineral potassium when they were grown on Aleksandrov medium.

An integrated application of rock P and K materials with co-inoculation of bacteria that solubilize them may provide faster and continuous supply of P and K for optimal plant growth (Girgis, 2008). Organic acids present in organic matter and/or exudates by microorganisms and plants can increase the liberation of potassium from minerals.

Dadarwal *et al.* (2009) conducted a field experiment during kharif season at Udaipur to evaluate the effect of integrated nutrient management in baby corn (*Zea mays* L.). Maximum plant height and dry matter accumulation were recorded under 75% NPK+2.25 tonnes vermicompost/ ha along with biofertilizers. Application of 75% NPK along with 2.25 tonnes vermicompost/ha+biofertilizers significantly increased the available N, P and K of soil after harvest of baby corn and recorded significantly higher net returns (Rs 26815/ha) and benefit: cost (2.83:1) than the rest of treatments.

Neupane *et al.* (2013) conducted a field experiment during *pre-kharif season* of 2008 and 2009 to assess the response of different sources of nitrogen and row spacing on yield and quality of baby corn *(Zea mays)* at Varanasi, Uttar Pradesh. Application of 75% N through urea + 25% N through FYM produced the highest yield than the other sources of N. Chlorophyll content in leaves, protein, carbohydrate and sugar contents and nutrient uptake in baby corn were significantly improved by the application of 75% N through urea + 25% N through FYM. Row spacing of 40 cm × 15 cm increased yield, quality parameters and nutrient uptake by baby corn.

Waffa and Mona (2015) carried out a field experiment in two winter seasons at Ismailia Agricultural Research Station, to study the impact of feldspar acidulation on potassium dissolution and pea production. Field experiment results revealed that available N and K in the experimental soil were increased significantly due to feldspar acidulation with different acids especially fulvic acid at high concentration (20%). They concluded that feldspar acidulation with fulvic acid at concentration (20%) had recorded the highest values of yield components (pods, straw and biological yield) as compared to either control or other treatments along with N and K total contents.

Mikajlo *et al.* (2015) conducted a laboratory experiment and demonstrate the effect of two types of plant growth promoting bacteria (PGPB) inoculums. *Lactuca sativa* (lettuce) was selected as a model plant. It was concluded that colonization increased as the result of PGPB inoculums. In addition, growth attibutes were increased with these bacteria.

Bahadur *et al.* (2016) evaluated the mineral release abilities of 10 rhizobacterial strains isolated from various crops grown in Indo-Gangetic plain (IGP) and their abilities to solubilize inorganic phosphorus and potassium from insoluble tri-calcium phosphate (TCP) and waste muscovite (WM).They found that rhizobacteria significantly solubilized different levels of inorganic P and fixed K. Some of the rhizo-bacterial strains have the ability to produce ammonia, indole-3-acetic acid (IAA), and hydrogen cyanide (HCN).

Bahadur *et al.* (2017) carried out an experiment to compare the ability of PSR and KSR of solubilizing different forms of insoluble P and K to make them available to plants for plant growth promotion and soil fertility maintenance. The MSR strains influenced nutrient availability and soil biodiversity and also regulate the interactions between plants and other beneficiary microflora. The PSR and KSR strains might be useful bio-inoculants for ecofriendly crop production in the soils with low P and K availabilities.

Machado *et al.* (2016) undertook a study to characterize the residue from ornamental rocks and evaluate the release of K from these residues following application of organic acids. Two organic acids (citric acid and malic acid), three ornamental rock residues (R_1, R_2 and R_3) and five organic acid rates (0, 5, 10, 20 and 40 mmol L^{-1}) were taken in study. Citric and malic acids promoted the release up to 4.86 and 4.34% of the total K content in the residue, respectively, reinforcing the role of organic acids in the weathering of minerals and in releasing K to the soil. The K quantities were, on average, 6.1% higher when extracted with citric acid compared to malic acid.

Prajapati (2016) evaluated two promising organisms (KSB-1 and KSB-7) capable of solubilization of both organic and inorganic potassium. In response to inoculation with these selected potassium solubilizing bacteria (KSB), significant increase in seed germination, root and shoot length, number of leaves and grain yield were observed over uninoculated control. The study demonstrated that the use of KSB having multifaceted beneficial traits would be highly effective for improving growth and yield of crops.

Impact of *Agrobacterium* sp. on Growth Parameters

Zhang and Kong (2014) described that many strains of *Agrobacterium tumefaciens Enterobacter cloacae, rhizobium pusense, Enterobacter aerogenes, Flavobacterium anhuiense* and *Burkholderia cepacia* bacteria were able to solubilize potassium ranging from 0.59 mg/L to 4.4mg/L. Potassium performs 4 four main roles for bacteria, like adjusting turgor pressure and osmotic solutes, regulating internal pH, and activating intracellular enzyme.

Impact of *Flavobacterium* sp. on Growth Parameters

A number of nitrogen fixing bacteria were isolated from forest phyllosphere of various plants on the basis of nitrogenase activity (Giri and Pati, 2004). Among them two best isolates were selected and identified as *Corynebacterium sp.* AN1 and *Flavobacterium sp.* TK2 which were able to reduce 88 and 132 n mol of acetylene (10^8 cells^{-1} h^{-1}) respectively. They were grown in large amount and sprayed on the phyllosphere of maize (*Zea mays*) as a substitute for nitrogen fertilizer. Marked improvement in growth and total nitrogen content of the plant were observed by the application of these nitrogen-fixing bacteria. An average 30-37% increase in yield was obtained, which was nearer to chemical fertilizer treatment. Comparatively better effect was obtained by application of *Flavobacterium* sp.

Soltani *et al.* (2010) found that *Flavobacterium* promotes characteristics such as phosphate solubilizing capacity, ability to use 1-Amino Cyclopropan-1-Carboxylate (ACC) as sole nitrogen source and production of auxin, siderophore, salicylic acid, chitinase and hydrogen cyanide. There was a significant negative correlation (r=-0.81**) between solubilized P and the final pH of the growth medium. In this study, all the isolates were able to produce auxin, ranging from 0.27 to 12.03 micro gml^{-1} averaged by 2.03. Considering the ability of the isolates to produce auxin and for P-solubilization, which facilitate growth and yield of different crop plants.

Sarson (2016) found that the culture inoculum of *Bacillus* PSB24 and *Flavobacterium* increased growth parameters like shoot and root and their fresh weight in tomato plants.

Yang *et al.* (2017) reported that the genus *Flavobacterium* may be copiotrophic and fast-growth bacteria and be able to exploit a transient niches for nutrition and others at the early growth stage of maize. The *Flavobacterium* at later stage increased the quantity and quality of organic carbon and interspecies competition for resources, showing rhizosphere has more impact on soil microorganisms in maize soil.

Impact of *Rhizobium sp.* on Growth Parameters

Jat (1996) conducted a field experiment to study the effect of weed management, fertilizer levels and *Rhizobium* inoculation on maize and soybean intercropping system. The treatments comprised 3 levels of fertilizer, i.e. 0, 50% (30 kg N, 20 kg P/ha) and 100% recommended dose of fertilizer (60 kg N, 40 kg P/ha); 2 levels of *Rhizobium* inoculation (with and without) to the intercrop soyabean; and 6 weed treatments (weedy control, 2 hand weedings at 25 and 40 days after sowing, fluchloralin at 1.0 kg/ha, pendimethalin at 1.0 kg/ha, metolachlor at 1.0 kg/ha and metribuzin at 0.5 kg/ha). The highest nutrient uptake was obtained under 2 hand weedings, followed by metolachlor and pendimethalin in both crops. Fertilizer levels and *Rhizobium* inoculation to soyabean seeds increased uptake of nutrients in soyabean but failed to show any effect on maize.

Sardana *et al.* (2006) conducted a field experiment for two consecutive winters under dryland conditions in the maize-lentil cropping sequence. The optimum seed rate for lentil was found to be 30 kg/ha, whereas the highest seed yield was obtained with row spacing of 25 cm. Seed inoculation with Rhizobium was found beneficial with yield increase of 20.3% over no inoculation. Seed yield increased with increasing doses of nitrogen and phosphorus. Application of 12.5 kg N+20 kg P_2O_5/ha increased the seed yield by 18.7% over 6.25 kg N+10 kg P_2O_5/ha, whereas application of 12.5 kg N+30 kg P_2O_5/ha increased the mean seed yield by 6.6% over 12.5 kg N+20 kg P_2O_5/ha.

Bano and Ilyas (2010) evaluated the growth promoting properties and phytohormone and bacteriocin production ability of *Rhizobium* and *Azospirillum* strains isolated from roots and rhizosphere of maize (at tillering and anthesis stages) grown under different moisture regimes in the field. The largest diameter of inhibition zone was produced by MRA5 and MSR5 respectively.

A field experiment was conducted to investigate effects of inoculation of legumes and cereals with rhizobium (Nyoki and Ndakidemi, 2016). Rhizobia inoculation and supplementation with phosphorus and potassium had positive significant effects on all parameters. It was recommended, to use rhizobia inoculants supplemented with optimum levels of phosphorus and potassium in intercropping systems for improving crop production.

Mia and Shamsuddin (2010) worked on biofertilizer technology and found that rhizobia could make association with graminaceous plants and plant nutrients like P, K, Ca, Mg and even Fe accumulation were observed. Therefore, further research in this area is needed to develop a sustainable biofertilizer technology for greater and environment friendly cereal production system.

An experiment was conducted to evaluate the effect of nitrogen (N) doses and *Rhizobium tropici* inoculation on field pea grown under no-tillage system (Mishra *et al*, 2010). Evaluations were made for the number of nodules per plant, nodule dry matter, N-leaf content, shoot dry matter, shoot-accumulated N, number of pods per plant, and yield. The evaluated variables were not affected by seed inoculation with *R. tropici*. Increasing doses of N fertilization decreased nodulation, and increased dry matter yield, N content and N accumulation in field pea aerial parts.

In a pot experiment with maize and soybean, the plants were inoculated with *Rhizobium* and/or arbuscular mycorrhizal fungi to study their effects on nitrogen uptake in the soybean/maize intercropping system (Shumin and Fan, 2011). Dual inoculation with *Glomus mosseae* and soybean *Rhizobium* SH212 significantly increased the biomass and nitrogen content of soybean and the associated maize plants. The results suggested that inoculation with both microorganisms in the intercropping system could improve soil nutrition efficiency and productivity of the intercropping system because of the synergistic effects of *Rhizobium* and arbuscular mycorrhizal fungi.

Hussain *et al.* (2014) found that rhizobia responded differently for improving physiology, nutrition and yield of maize under field conditions. Maize seeds (cv. Neelum) were inoculated with *Rhizobium phaseoli* (strains RS-1 and RS-3) and *Mesorhizobium ciceri* (strains RS-8 and RS-12). Plants inoculated with RS-3 showed significant increase in plant height, fresh biomass, cob yield, grain yield, grain P, and shoot K contents over control whereas RS-1 inoculated plants showed an increase in the photosynthetic rate, stomatal conductance, water use efficiency, mesophyll conductance, and intrinsic/photosynthetic water use efficiency over control. RS-8 inoculated plants showed the highest 1000 grain weight, sub-stomatal conductance and relative water content. However, the highest amount of crude protein, N in shoot/grain and shoot K contents were recorded in the RS-12 inoculated plots.

Impact of *Trichoderma* on Growth Parameters

Kowalska *et al.* (2011) experimented with *Trichoderma sp.* in nearly all soils and other habitats and found that most of *Trichoderma* strains were efficient for control of some pathogens while some strains induced plant native defence mechanisms. Treatments with microorganism-antagonist at concentration 10 gL^{-1} were applied as a foliar spray three times during the growing season. *Trichoderma* caused bigger and more vigorous growth. The possibility of use of *T. asperellum* as biological control agent for post-harvest diseases and for prolongation of storage time was observed until 7 days after harvest. In the second season of research, significantly higher yield of the treated plants (30.2%) was obtained in comparison to the untreated plants. Also the weight of aboveground part of plants (24.0%) and number of runners were increased.

Akrami *et al.* (2012) investigated the protective effects of *Trichoderma harzianum* (T-1) and *Trichoderma asperellum* (T-2) for controlling *Fusarium* rot of bean. Common bean roots were treated with *T. harzianum* (T-1) and *T. asperellum* (T-2) individually and in combination with each other and planted in soil artificially infested with *F. solani* pathogen. The findings indicated that prepared conidial suspensions either in water and in 10% sugar solution effectively reduced the colonization of the *F. solani*.

A study was conducted to evaluate the performance of three rhizosphere competent microbial strains, viz., *Pseudomonas fluorescens* OKC, *Trichoderma asperellum* T42 and *Rhizobium sp.* RH4, individually and in combination in bioprimed seeds of chickpea and rajma (Yadav *et al.*, 2013). Seeds were sown in pots and fields and the results demonstrated that bioprimed seeds had higher germination percentage and better plant growth in both the crops. It was also observed that the combined application of the microbes enhanced seed germination and plant growth better than their individual application. All combinations with *Trichoderma* showed better results than others and the triple microbial combination demonstrated the best results in terms of seed germination and seedling growth in both chickpea and rajma.

Zhao *et al.* (2014) found that iron (Fe) deficiency was a major plant nutritional disorder in many parts of the world, particularly in areas with saline soils. Among the numerous root-associated microbes that are beneficial for plant nutrient uptake, *Trichoderma sp.* has been found to be the most effective rhizosphere fungi for enhancing plant growth and plant resistance to biotic and abiotic stresses. To investigate the mode of action of *Trichoderma* on insoluble Fe in the soil, which is difficult for plants to absorb and utilize, a high siderophore-producing strain of *Trichoderma* T6, was isolated from the rhizosphere of cucumber plants. The strain was identified as *T. asperellum* based on the morphological features and molecular phylogenetic analyses. Applying strain T6 to sterile soil could increase soil levels of Fe^{2+} and siderophores and Fe^{2+} and Fe^{3+}-chelate reductase (FCR) activity in cucumber tissues.

Mahmoud *et al.* (2015) evaluated the antagonistic activity of 30 isolates of *T. asperellum* against 4 different isolates of FOL. Production of extracellular cell wall degrading enzymes of the antagonistic isolates was also measured. The random amplified polymorphic DNA (RAPD) method was applied to assess the genetic variability among the *T. asperellum* isolates. All the *T. asperellum* isolates significantly reduced the mycelial growth of FOL isolates but the extent of reduction in growth varied significantly. There was a correlation between the antagonistic capacity of *T. asperellum* isolates towards FOL and their lytic enzyme production. *Trichoderma* isolates and their biochemical capabilities are required for the selection of effective indigenous fungal strains used as biocontrol agents.

Gilberto *et al.* (2015) evaluated the growth of onion bulbs and the content of flavonoids and phenolic compounds, when the onion plants were inoculated with *Trichoderma asperellum* and grown with different doses of mineral fertilizer. Plants were grown in a greenhouse with 100% fertilizer, after 150 days, bulb mass and the content of phenolic compounds and flavonoids were measured. The *T. asperellum* isolate from onion (T0), had the greatest capacity for growth promotion, production of indole acetic acid (IAA) and induction of phenolic compounds and flavonoids.

Singh *et al.* (2015) suggested that *Trichoderma asperellum* T42 can be used as plant growth promoting fungus which had positive effects on seed germination, plant nutrient uptake and thus helps in improving plant growth and yield of pea. Apart from that, induced root and shoot development, increased photosynthetic pigment (chlorophyll), carotenoid, total sugar and protein content were observed as compared to control plants.

Singh *et al.* (2016) studied on bioprimed seeds of six vegetable crops (tomato, brinjal, chilli, okra, ridge gourd and guar) with different spore doses of *Trichoderma asperellum* BHUT8 ranging from 10^2 to 10^8 spores ml$''^1$ and the effect of biopriming was seen on seed germination and development. Biopriming with *T. asperellum* BHUT8 triggered various defense responses such as high phenylpropanoid activities and lignifications in bioprimed tomato seedlings compared to the non-bioprimed tomato seedlings demonstrating possible use of BHUT8 against phytopathogens.

Impact of Microbial Innoculum on Growth Attributes

The effects of the inoculation of *Rhizobium* and phosphate solubilizing bacterium (PSB; *Bacillus megaterium* var. *phosphaticum*), singly or in combination gave better result than the uninoculated control (Sengupta *et al.*, 2002; Marimuthu *et al.*, 2002; Mathew and Hameed, 2003; Purbey and Sen, 2005).

Inoculation of *Rhizobium* and PSB recorded significantly higher values of fresh root nodule weight/plant, leaf area index, yield attributes and yield and uptake of nitrogen and phosphorus over uninoculated control after wheat (Beg and Singh, 2009).

Durai *et al.* (2002) reported that the plant height and the number of branches plant^{-1} of moongbean were significantly influenced by phosphorus application in combination with PSB and the highest plant height of 42.7 cm was recorded with the application of 40 kg P_2O_5 ha^{-1}.

Maximum plant height (69.93 cm) was recorded in plots where seed was treated with *Rhizobium phaseoli* and fertilizer @ 50-50 kg N P ha^{-1}. Hossain (2011) and Ashraf *et al.* (2003) who reported an increase in plant height by seed inoculation and NPK application in moong.

Singh *et al.* (2018) conducted an experiment to study the effect of P fertilizers (at 0, 15, 30, 45 and 60 kg P_2O_5 ha^{-1}) and biofertilizers (*Rhizobium sp.*); phosphate solubilizing bacteria (PSB) and combination of *Rhizobium* +

PSB on the growth and yield of moongbean. All biofertilizers treatments increased growth and yield characters, except pod length and test weight. The highest values for all the parameters (dry matter accumulation m^{-1} row at 50 days after sowing and at harvest; branches $plant^{-1}$ at harvest; number of nodules $plant^{-1}$, pods $plant^{-1}$) were obtained with *Rhizobium* + PSB.

Seerat *et al.* (2004) conducted a field experiment during the summer season of 2000-01 at the Deemed University, Allahabad, after sorghum crop to see the effect of phosphorus status and biofertilizers on the yield of moongbean. The combined application of phosphorus at 60 kg ha^{-1} along with *Rhizobium* resulted in significantly higher plant height (cm) and number of branch $plant^{-1}$.

Bhuiyan and Mian (2007) recorded the highest nodule number, dry weight of nodule, biomass production and seed yield in BARI Mung-2 variety with *Bradyrhizobium* inoculation at the Bangladesh Agricultural University farm, Mymensingh.

At National Pulses Research Centre, Tamil Nadu, Vijila and Jabaraj (2008) compared seven strains of *Rhizobium* for their symbiotic performance with the host legume after maize crop. The rhizobial strain, VAM 3 obtained from the host grown under acid soil performed better than other strains. This acid tolerant strain demonstrated a comparative advantage over acid sensitive strain in their ability to nodulate and thereby promoting the growth and yield of moongbean. Combined inoculation of this strain with phosphobacteria resulted in improvement of crop yield over single inoculation in moong under acid soil condition.

Vikram *et al.* (2008) obtained from the inoculation of moongbean seeds with PSBV-14 the highest nodule number, nodule dry weight, shoot dry matter and total dry matter after 45 days of sowing after rice crop. On the other hand, treatment receiving the inoculation of PSBV-13 recorded the highest root length, root dry matter, P content and P uptake in root and shoot in moongbean plants.

Kumawat *et al.* (2010) observed favourable response on moongbean to biofertilizers under different fertility levels. Inoculation of *Rhizobium* + PSB and application of 15 kg N+20 P_2O_5 kg ha^{-1} significantly increased the number of branches $plant^{-1}$ and root nodules $plant^{-1}$.

Applications of 2 percent DAP along with bio-fertilizers (*Rhizobium* + Phosphobacteria) + residual effect of inorganic fertilizers and organic manures significantly increased the growth, yield attributes and grain yield of moongbean at Tamilnadu (Anu Lavanya and Ganapathy, 2011).

Nazir *et al.* (2011) reported combined inoculation of *Rhizobium* + PSB slightly improved plant height, dry matter production, number and weight of nodules $plant^{-1}$ of black gram than *Rhizobium* and PSB inoculated separately after wheat crop.

Mondal *et al.* (2013) revealed that application of biofertilizer and urea was more effective in promoting plant growth and yield attributes of moong bean than sole application of biofertilizer or urea. Among the fertilizer combinations, biofertilizer with recommended triple super phosphate, muriate of potash, gypsum and one-third urea exhibited superiority in plant height, number of branches plant^{-1}, leaf area plant^{-1}, number of nodules plant^{-1}, chlorophyll content in leaves, total dry mass plant^{-1}, absolute growth rate over other fertilizer treatments. Therefore, biofertilizer with 13 kg urea ha^{-1} may be recommended for increasing seed yield of moongbean after maize crop.

During the lag phase growth parameters of moongbean, *viz.* plant height, number of functional leaves plant^{-1}, number of branches plant^{-1} and drymatter accumulation showed significant improvement by the application of RDF (25-50-00 kg N + P_2O_5 + K_2O ha^{-1}) with biofertilizers (*Rhizobium* and PSB @ 25g each kg^{-1} seeds), RDF alone and 75% RDF with biofertilizers at Dapoli, Maharashtra (Gorade *et al.*, 2014). The increase in various growth parameters due to balanced nutrition in moongbean as a residual crop of wheat were also reported by Rudreshapa and Halikatti (2002) and Das *et al.* (2002).

Mohanty *et al.* (2015) on sandy clay loam soils of Mayurbhanj found that moong plants supplied with 50% RDF + bio fertilizers proved superior to other treatments by registering higher plant height, more number of primary branches/plant and nodules/plant after the preceeding crop of maize.

Sarikhani *et al.* (2018) isolated and characterize the K releasing bacteria (KRB) and to evaluate their contribution to the solubilization of K from muscovite and biotite, and to the assimilation of released K by tomato in a pot culture experiment. Results of the pot culture experiment showed that the concentration and content of K in plant tissue were considerably more than those in any of the controls with no living organisms present. Results revealed that significantly more biomass was accumulated and K acquired in most pots treated with bacterial strains than in the control, especially for *Pseudomonas* sp. strain S10 3. This treatment increased K concentation and content by more than 50 and 70%, respectively, in tomato aerial tissue. Further research is necessary to examine the effects of these bacterial strains on the mobilization of K bearing minerals under field conditions

Impact of Microbial Innoculum on yield Attributes

Introduction of bio inoculants in cereal-based cropping systems saved the cost of fertilizer nutrients to the tune of Rs. 350 ha^{-1}. The NPK fertilizer substitution in rice by incorporating moongbean haulms was 20-30 kg ha^{-1} (Palaniappan *et al.*, 1990).

Grain legumes are grown in rice-based cropping systems for protein, fodder and green manure purpose. It is found that about 18 grain legume species are important in various rice farming situations of Asia. In the irrigated environment of tropics and subtropics, green legumes can be grown in rotation with one or more rice crops per year (Buresh and Datta, 1991).

Growing a short-duration grain legume like moongbean, black gram, or cowpea and incorporating the residues into the soil after harvesting the grains/pods is suggested not only for increasing the system productivity but also for making a considerable saving on chemical fertilizer (Reddy, 2001).

Manivannan *et al.* (2002) revealed that *Rhizobium* seed treatment and foliar application of N, P, K and chelated micronutrients (microsol) at 15, 30 and 45 DAS resulted in significant increase in growth and yield parameters of urdbean after rice crop.

Introduction of a grain legume or green manure crop in a cereal based system has been found quite promising in enhancing crop yield and fertilizer saving (Kachroo and Dixit, 2005).

Deshmukh *et al.* (2013) reported that the yield contributing characters og moongbean *viz.*, number of pods plant^{-1}, number of seeds pod^{-1}, test weight (g), grain and straw yield increased significantly due to the application of 75% RDF + bio fertilizers before flowering with 150-60-60-40-25 kg of NPKS and Zn of the previous maize.

Impact of Microbial Innoculum on Soil Fertility

Application of Phosphobacteria made the insoluble phosphates present in the soil into soluble forms by secreting organic acids resulting in effective solubilization and utilization of phosphorus. These findings are in agreement with Subramani and Solaimalai (2000) and Sirinivasa Perumal and Sundari (2004).

Davari *et al.* (2012) at IARI, New Delhi, concluded that all combinations of organic manures and biofertilizers significantly increased N, P and K concentration in mung bean grain over the control. Combinations of organic manures and biofertilizers resulted in significantly (p = 0.05) higher N, P and K uptake by mung bean grain than the control.

For obtaining higher yields by sustaining soil fertility in terms of available N, P_2O_5, moongbean (Phule mung-2) be grown during summer succeeding crop with sorghum as a main crop with the application of RDF (25:50:00 kg N : P_2O_5 : K_2O ha^{-1}) along with seed inoculation of *Rhizobium* and PSB biofertilizers (@ 25g each kg^{-1} seeds (Gorade *et al.*, 2014).

Combined application of organic manures with *Rhizobium* + PSB + *Trichoderma* increased nutrient content in soil and nutrient uptake by plant (Das and Singh, 2014) in moong exhibited higher yield after rice crop. Similar findings were also reported by Kumpawat (2010), Vadgave (2010) and Prajapati (2014).

Impact of Microbial Innoculum on Soil Microbial Status

Kandeler *et al.* (1999) reported soil management influences soil microorganisms and soil microbial processes through changes in the quantity and quality of plant residues in the soil profile.

Organic compounds produced by microorganisms such as acetate, citrate and oxalate can increase mineral dissolution rates in laboratory experiments and in the soil reported by [Sheng *et al.* (2003), Badr *et al.* (2006) and Styriakova *et al.* (2003)].

Sheng and He (2006) reported that solubilization of illite and feldspar by microorganism is due to the production of organic acids like oxalic acid and tartaric acids and also due to production of capsular polysaccharides which helps in dissolution of minerals to release potassium.

Singh *et al.* (2015) reported that crop residue retention and biofertiliser application can substitute a significant part of fertilizer, as the rice straw at maturity contains over 80% of the total plant NPK. The enzymatic activities in the soil are mainly of microbial origin, being derived from intracellular, cell-associated or free enzymes. A unique balance of chemical, physical, and biological (including microbial especially enzyme activities) components contribute to maintaining soil health (Das and Varma, 2011).

Enzymes may respond to changes in soil management more quickly than other soil variables and, therefore, enzymes might be useful as early indicators of biological change (Bandick and Dick, 1999).

The microbial and enzymatic activities were stimulated by addition of crop residue and small doses of N, while removal of residue, conventional tillage and a large amount of N exert weaker or negative effect on these biological activities [Marinori *et al.* (2000); Singh *et al.* (2009a)].

Ogunmwonyi *et al.* (2008) observed that the total bacterial and fungal counts of the soil samples. A pH meter was used to monitor soil pH while isolates were identified by their cultural, morphological and biochemical characteristics using established procedures. Bacterial counts were in the order of 10^5-10^7 cfu/g of soil, while fungal counts were in the order of 10^5-10^7 cfu/g of soil. Bacterial and fungal abundance were typical of an environment with high species richness and functional diversity.

Crop Residues and their Scope in India

Crop residues, in general are parts of the plants left in the field after crops have been harvested and threshed. The recycling of crop residues has the advantage of converting the surplus farm waste into a useful product for meeting the nutrient requirement of crops. It also maintains the soil physical and chemical condition (Powel and Unger, 1997) and improves the overall ecological balance of the crop production system. Application of organic matter in the form of plant residues has long been known to improve the properties of soils, especially the soil organic matter content (Blevins and Frye, 1993). Crop residues left on the soil surface protect the soil against crusting, surface sealing, and detachment by intercepting and buffering the kinetic energy of rainfall and runoff and increasing infiltration rate (Lentz and Bjorneberg, 2003).

Ministry of New and Renewable Energy (MNRE, 2009), Govt. of India estimated that about 500 million tonnes of crop residue is generated every year in India. However, India has large variability in crop residue generation and their use depending on the cropping intensity, productivity and crops grown in different states of India. Residue generation was highest in Uttar Pradesh (60 Mt) followed by Punjab (51 Mt) and Maharashtra (46 Mt). Among different crops, cereals generate 352 Mt of residue followed by fibres (66 Mt), oilseed (29 Mt), pulses (13 Mt) and sugarcane (12 Mt).

Cereals (rice, wheat, maize, millets) contribute 70% residues while maize contributes (23421.3 KT/year) of crop residues (MNRE, 2009). If this residue is not returned to the soil, this may cause mining of soil for major nutrients leading to net negative balance and multi-nutrient deficiencies in crops. This is one of the reasons for the yield decline in the IGP region. Farmers do not incorporate straw in the crop field because of its slow degradation rate, disease infestation, unstable nutrients, and reduced yield from short-term negative effect of nitrogen immobilization (Pandey *et al.*, 2009).

They usually dispose of it through open field burning. As a consequence, carbon dioxide, carbon monoxide, methane, nitrous oxide and sulphur dioxide are emitted into the atmosphere. This process also emits harmful air pollutants, which have toxic properties and are notably, potential carcinogens that can cause harmful effects on human health (Gadde *et al.*, 2009).

There has been increased realization that crop residue is a source of nutrients and organic material for farmers. In addition to N, P and K residue incorporation also helps overcome deficiencies of other nutrients, *viz.*, S, Zn and B which are widespread in the IGP region (Prasad, 2005).

Residual impact of KSB and *Trichoderma* on Moongbean

Beary *et al.* (2002) observed that inoculation of fungal-bacterial consortium accelerated decomposition of sugarcane crop residue. The consortium of different hypercellulytic fungal culture can be used to lower C: N ratio of crop residue at a faster rate.

The microbial consortium of four lignocellulolytic fungi can be used for rapid bio-conversion of agro-waste using organic inputs (ICAR NEWS., 2008). Residue application improved the physical condition of soil for better germination and seedling establishment. A better soil physical condition provides more plant nutrients and source of energy for soil microbes. Crop residues left on soil surface protect the soil against crusting and surface sealing, reduce soil compaction and temperature, conserve soil moisture, aggregation and macro-porosity and enhance root growth (Blanco- Canqui and Lal, 2006; Singh and Dhar, 2011).

Amgain *et al.* (2013) assessed the effect of residue management practices on productivity and profitability of moong followed by winter-season crops viz., wheat, chickpea and mustard and concluded that moong should be followed by chickpea/mustard along with residue retention with spray of compost culture of crops/*Leucaena* twigs for higher productivity and profitability under zero-till dryland conditions of North-Western India.

Residual impact on Microbial Biomass Carbon (MBC)

The soil microbial biomass carbon (SMBC) is a small but key component of the active soil organic matter (SOM) pool and serves as a source and sink of soil nutrients (Smith and Paul, 1990). Residue application increased the microbial population, MBC and microbial activity by 10.2%, after harvest of 2nd maize crop (Chandra, 2011). The MBC and MBN values significantly increased from CRI to flowering stage of wheat and then dropped significantly at the harvest stage due to low availability of substrate carbon arising out of poor root exudation at crop maturity (Gaind and Nain, 2011). Dong *et al.* (2009) reported that the mean annual MBC was the highest in no-tillage with residue, while lowest in conventional tillage.

The availability of N, P, K, S, soil MBC, dehydrogenase assay and productivity of sorghum and wheat was significantly increased with the integrated application of organic manure and mineral fertilizer over control (Katkar *et al.*, 2011). Long-term fertilization greatly increased SMBC and microbial activity in soil (Chu *et al.*, 2007).

Saini *et al.* (2005) reported that application of fertilizer nutrients along with FYM+ use of nitrogen fixers+ phosphate solubilizers and VAM increased the MBC, N and P contents in the rhizosphere and were maximum at 30 days and decreased subsequently (at 60 days or harvest) in soybean-winter maize sequence.

Impact of Fungus on Residue Decomposition

The role of lygnolytic and cellulolytic, saprophytic micro-organisms like *Trichoderma* species (*T. harzianum or T. viridae*) would be of immense importance and it has been demonstrated that *T. harzianum* fungus with *Clostridium butyricum* bacteria could decompose N as high as 12 mg/g straw (Lynch and Harper, 1985).

PMC, a by-product of sugar industry contains adequate quantity of mono and dimer of the carbohydrates for growth of microbes and hence fungus *Trichoderma* exhibited more response in degrading this organic material (Kanso *et al.*, 1999).

In situ decomposition of the crop residues viz. cane trash, paddy trash, maize trash left after mechanical or combine harvesting in the field by the use of *T. asperellum* elevates soil fertility status and physico-chemical and microbial condition of the soil for sustainable crop production besides safeguarding the environment being intoxicated by hazardous burning impacts (Freeman *et al.*, 2004).

Sharma *et al.* (2012) performed experiment with urea and dung treatments, inoculation by fungi *Trichoderma* increased N, P, K, S content in the resultant compost consistently in either of the residues having highest at 90 days. Likewise, organic-C and C:N ratio decrease substantially in the residues and exhibited minimum at the end of composting. Degradation of the crop residues involved narrowing down of the C:N ratio by urea solution applied followed by microbial decomposition by the *Trichoderma*. This study can be subjected to mass scale composting of rural or urban wastes and can be extended to the in situ decomposition of the crop residues viz. cane, paddy and wheat trashes left after mechanical or combine harvesting in the field and thus would elevate soil fertility for sustainable crop production safeguarding the environment.

Ogireddy *et al.* (2019) studied on the residue decomposition simple substrates like carbohydrates which was degraded by bacteria, but in later stages degradation of complex constituents viz., cellulose, lignin needs microbes which was capable of secreting enzymes like cellulase, acting on complex organic substrates and found cellulolytic micro-organisms like *Trichoderma* have the potential impact as microbial inoculants to enhance the rate of decomposition as well as alleviate the effect of residue burning.

Effect of Microbial Strains on Economics

Savaliya *et al.* (2017) showed higher values of growth and yield attributes *viz.*, dry matter per plant, effective tillers and test weight were registered with application of 45 kg K_2O/ha + KSB seed inoculation, resultantly gave higher grain and straw yield of 40.8 and 60.8q/ha respectively along with higher net return (₹46946/ha) and B:C (2.15) over the control.

Kumar *et al.* (2014) conducted experiment to find out the effect of different combinations of vermicompost, biofertilizers and chemical fertilizers on growth, productivity and economics in chickpea. Application of RDF + 5.0 ton/ha VC + Rhizobium + PSB significantly increased growth and yield attributes of chickpea over control. Maximum net profit (₹40086) and benefit cost ratio (2.12) was recorded by the application of RDF +3.0 ton/ha VC + Rhizobium + PSB on control.

Rahaman and Merwad (2016) conducted a field trial to assess the application of 95 kg K ha^{-1} on maize (*Zea mays*) through potassium sulphate

(KS) and potassium feldspar (KF) combined with potassium dissolving bacteria individually or in different combinations. 50% KS + 50% KF (K_3) gave the highest gross return (₹12783) and maximum net return (₹11271).

Davari *et al.* (2012) found that the application of FYM + crop residue + biofertilisers was the most economical treatment with respect to increasing net profit. The combination resulted in improved grain yield by mung bean over the control by 47% and net return by 27%.

Sharma and Banik (2014) observed that application of 50% RDF+ Arbuscular Mycorrhiza (AM) + Azospirilllum to baby corn was more economical with maximum net return (Rs. 59889) and B:C ratio (4.08) and higher cob and green fodder yield.

Kaur and Reddy (2015) conducted a field trial to test the effects of two phosphate-solubilizing bacteria PSB-3 and PSB-5, inoculated singly or together with rock phosphate (RP) fertilization on maize and wheat. The combined use of PSB inoculation and RP fertilization was more economical because of minimal cost and maximum returns. These results suggested that PSB inoculation along with RP fertilization would be an appropriate substitute for chemical phosphatic fertilizer in sustainable agriculture systems.

Kumhar *et al.* (2014) evaluated the cost effective mass production of local strain KBN-24 (*Trichoderma viride*) for large scale adoption. Results indicated that the locally available food grains like rice and wheat were comparatively cheaper and serve as convenient substrates for the mass multiplication of *Trichoderma viride.* Cost of synthetic media varied from Rs. 0.15 to 15.11 whereas in case of mass multiplication with the use of food grains, the cost of production per gram of fresh biomass ranged from Rs. 0.01 to 0.08 only indicating its economic viability.

Methodology for impact of KSB and *Trichoderma* on Baby Corn and Moongbean

The detailed methodology and experimental protocol have been given in this chapter for study of *Eco-friendly Production of Baby Corn and Moongbean.* The experiment was conducted during the rabi seasons of 2017-18 and 2018-19 at the Agricultural Research Farm, Institute of Agricultural Sciences, Banaras Hindu University, Varanasi, Uttar Pradesh (India). Detail account of the methodology used, experimental procedures followed and the techniques adopted during the course of study are described in this chapter.

Experimental site

The Agricultural Research Farm is situated at a distance of about 10 km from Varanasi Cant railway station. Flanked by left bank of the river Ganges it is situated at the Southern end of Varanasi city. Geographically the farm lies at 25° 18′N latitude and 88° 03′E longitude and at an altitude of 128.93 meters above the mean sea level. The experimental site was homogeneous in fertility with even topography, uniform textural make up having assured irrigation and other required facilities. Proper drainage facility was also available in order to remove the excess water if any, during the experimental period.

Weather and Climate

Broadly speaking climate of Varanasi district is sub-tropical with extremes of weather conditions i.e. extremely hot summers and cold winters. Specifically this region falls in semi-arid to sub-humid type of climate. The temperature begins to rise from end of February and reaches its maximum by May and June but has a tendency to decrease from July onwards touching the minimum in December/January. The maximum temperature usually fluctuates between 14.5°C to 42.8°C while minimum temperature varies from 6.2 to 28.7°C. Occasionally extreme of minimum and maximum temperature variations are also realized. The period between March and May remains generally dry. The onset of monsoon in this region normally takes place during third week of June and ceases by the end of September or sometimes up to first week of October. The region also experiences (although not regularly) winter showers due to cyclonic rains in the months of January and February. The average relative humidity of the area is 68.1 percent with a maximum of 81 percent during July to September and a minimum of 38 per cent during April to early June. The meteorological data during the experimental period for both the years were recorded week wise from the meteorological observatory of the Research Farm, and presented in Table 3.1 and Table 3.2 and graphically shown in figure. 3.1 and figure. 3.2.

Rainfall (mm)

Total rainfall received during 2017-18 and 2018-19 was 1008.9 mm and 1248.3 mm, respectively which was 19.178% higher in 2015-16 than 2014-15. The total rainfall received during the first experimental year (November 2018 to April 2019) was 124.1 mm where the crop of baby corn (DKC 9108) received 69.8 mm and the crop of moong (HUM 16) received 54.3 mm rainfall. During second year of experimentation (2018-19) the crop of baby corn (DKC 9108) received 46.3 mm while, moong crop received 13.0 mm rainfall. The distribution of the rainfall obviously indicated that the highest rainfall received in the month of January (33.1 mm) of the first year of experimentation while it was very less rainfall in the second year during experimentation. The number of rainy weeks during first and second year remained 5 weeks, when experimental crop faced varied pattern of distribution, intensity and amount of rainfall. The distribution pattern of rainfall was irregular as depicted during 2017-18 and 2018-19.

Temperature (°C)

The weekly mean maximum temperature ranged from 14.5 to 42.8°C with an average of 28.65°C during the first experimental year (2018-19). During baby corn growing period it ranged from 14.5 to 34.1°C, while succeeding moong experienced comparatively warmer temperature ranging from 33.9°C to 42.8°C. On the other hand, the weekly mean maximum temperature ranged from 38.1°C to 41.4°C with an average of 39.75°C during the second year (2018-19). It ranged from 19-35.5°C during the crop growth period of baby corn, while moong had comparatively higher temperature ranging from 38.3-41.4°C. The weekly mean minimum temperature ranged from 6.2°C to 20.9°C with an average of 13.55°C during the first experimental year (2018-19) and during baby corn growing period it varied between 6.2 to 20.9°C while moong experienced temperature ranging from 20.3 to 28.7°C during the first experimental year (2018-19). Similarly the weekly mean minimum temperature ranged from 7.2 to 18.4°C with an average of 12.18°C during the second year (2018-19). The mean fluctuation in the maximum and minimum temperature varied during both the years.

Table 3.1: Weekly meteorological data recorded at Agricultural research farm during crop season 2017-18

Week No.	Month and Date	Rainfall (mm)	Temperature (°C)		R.H. (%)		Wind Speed km/hr	Sunshine (h day^{-1})	Evaporation (mm day^{-1})
			Max	Min	Max	Min			
*47	Nov 19-25	0.0	26.9	11.0	89	36	1.3	7.2	1.7
48	26-02	0.0	27.8	11.9	84	49	1.0	7.3	1.9
49	Dec 03-09	0.0	24.6	9.4	85	45	2.5	5.5	1.7
50	10-16	2.8	21.2	11.5	89	58	2.0	3.0	1.6
51	17-23	0.0	19.3	8.1	94	54	2.0	3.7	0.9
52	24-31	0.0	17.9	6.2	93	65	1.4	2.9	0.9
1	Jan 01-07	33.1	20.0	13.3	96	74	3.7	2.8	0.8
2	08-14	0.0	14.6	8.3	90	77	3.1	1.8	0.8
3	15-21	0.0	14.5	7.8	91	74	2.4	1.0	0.5
4	22-28	10.6	19.9	11.8	94	69	2.0	3.5	0.7
5	29-04	3.5	22.1	10.2	86	63	2.3	5.2	1.2
6	Feb 05-11	0.0	22.5	11.0	88	56	2.3	6.6	1.8
7	12-18	0.0	25.6	13.1	84	52	2.2	6.9	2.2
8	19-25	0.0	29.3	14.9	87	48	1.9	7.2	2.7
9	26-04	11.8	25.6	17.4	89	62	3.2	3.1	2.5
10	Mar 05-11	0.0	28.0	13.9	80	38	3.6	9.5	3.2
11	12-18	8.0	28.1	16.3	79	49	3.7	6.9	3.4
12	19-25	0.0	32.2	16.7	69	38	3.7	9.8	4.6

(Table Contd…)

Week No.	Month and Date	Rainfall (mm)	Temperature (°C)		R.H. (%)		Wind Speed km/hr	Sunshine (h day^{-1})	Evaporation (mm day^{-1})
			Max	Min	Max	Min			
*13	26-01	0.0	34.1	20.9	74	40	2.4	6.9	3.7
**14	Apr 02-08	7.0	35.2	20.3	60	39	3.4	8.2	4.9
15	09-15	29.9	33.9	20.6	64	44	4.0	7.6	4.5
16	16-22	24.4	36.6	23.2	68	36	3.8	8.2	5.4
17	23-29	0.0	35.0	24.8	68	44	7.2	6.9	6.4
18	30-06	0.0	39.0	23.6	67	37	3.8	9.7	6.0
19	May 07-13	0.0	39.6	27.2	63	40	3.8	7.2	6.0
20	14-20	0.0	38.7	27.1	61	37	3.9	8.0	6.7
21	21-27	0.0	42.8	27.6	57	33	5.5	9.4	7.9
22	28-03	0.0	42.1	28.7	62	32	3.6	7.6	7.0
**23	Jun 04-10	0.0	42.6	28.2	59	35	3.3	8.0	6.7

*Growing period of baby corn, **Growing period of moong

Table 3.2. Weekly meteorological data recorded at Agricultural research farm during crop season 2018-19

Week No.	Month and Date	Rainfall (mm)	Temperature (°C)		R.H. (%)		Wind Speed km/hr	Sunshine (h day^{-1})	Evaporation (mm day^{-1})
			Max	Min	Max	Min			
*47	Nov 19-25	0.0	28.7	16.2	90	49	0.7	4.4	1.4
48	26-02	0.0	28.4	17.2	86	53	1.1	4.3	2.1
49	Dec 03-09	0.8	24.6	14.8	93	62	1.0	2.2	1.4
50	10-16	0.0	22.7	11.4	92	56	2.6	3.7	1.5
51	17-23	0.0	22.0	8.2	91	43	1.5	3.8	1.4
52	24-31	0.0	22.8	8.0	82	37	2.5	5.4	1.6
1	Jan 01-07	0.0	24.3	9.6	94	47	4.2	2.5	1.2
2	08-14	0.0	25.0	10.7	85	45	1.9	5.9	1.7
3	15-21	7.7	19.0	11.0	94	69	1.9	0.6	0.9
4	22-28	0.0	21.7	7.2	85	43	2.0	5.2	1.6
5	29-04	0.0	24.7	11.9	79	50	2.0	6.5	2.1
6	Feb 05-11	0.0	24.5	9.6	83	52	2.3	6.3	2.2
7	12-18	2.4	27.1	13.5	85	57	1.7	6.3	2.2
8	19-25	0.0	28.6	14.9	77	44	4.0	8.5	3.6
9	26-04	0.0	29.9	16.2	85	51	1.4	6.4	2.7
10	Mar 05-11	19.2	30.9	17.9	77	46	2.4	7.6	3.3
11	12-18	16.2	28.9	16.6	73	51	3.5	6.4	3.6
12	19-25	0.0	33.6	17.3	61	26	3.8	9.6	4.6

(Table Contd...)

Week No.	Month and Date	Rainfall (mm)	Temperature (°C)		R.H. (%)		Wind Speed km/hr	Sunshine (h day^{-1})	Evaporation (mm day^{-1})
			Max	Min	Max	Min			
*13	26-01	0.0	35.5	18.4	58	34	2.0	9.0	4.6
**14	Apr 02-08	0.0	38.3	23.1	63	26	3.5	7.9	5.9
15	09-15	0.0	39.2	22.3	42	19	5.0	8.4	7.9
16	16-22	0.0	41.4	23.9	65	22	4.3	8.7	8.4
17	23-29	0.0	41.3	22.2	64	15	4.8	9.3	8.4
18	30-06	0.0	39.6	26.5	62	24	3.6	6.6	6.7
19	May 07-13	10.6	38.6	25.2	69	33	3.1	8.4	6.6
20	14-20	0.0	41.3	27.6	63	28	4.1	8.4	7.3
21	21-27	0.0	38.4	25.1	68	38	7.3	7.2	8.1
22	28-03	0.0	38.1	26.1	64	39	3.6	7.4	6.8
**23	Jun 04-10	2.4	40.4	29.9	61	36	5.5	8.2	8.7

*Growing period of baby corn, **Growing period of moong

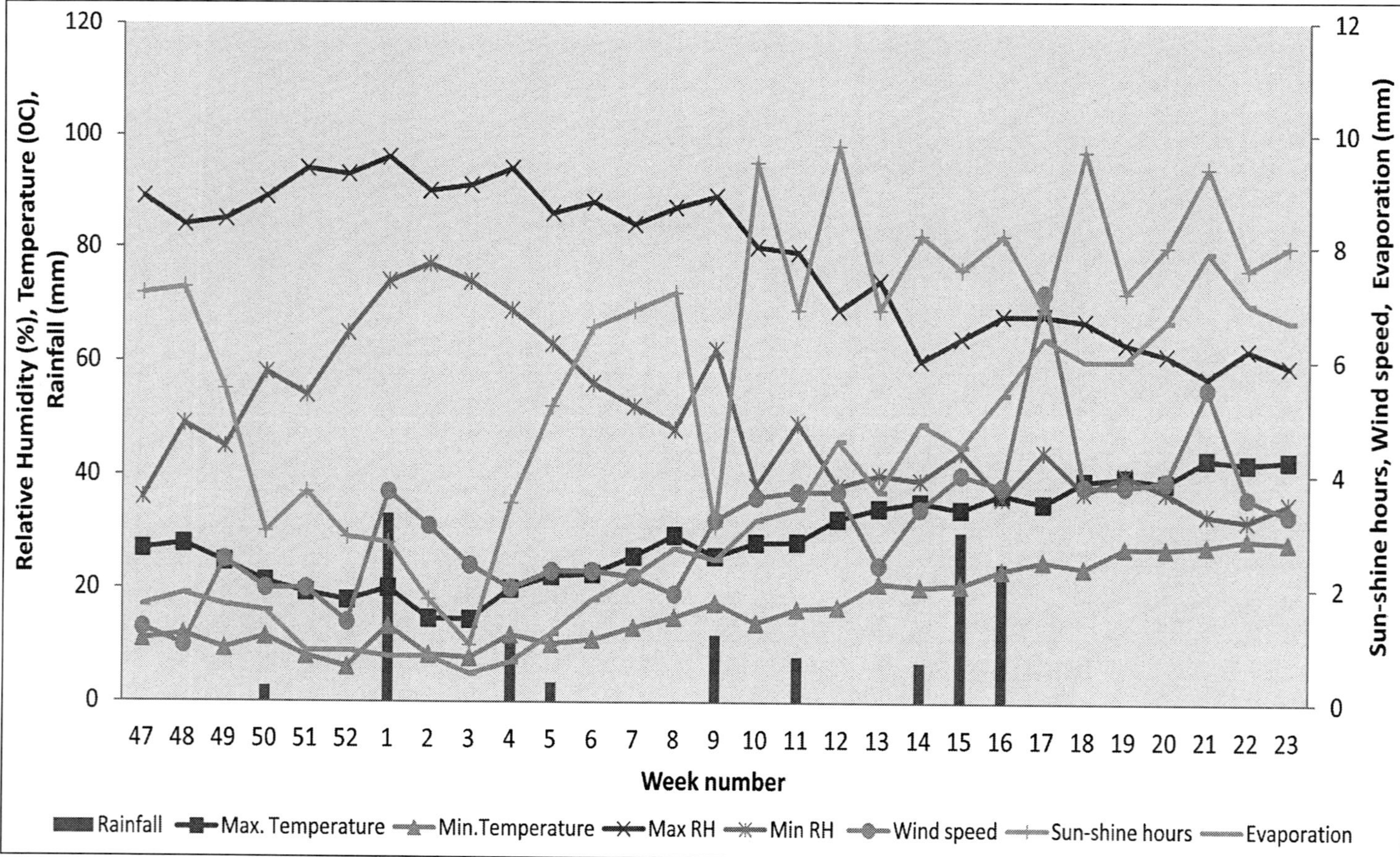

Fig. 3.1: Meteorological data at B.H.U. Agricultural farm during the crop season of 2017-18

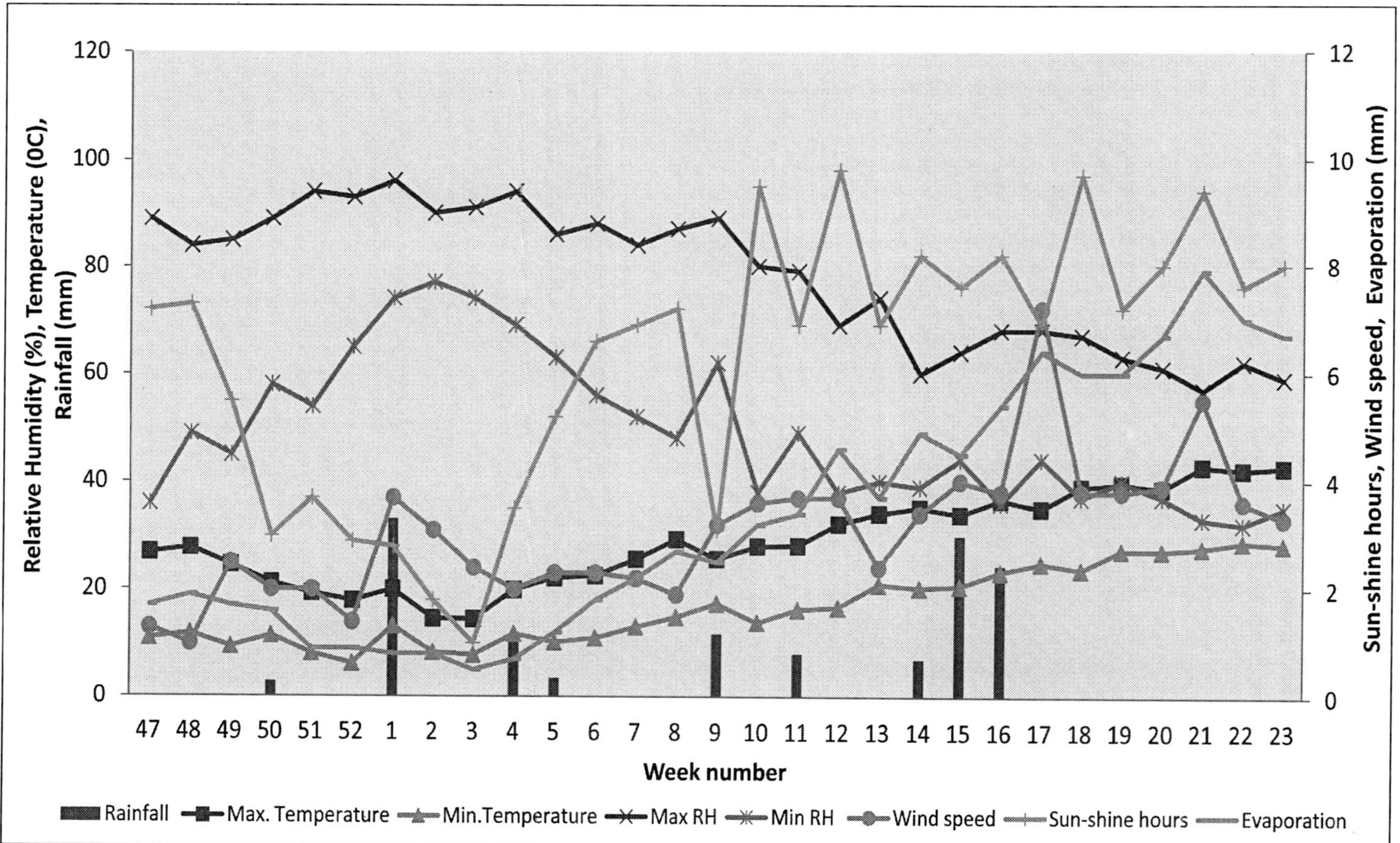

Fig. 3.2: Meteorological data at B.H.U. Agricultural farm during the crop season of 2018-19

Relative Humidity (RH) (%)

The weekly mean maximum relative humidity during the first experimental year (2018-19) ranged from 57 to 96 per cent with an average of 76.5 per cent and it ranged from 69 to 96 per cent during the crop cycle of baby corn and 57 to 68 per cent in case of moong during the year 2018-19. The weekly mean maximum relative humidity during the second year (2018-19), ranged from 36 to 77 per cent with an average of 56.5 per cent, during baby corn growth period and 32 to 44 per cent during moong crop in 2015-16. The weekly mean minimum relative humidity during the first experimental year (2018-19) ranged from 29 to 94 per cent with an average of 61.5 per cent. The crop of baby corn faced 58 to 94 per cent, while the crop of moong sustained 29 to 68 per cent of weekly mean minimum relative humidity during 2018-19. The relative humidity indicated considerable variation throughout the growing season during both the years. Data also indicated that the second year was comparatively more humid as compared to the first year for baby corn.

Sun-shine duration (hrs day^{-1})

The average duration of bright sunshine during the year 2018-19 was 6.24 hr day^{-1} which varied during the crop growth period. It was 5.21 hr day^{-1} for baby corn and approx. 8.08 hr day^{-1} for moong. The average duration of bright sunshine hrs during the year 2018-19 was little bit higher by 6.29 hr day^{-1} and it varied markedly during the crop growth period. It was 5.31 hr day^{-1} for baby corn crop and 8.05 hr day^{-1} for the growth period of moong. The average sunshine hours per day showed a variation of 1.0 to 9.7 hrs and 0.6 to 9.3 hrs in 2017-18 and 2018-19 respectively during the period of investigation.

Evaporation

The evaporation data recorded from United States Weather Bureau Class A Pan Evaporimeter revealed that there was mean weekly evaporation of 1.94 mm day^{-1} during the crop cycle of baby corn (DKC 9108) and 6.15 mm day^{-1} during the cultivation of moong for the experimental year 2018. The crop of baby corn in the second year of investigation experienced 2.30 mm day^{-1} which is very low in case of baby corn but it was markedly higher for moong which was 8.70 mm day^{-1} in the year 2018-19. The total evaporation during crop growth period was 85.6 mm in the year 2018-19 and 118.5 mm in the year 2018-19 indicating more evaporation during second year as compared to first year.

Soil Characteristics

To evaluate the fertility status of the soil, random soil samples from two place from each plot were collected as per the methodology of Black *et al.* (1965) from a depth of 0-30 cm from the experimental field with the help of screw auger prior to the experimentation. All the possible technical precautions as prescribed for standard soil sampling were taken. Tagged samples were brought to the laboratory, air-dried, grounded and sieved through 20 mm mesh. The processed and prepared samples were analyzed for physical, chemical and microbiological characteristics of soil. Soil of the experimental site was sandy clay loam in texture, deep, well drained, moderate in fertility with low in available nitrogen, medium available phosphorus and potassium along with neutral reaction. The soil was having optimum range of pH and EC that favoured better crop management.

Table 3.3: Physical and chemical properties of experimental soil

Particulars	Value		Method employed
	2017-18	2018-19	
Soil properties (%)			
Mechanical analysis			
Sand	46.75	46.54	Hydrometric method (Bouyoucos, 1962)
Silt	30.69	30.82	
Clay	23.49	23.57	
Textural class	Sandy clay loam		
Taxonomy	Ustochrept		
Physical analysis			
Bulk density (Mg m^{-3})	1.39	1.37	Core Sampler (Piper, 1966)
Field capacity (%) Depth (0-30 cm)	19.7	19.56	Keen's box (Black *et al.*, 1965)
Permanent Wilting (%) Depth (0-30 cm)	6.3	6.1	Briggs and Shantz (1912)
Chemical analysis			
Soil pH (1:2.5 soil : water suspension)	7.36	7.39	Glass electrode pH meter (Jackson, 1973)
Electrical Conductivity (dSm^{-1} at 25°C)	0.32	0.31	Systronics electrical conductivity meter (Jackson, 1973)
Organic Carbon (%)	0.38	0.41	Walkley and Black method (Jackson, 1973)
Available Nitrogen (N kg ha^{-1})	192.21	194.67	Alkaline permanganate method (Subbiah and Asija, 1956)
Available Phosphorus	18.01	18.85	0.5 M $NaHCO_3$ Olsen's Colorimetric method (Olsen *et al.*, 1954)
Available Potassium (K kg ha^{-1})	196.06	199.88	Flame Photometer method (Jackson, 1973)

(Table Contd...)

Particulars	Value		Method employed
	2017-18	2018-19	
Microbiological analysis			
Total Bacteria (Cfu/g of soil)	166.47×10^6	174.12×10^6	Nutrient Agar medium for total bacterial counts (Miles and Misra,1938)
Total Actinomycetes (Cfu/g of soil)	53.21×10^4	54.25×10^4	Kenknight and Munaier's medium (Subba Rao,1999)
Total Fungi (Cfu/g of soil)	36.45×10^4	38.11×10^4	Martin rose bengal medium (Martin, 1950)
Soil microbial biomass carbon (μg C g^{-1} soil)	124.85	126.11	Fumigation extraction method (Vance,1987)

Besides Mechanical, physical and chemical analyses, the microbiological analyses also inferred that soil was having good fertility status with maximum no. of colony forming unit per gram of soil. The fertility status has been found to be increased leading to more no. of total bacteria, total actinomycetes during the second year of investigating the experimental site.

On the basis of above analyses it could be inferred that it was low in organic carbon and nitrogen, but medium in phosphorus and potassium. However, soil was having optimum range of pH and EC that favoured better crop management during both the year of investigation.

Cropping History of the Experimental Field

The productive potentials of the experimental field can be judged from the cropping history. The details of the cropping history of the experimental site preceding the period up to last 6 years are given below (Table 3.4)

Table 3.4: Cropping history of the experimental field

Year	Kharif	Rabi
2011-2012	Rice	Wheat
2012-2013	Rice	Wheat
2013-2014	Rice	Wheat
2014-2015	Rice	Wheat
2015-2016	Rice	Wheat
2016-2017	Rice	Baby corn*
2017-2018	Moongbean*	Babycorn*
2018-2019	Moongbean*	–

*Experimental crops

Experimental details

The experiment was laid out in a split plot design with 4 fertility levels (F_1, F_2, F_3 and F_4) in main plot and 4 strains (three bacterial strains of

KSB *i.e.* S_1, S_2, S_3) and one fungal strain of *Trichoderma i.e.* (S_4) as a seed treatment in sub plot for baby corn. Treatments were allocated to each plot randomly and replicated four times. Main plot and sub plot treatments were randomized separately. The experimental details are given below and layout plan are depicted in figure 3.3.

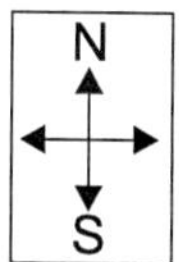

MIC					
R_1		R_2	R_3		R_4
F_2S_2		F_1S_1	F_3S_3		F_4S_4
F_2S_4		F_1S_2	F_3S_1		F_4S_3
F_2S_3		F_1S_4	F_3S_2		F_4S_1
F_2S_1		F_1S_3	F_3S_4		F_4S_2
F_1S_4		F_4S_3	F_2S_2		F_3S_3
F_1S_2		F_4S_4	F_2S_1		F_3S_1
F_1S_1		F_4S_2	F_2S_3		F_3S_4
F_1S_2	SIC	F_4S_1	F_2S_4	SIC	F_3S_3
F_3S_1		F_2S_3	F_4S_2		F_1S_4
F_3S_3		F_2S_4	F_4S_1		F_1S_2
F_3S_4		F_2S_2	F_4S_3		F_1S_1
F_3S_2		F_2S_1	F_4S_4		F_1S_3
F_4S_2		F_3S_4	F_1S_3		F_2S_1
F_4S_1		F_3S_2	F_1S_4		F_2S_3
F_4S_3		F_3S_1	F_1S_2		F_2S_4
F_4S_4		F_3S_3	F_1S_1		F_2S_2

F_1 100% NP+25% K
F_2 100% NP+50 K
F_3 100% NP+75% K
F_4 100% NPK
RDF 150 N+ 80 P_2O_5 + 80 K_2O

S_1 *Agrobacterium sp.*
S_2 *Flavobacterium sp.*
S_3 *Rhizobium sp.*
S_4 *Trichoderma sp.*

Fig. 3.3: Lay out of the experimental field

1st trial: Baby corn

(A) Fertility levels (RDF)	**Symbol**
(i) 100% NP+25% K	F_1
(ii) 100% NP+50% K	F_2
(iii) 100% NP+75% K	F_3
(iv) 100% NPK	F_4

Recommended dose of fertilizers (RDF) 150N+80P_2O_5+80K_2O+ 40S + 10Zn kg ha^{-1}

(B) Strains applied (CFU)	**Symbol**
(i) *Agrobacterium* sp.	S_1
(ii) *Flavobacterium* sp.	S_2
(iii) *Rhizobium* sp.	S_3
(iv) *Trichoderma* sp.	S_4

Treatment details

Main plot treatment	Fertility levels = 4
Sub plot treatment	Strains applied = 4
No. of treatment combinations	16
No. of replication	4
Total no. of plots	64
Plot size	4.0m × 2.8m.
Spacing	40×10 cm^2

Irrigation Channel

Main irrigation channels	0.75 m
Sub irrigation channels	0.50 m
Experimental design	Split - Plot Design

Treatment Combinations

T_1 =	F_1S_1	T_9 =	F_1S_3
T_2 =	F_2S_1	T_{10} =	F_2S_3
T_3 =	F_3S_1	T_{11} =	F_3S_3
T_4 =	F_4S_1	T_{12} =	F_4S_3
T_5 =	F_1S_2	T_{13} =	F_1S_4
T_6 =	F_2S_2	T_{14} =	F_2S_4
T_7 =	F_3S_2	T_{15} =	F_3S_4
T_8 =	F_4S_2	T_{16} =	F_4S_4

Baby corn (Experiment 1)

Calendar of Operation and Cultural Practices

Details of field operations for baby corn during the entire period of experimentation are described below and summary of that is given in Table 3.5.

Table 3.5: Details of field operations carried out for baby corn experiment

S.No.	Operations	Date	
		2017-18	**2018-19**
1.	Pre sowing irrigation	23.11.17	21.11.18
2.	Land preparation	25.11.17	23.11.18
3.	Harrowing and planking	25.11.17	23.11.18
4.	Lay out preparation	27.11.17	24.11.18
5.	Fertilizer application		
	(a) Basal application	28.11.17	26.11.18
	(b) Top dressing	09.01.18	04.01.18
6.	Seed sowing	28.11.18	26.11.18
7.	Gap filling and thinning	30.12.18	29.12.18
8.	Weeding	01.01.18-05.01.18	05.01.19-09.01.19
9.	Earthing up	09.01.18	12.01.19
10.	Irrigation		
	(a) 1st	03.12.18	05.12.19
	(b) 2nd	29.12.18	22.12.19
	(c) 3rd	28.01.18	15.01.19
	(d) 4th	05.03.18	02.03.19
11.	Detasseling	01.03.18-05.03.18	04.03.19-09.03.19
12.	Cob plucking	06.03.18-24.03.18	10.03.19-28.03.19
13.	Harvesting (stover)	26.03.18	30.03.19

Field Preparation

The experimental trial was conducted in a rectangular plot having even topography with homogenous fertility. Pre-sowing irrigation was given two days before land preparation and land was prepared to achieve a good tilth by ploughing with tractor drawn disc plough followed by harrowing to flush out stubbles and weeds of previous crop and planking in criss-cross manner to break the clods of the field and was leveled uniformly prior to set a good seedbed. Thereafter, layout was done as per scheduled plan of the experimental design.

Variety used

Baby Corn Variety

DKC 9108 is variety is dekalb hybrid released from Monsanto. The seeds of dekalb are characterized as high yielding, drought tolerant, and resist diseases such as leaf rust, Maize Streak Virus (MSV), Grey Leaf Spot (GLS), and diplodia. Dekalb hybrids are responsive to good management and thus yields can be enhanced by adopting good agronomic practices.

The characteristics of DKC 9108 seeds are mentioned below:

- DKC 9108 is recommended for the spring planting season.
- Seeds possess golden yellow colour.
- Not sensitive to planting dates.
- Wide leaf angle between blade and stem.
- Early anthesis.
- Off white coloration of glumes of cob with good husk cover.
- Long uniform cylindrical cob with excellent tip filling,
- Tall plant length with Good standabilty.
- Compact cobs with excellent tip-filling with high shelling recovery.
- Stay green at harvest and good heat tolerance level.
- Early - medium maturity hybrid 115-120 days.
- Good tolerance to disease (GLS, MSV, blight, rust and cob rot)
- Double or sometimes triple cobbing.
- Sweet in taste with TSS about 16%.
- Prolific hybrid with high yield potential.

Seed and sowing

Baby corn

25 number of seeds were tested in petriplates, moistened and placed for overnight. On the next day counting is done to ensure the germination (%) of this variety. Then the required amount of seed per plot as per the treatment were calculated weighed. Seeds were sown on the ridge made from kudal at a spacing of 40×10 cm^2 and at a depth of 4-5 cm. Seed rate was kept 40 kg/ha for the variety DKC 9108. The date of sowing varied due to 65% of seed mortality in first year of sowing during November, so the crop was resown on 14th of March, where more than 90% of the crop established and remaining 10% had been gapfilled. In the second year of experimentation, the crop was sown on the scheduled date *i.e.* 26th of November.

Fertilizer

Sources of Fertilizer

Nitrogen	:	Urea (N- 46%) and Di- ammonium phosphate
Phosphorus	:	DAP (P_2O_5- 46% and N-18%) Di- ammonium Phosphate
Potassium	:	MOP (K_2O-60%) Muriate of potash

Application of Fertilizer

The sources of the nutrient applied for N, P and K as per treatment were urea, DAP and MOP respectively. Half of the recommended dose of nitrogen and full doses of P, K and Zn were applied as basal and the one-fourth amount of nitrogen was top dressed through urea at tillering stage of the crop at optimum soil moisture condition and rest amount was applied at knee high stage.

Strains

Three strains of KSBs (potassium solubilizing bacteria) and one fungal strain were used as seed innoculants during both the years of investigation.

Agrobacterium tumefaciens	:	KSB 17 isolates Gene bank accession no. **KJ410660** was obtained from Deptt. of Soil Sc. and Agril. Chemistry, B.H.U, Varanasi
Flavobacterium anhuiense	:	KSB 43 isolates Gene bank accession no. **KJ410663** was obtained from Deptt. of Soil Sc. and Agril. Chemistry, B.H.U, Varanasi
Rhizobium pusense	:	KSB 55 isolates Gene bank accession no. **KJ410661** was obtained from Deptt. of Soil Sc. and Agril. Chemistry, B.H.U, Varanasi
Trichoderma asperellum	:	T 42 isolates Gene bank accession no. **JN128894** isolates was obtained from Deptt. of Mycology and Pl. Pathology, B.H.U, Varanasi

(Ref: www.ncbi.nlm.nih.gov)

Mode of action of potassium solubilizing bacteria (KSB)

KSB could dissolve fixed form of minerals and release K through the production of organic and inorganic acids, acidolysis, polysaccharides, complexolysis, chelation, and exchange reactions. The cells of KSB on reaching the soil get activated and produce fresh batches of active cells. These cells grow and multiply by utilizing carbon source in the soil or from root exudates. During their growth, they solubilize the fixed potash in the soil and make it available to the plant in an easily usable form.

Dose and method of application

Seed treatment: Mix 50 ml of potassium solubilizing bacteria (KSB) with seeds alongwith 3 ml of gum acacia for 5 kg seeds for 6-8 hrs before sowing.

Properties

- It solubilizes the potash locked up in the soil into a simpler form and makes it available directly to the plants.
- It helps to prevent soil erosion and improves the soil texture and fertility.
- KSB helps to enrich soil micro-flora.

Benefits

- KSB enhances the potash uptake in plants leading to higher productivity.
- It helps to save up to 30% of normal potash fertilizer cost.
- It does not disturb the ecological balance.
- It improves the plants immune system.

Mode of action of *Trichoderma*

Trichoderma sp. is a very effective biological mean for plant disease management especially the soil born. It reduces growth, survival or infections caused by pathogens by different mechanisms like competition, antibiosis, mycoparasitism, hyphal interactions, and enzyme secretion. These fungi colonize the root epidermis and outer cortical layers and release bioactive molecules that cause walling off of the *Trichoderma thallus*. At the same time, the transcriptome and the proteome of plants are substantially altered. As a consequence, in addition to induction of pathways for resistance in plants, increased plant growth and nutrient uptake occur.

Dose and method of application

Seed treatment: Mix 50 ml of *Trichoderma* with seeds along with 3 ml of gum acacia for 5 kg seeds for 6-8 hrs before sowing.

Properties of *Trichoderma*

- Control of root and foliar pathogens
  - ➢ ¾ Induced resistance
  - ➢ ¾ Biological control of diseases by direct attack of plant pathogenic fungi
- Changes in the microfloral composition on roots
- Enhanced nutrient uptake, including but not limited to nitrogen
- Enhanced solubilization of soil nutrients
- Enhanced root development

- Increased root hair formation
- Deeper rooting

Benefits of *Trichoderma*

- **Disease control** - It is a potent biocontrol agent and used extensively for soil born diseases
- **Plant growth promoter** - These strains with plants increases the number of deep roots, thereby increasing the plant's ability to resist drought.
- **Biochemical elicitors of disease** - The strains are known to induce resistance in plants.
- **Transgenic plants** - It increased resistance to fungal growth.
- **Bioremediation** - The strain plays an important role in the bioremediation of soil that are contaminated with pesticides and herbicides.

Irrigation

First light irrigation was applied at 8 and 9 DAS (days after sowing) in the first and second year respectively and subsequent irrigations were given at 12 to 15 days interval or according to requirement of the crop during both the years when depletion of soil moisture was observed due to high evaporation and no rains. Overall, the crop received 4 post sowing irrigations during both first and second year.

Gap filling and thinning

Gap filling was done by transplanting the baby corn seedling of same physiological age in experimental field within 10 to 12 DAS to maintain the optimum plant population, wherever necessary. Subsequently thinning was practiced which allowed plenty of growing rooms for the plants as per their proper growth requirements (moisture, nutrients, light, etc.)

Earthing

Earthing up was done at 30 DAS coinciding with knee high stage to prevent any crop lodging and provide anchorage to root.

Weed control and interculture operations

Hand weedings were done at 25 to 30 DAS to remove the weeds and this was followed by light scrapping to provide proper aeration to the plant roots during both the years.

Protection measures

Application of Furadon @ 5 kg ha^{-1} at the tip of the stem was done to control shoot borers (*Chilo partellus* and *Sesamia inferens*) at 25 DAS uniformly during both the years of investigation.

Detasseling

Removal of tassels from baby corn plant by holding the tassels firmly with hand by giving an upward jerk and breaking it at the neck from all the plants immediately after their appearance is known as detasseling. It was an important practice in baby corn cultivation to avoid any pollination and subsequent fertilization. This operation is necessary for getting good quality baby corn.

Harvesting

The baby corns were removed at green stage from net plot area of each plot. The weight of green cobs and baby corn plot^{-1} were recorded and expressed in kg and finally converted into in q ha^{-1}. After removing green cobs from the plant, green fodder was harvested and weight was taken per plot in kg and expressed in q ha^{-1}.

Sampling procedure and observation

An appropriate sample is one that provides an estimate or a sample value which is as close as possible to the value that would have been obtained had all plants in the plot been measured to get the plot value. The difference between the sample value and plot value constitutes sampling error and a good sampling technique is one that gives a small sampling error. Error of any sample estimates generally decreases with the size of sampling and number of sampling unit per plot and the sampling design. However, an increase in either the size or the number of sampling unit almost always results in an increase in cost. Therefore, the choices of an appropriate sampling technique is primarily concerned with maintaining the proper balance between the sizes of the sampling unit and design to achieve the maximum precision at minimum cost. Single plot as a sampling unit and five plants per plot are considered appropriate number of plants as a sample size and is to be followed by random sampling techniques (Gomez and Gomez, 1984) for recording growth and yield attributes of the test crop. However, for dry matter plant^{-1}, destructive sampling was done from the sampling rows.

Biometric observations

Growth characters

Observation on growth characters *viz.*, initial plant stand per unit area, plant height (cm), number of leaves plant^{-1}, leaf area index (LAI), chlorophyll content and dry weight plant^{-1} (g) at 20,40,60,80 DAS and at harvest were recorded during both the years of experimentation.

Initial plant stand m^{-2}

The initial plant populations were recorded at 20 DAS from each plot and converted into plant per m^{2} and subjected to statistical analysis.

Final plants stand m^{-2}

The final plant population were recorded from each plot at the time of cob harvest, converted to plant per m^2 and subjected to statistical analysis.

Plant height (cm)

The height was measured from five randomly selected plants (with tag marked on it) from base to tip of flag leaf of sampling area, preferentially from third row at successive stages of crop growth starting from 20, 40, 60, 80 DAS to harvest. Plant height of the baby corn was recorded with the help of meter scale from base of plant to the tip of upper most leaf of the plant, averaged and expressed in cm.

Number of leaves plant^{-1}

The number of functional (usually green) leaves plant^{-1} was counted at 20, 40, 60, 80 DAS and at harvest and expressed as average number of leaves plant^{-1}.

Leaf area (cm^2)

The length and width (at the broadest point) of leaves were recorded, and manipulated by a conversion factor(k) of 0.73308 to get the actual leaf area (McKee, 1964) and then multiplied by the number of leaves to get the total leaf area plant^{-1}.

Leaf Area Index

Myneni *et al.* (1997) defined LAI as the maximum projected leaf area per unit ground area. Leaf area index was computed for each treatment using the formula given below:

$$LAI = \frac{\text{Total leaf area per plant}}{\text{Land area occupied by plant}}$$

Chlorophyll Content

The SPAD (Soil Plant Analysis Development) -502 chlorophyll/ SPAD meter (Minolta corporation Ramsey, N.J.) was used for rapid and non-destructive estimation of extractable chlorophyll in leaves at 30 and 45 DAS. This instrument uses a silicon photo-iodide for transmittance of light emitted by two lights emitting diode-through leaf sample, one with peak emittance at 650 nm, where absorbance by chlorophyll is high and relatively unaffected by carotene and another with peak emittance at 950 nm, where absorbance by chlorophyll is negligible. The SPAD reading is correlated with leaf chlorophyll concentration and calculated from the transmittance through leaf tissue at these two wavelengths. It is a simple portable, diagnostic tool, which measures relative greenness/chlorophyll content of leaves. For taking SPAD reading, topmost fully expanded leaf from sample plants (three plants from centre three rows) were selected and expressed in SPAD unit.

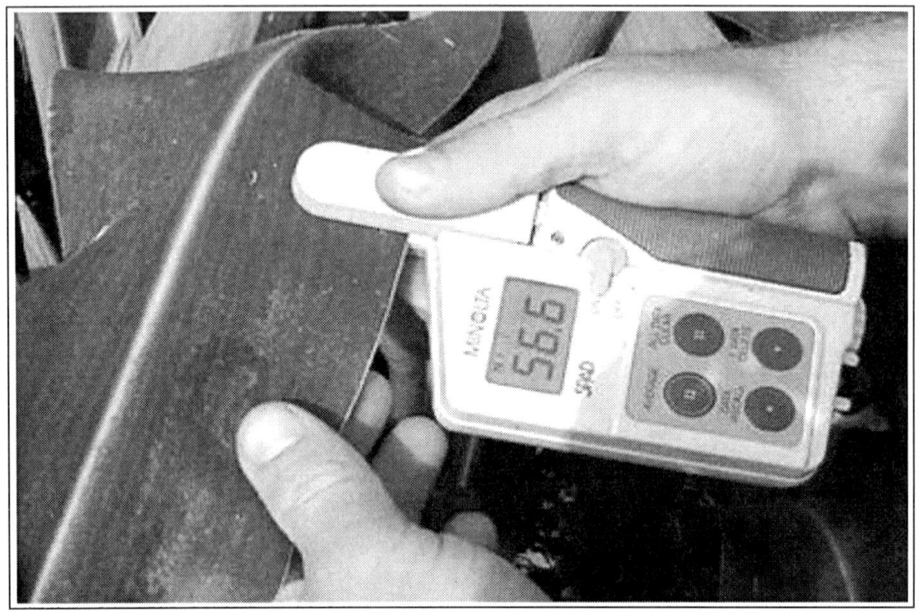

Fig. 3.4

Dry matter production plant^{-1} (g)

Five plants were selected randomly (at 20, 40, 60, 80 DAS and at harvest) from sampling area preferentially from third row of each plot and were cut from the base, sun dried and then transferred to a thermostatically controlled dry oven, regulated at a temperature of 70°C for 48 hours and weighed to work out the dry matter production plant^{-1}.

Yield and yield attributes

Baby corn length (cm)

Five cobs were selected from the tagged plants in each harvest randomly and the length of each baby corn was measured after dehusking the cob. Baby corn length was computed by averaging the mean of all harvest.

Baby corn girth (cm)

The girth of each of five randomly selected baby cob used for measuring the baby corn length in each harvest measured after dehusking with vernier caliper and then average baby corn girth was worked out treatment wise.

Barren plants m^{-2}

Number of plants not bearing baby corns were counted from each plot separately and finally converted into per m^{2}.

Number of cobs plant^{-1}

Five plants in each plot tagged for recording growth observations were used for this purpose and total number of cobs from each plant were recorded up to final harvest of crop and averaged to get number of cobs plant^{-1}.

Number of cobs ha^{-1}

Total number of cobs from each plot per picking/plucking were calculated and recorded up to final harvest of crop and averaged to get number of cob ha^{-1}. The picking/plucking was done on regular basis upto final harvest and denoted as 1st plucking, 2nd plucking etc. till harvest. The average interval of plucking was maintained at 3 days.

Baby corn (with husk) weight (g) cob^{-1}

Just after picking/plucking, the weight of baby corn with husk were recorded for the same five tagged plant for each harvest individually, summed and averaged for determination of baby corn weight plant^{-1} (g).

Baby corn (without husk) weight (g) cob^{-1}

The cobs of each harvest were dehusked and their fresh weights were recorded, averaged and expressed as baby corn (without husk) weight (g) plant^{-1}.

Baby corn (with husk): baby corn (without husk) ratio

Total baby corn (with husk) weight and baby corn (without husk) weight recorded separately from each plot were used for calculating their ratio.

Baby corn (with husk) and baby corn (without husk) yield (q ha^{-1})

The baby corn (with husk) and baby corn (without husk) yield obtained and summed for total yield were expressed separately in kg plot^{-1} and presented in q ha^{-1}.

Stover yield (q ha^{-1})

The plants were cut at ground level after removal of cobs and stover yield was noted in kg plot^{-1} and converted into q ha^{-1}. The whole stover after harvesting was chopped into small pieces and spread over each plot uniformly and incorporated into the soil.

Soil analysis

The soil samples collected before sowing and after harvesting of the crops were air dried and powdered in a mortar to pass through a 2 mm sieve. They were then stored in labeled and scaled polythene bags for chemical estimation. The physical and chemical properties were determined by methods given in table 3.3.

Qualitative studies

Plant analysis

Treatment wise from each plot, the plant samples (baby corn and stover) were collected for chemical estimation of N, P and K. The leaves, stem and baby corn were dried in an oven at 65 ± 5 °C and then ground thoroughly in a Willey mill to pass through 30 mesh sieve. The powdered materials were collected in butter paper bag for chemical analysis.

Nitrogen content (%) in baby corn and stover

Nitrogen content was estimated using the modified Kjeldahl method (Jackson, 1973).

Phosphorus content (%) in baby corn and stover

Phosphorus was estimated by Vanado-molybdo-phosphoric acid yellow colour method using the Barton's reagent as suggested by Jackson (1973).

Potassium content (%) in baby corn and stover

The potassium was determined with the help of flame photometer (Jackson, 1958).

Nutrient removal (kg ha^{-1})

The nutrient removal (kg ha^{-1}) by baby corn and stover were obtained by multiplying baby corn and fodder dry yield with their respective nutrient content (%). Since fresh baby corn and its fodder contain very high amount of moisture, fresh baby corn as well as stover were converted into dry yield. The total nutrient removal was determined by their summation. Total N, P and K removal were calculated for each treatment separately and expressed in kg ha^{-1}.

Protein content

Protein content in baby cob and stover were worked out by multiplying the nitrogen content with the factor 6.25 (Humphries, 1956).

Carbohydrate content

The carbohydrate content in baby corn was estimated by Anthron method as per the methodology of Hedge and Hofreiter (1962).

Sugar content

The sugar content in baby corn was determined as per method described by Dubois *et al.* (1956).

Starch content

The starch content in baby corn was determined as per method described by Dekker and Richards, (1971).

Moong (Experiment 2)

2nd trial: Moong

Moong was planted in the same lay out after harvesting of baby corn without any fertilizer to observe the residual effect.

Year of experimentation	Consecutive two years *i.e.* 2017-18 and 2018-19
No. of treatment combinations	16
No. of replication	4
Total no. of plots	64
Plot size	4.0 × 2.8m^2
Experimental design	Split- Plot Design
Crop	Moong
Moong variety	Hindu University Moong-16(HUM-16)

Calendar of operation and cultural practices

Details of field operations for moong during the entire period of experimentation are described below and presented in table 3.6.

Table 3.6: Details of operations carried out in moong experiment

S.No.	Operations	Date	
		2018	2019
1.	Glyphosate application	01.04.18	02.04.19
2.	Seed sowing	06.04.18	07.04.19
3.	Gap filling	14.04.18	15.04.19
4.	Thinning	18.04.18	17.04.19
5.	Furadon granules	19.04.18	21.04.19
6.	Hand weeding	27.04.18-29.04.18	28.04.19-30.04.19
7.	Irrigation	As and when needed	As and when needed
8.	Harvesting	08.06.18	09.06.19
9.	Threshing	10.06.18	11.06.19

Field preparation and residual application

After harvesting of baby corn the whole plant biomass of each plot was chopped and distributed between rows and then glyphosate was applied to control annual and perennial grasses and broad-leaved weeds. Like that of the first crop the row were opened with kudal and the seeds of moong (HUM-16) were dibbled.

Seed sowing

25 seeds were tested in petri-dish before sowing to ascertain its germination (%) and viability and after that required amount of seed per plot was calculated and weighed. Seeds were sown by opening rows with

kudal, at 30 cm spacing of the field. The seeds of moong (HUM-16) were dibbled on 16th September 2018 and 23rd April 2019. The sowing of moong in the first year was delayed by three months because of continuous rainfall.

Gap filling and thinning

Gap filling was taken up 8 days after sowing to maintain optimum plant population, while thinning was carried out 12 days after sowing by retaining the healthy seedling.

Hand weeding

The weeds were removed by one manual weeding at four week crop stage during both the years of investigation.

Irrigation

The crop was irrigated as and when required.

Plant protection

Furadon granules (at the rate of 5 kg ha^{-1}) were applied into the whorls of each plant at 43 days after sowing to control the incidence of shoot fly.

Harvesting and threshing

The plants from net plot were cut close to the ground level and pods were separated. The pods from net plot were sun-dried, threshed and grain yield per plot was recorded after 7 days of sun drying. The stover was harvested and weight was taken and expressed in q ha^{-1}.

Yield attributes and yield

No. of pods per plant (g)

The grains from the sun dried ears of five plants were separated and the weight of the grains was recorded. The average grain weight per plant was expressed as gram per plant.

Test weight (g)

Thousand grains from each treatment were counted randomly weighed and expressed in g.

Number of grains per pod

Grain number pod^{-1} was calculated by counting the number of grains from the sun dried five pods and the average grain number pod^{-1} was recorded.

Grain yield (q ha $^{-1}$)

Plants from each net plot were harvested at physiological maturity and ear heads were separated, air dried, threshed, cleaned and weighed. Grain yield ha^{-1} was worked out and expressed in q ha^{-1}

Stover yield (q ha^{-1})

Stover yield of moong was recorded after harvesting the stalks from each net plot except grain and expressed on per hectare basis.

Chemical analyses of plant samples

Collection and preparation of plant samples

The plant samples (grain and green fodder) were collected for chemical estimation of N, P and K. The green fodder samples and grain were dried in an oven at 65 ± 5 °C and then ground thoroughly in a Willey mill to pass through 30 mesh sieves. The powdered material collected in butter paper bag was used for chemical analyses.

Nitrogen content in grain and straw (%)

Nitrogen content was estimated using the modified Kjeldahl method Jackson (1973).

Phosphorus content in grain and straw (%)

Phosphorus was estimated by Vanado-molybdo-phosphoric acid yellow colour method using the Barton's reagent as suggested by Jackson (1973).

Potassium content in grain and straw (%)

The potassium was determined with the help of flame photometer (Jackson, 1958).

Nutrient removal by grain and straw of crop (kg ha^{-1})

Removal of N, P, K (kg ha^{-1}) by moong grain and straw were estimated by multiplying moong grain and straw dry yield with their respective nutrient content (%) and total nutrient removal was determined by their summation.

Soil analysis

Preparation of soil samples

The physico-chemical properties of the experimental field were worked out before the beginning of the study. Random soil samples (Black *et al.*, 1965) after harvest of the crops were collected from the depth of 0-30 cm and brought to the laboratory, air dried and crushed to pass through 20 mm mesh sieve. Representative samples were taken for analyses and the results are presented in table 3.3.

Microbial population (Cfu/g of soil)

Microbiological studies in respect of total bacterial, actinomycetes and fungal count were carried out using standard plate count technique (Wollum, 1982).The microbial population estimation was done before sowing of baby corn, at 60 DAS and after harvest of baby corn followed by before sowing of moong, 60 DAS and at harvest of moong during both the years of experimentation.

Serial dilution method

Fresh soil samples from two places of each plot were taken in a laboratory for serial dilution. One gram of each of the moist soil sample was transferred to 99 mL sterilized distilled water blank under aseptic conditions resulting in 10^{-2} dilution. From this dilution blank, 1 mL was taken and added to 9 mL of dilution blank to make further serial dilutions upto 10^{-6}.

For enumerating microbial population of soil, standard pour plate method was used after serial dilution. The media used for total bacteria, actinomycties and fungi were Nutrient Agar, Rose Bengal Agar and Ken knight and Munnier's Agar repectively.

Temperature and time of incubation for different nutrient media:

S. No.	Media used	Temperature range (°C)	Incubation period (Days)
1.	Nutrient Agar	30-32	4-6
2.	Rose Bengal	28	2
3.	Ken knight and Munniar's Agar	28	7-10

Calculation of microbial count: average no. of colonies per plate for a given dilution was multiplied by dilution factor to obtain the viable count or cfu per gram soil.

Soil microbial biomass carbon (μg C g^{-1} soil)

Soil microbial biomass carbon (SMBC) was determined by Fumigation –extraction method as per the procedure given by Vance et al. (1987). The SMBC estimation was done before sowing of baby corn, at 60 DAS and after harvest of baby corn followed by before sowing of moong, 60 DAS and at harvest of moong during both the years of experimentation.

Twenty g soil (air dried) was fumigated with 50 mL of ethanol free chloroform in a desiccator. Ethanol free chloroform was prepared by passing 100 ml chloroform where a clear distinct zone was visible in a separating funnel. After 24 hrs fumigation at 25°C, chloroform was removed by repeated evacuations. The fumigated soil samples were extracted with 80 mL of 0.5 M K_2SO_4 for 30 min. on a rotary shaker at 160 rpm and filtered. 8ml of filtrate was refluxed with 2 ml of $K_2Cr_2O_7$ and 15 ml of diacid mixture (H_2SO_4:H_3PO_4::2:1) for half an hour on hot plate at 150 °C with three drops of phenanthroline indicator solution. After cooling the mixture was titrated with FAS solution. Similar procedure was followed for non- fumigated soil samples also.

SMBC(μg C g^{-1} soil) = Extractable C in fumigated soil- Extractable C in non-fumigated soil.

Statistical analyses

The data collected from the experiment at harvest were subjected to statistical analyses as described by Gomez and Gomez (1984). The level of significance used for 'F' tests was P=0.05. Year wise data as well as pooled data were analyzed. Critical Difference (CD) values were calculated at 5 per cent probability level, where the F test was found to be significant. The results are presented in tabular forms and wherever necessary, depicted in figures.

Economics

The price of inputs and market price of the output (current) of crops were considered to work out the cost of cultivation and gross returns. The net return ha^{-1} was calculated by deducting the cost of cultivation ha^{-1} from gross income.

Benefit: Cost ratio was worked out as follows:

$$\text{B: C ratio} = \frac{\text{Cost of cultivation a input (₹ ha}^{-1}\text{)}}{\text{Gross income output a (₹ ha}^{-1}\text{)}}$$

Experimental Case Study for KSB and *Trichoderma* on Baby Corn and its Residual Studies on Moongbean

The detailed description of experimental findings are discussed in this chapter. All experiments were carried out during the rabi seasons of 2017-18 and 2018-19 at the agricultural research farm of Banaras Hindu University. In this chapter, an attempt has been made to ascertain the degree of variation exhibited by various parameters of plant and soil characters due to treatment variables. The data have been statistically analyzed and incorporated at appropriate places in tables. Data on the growth, yield parameters, yield, quality and removal of N, P and K by the crop as well as nutrient status of the experimental site were recorded at the respective stages (20, 40, 60, 80 and at harvest) and presented accordingly. Residual effects of the treatments were noted on the yield attributes and yield of moongbean and nutrient status of the soil after harvesting of the crop. Economics of both baby corn and succeeding crop of moongbean were also worked out and the data thus obtained were analyzed using standard statistical procedure. Main effects were described first and interaction effects (if significant) were narrated thereafter.

Baby corn

Growth Characters

Initial and Final Plant Stand

Fertilizer Levels

Data presented in table 4.1 indicated that the initial plant stand of baby corn differed significantly under different fertility levels during both the years.

Table 4.1: Effect of fertility levels and microbial strains on initial plant stand, final plant stand, barren plant (m^{-2}) and barrenness (%) of baby corn

Treatments	Initial plant stand (m^{-2})		Final plant stand (m^{-2})		Barren plant (m^{-2})		Barrenness (%)	
	2017-18	2018-19	017-18	2018-19	2017-18	2018-19	2017-18	2018-19
Fertility levels (RDF)								
F_1 (100%NP+25%K)	12.63	12.79	11.59	11.67	0.60	0.55	5.20	4.71
F_2 (100%NP+50%K)	12.64	12.81	11.65	11.71	0.56	0.51	4.83	4.36
F_3 (100%NP+75%K)	12.82	12.90	11.73	11.82	0.51	0.46	4.36	3.90
F_4 (100% NPK)	12.84	12.94	11.78	11.87	0.49	0.44	4.12	3.70
SEm±	0.01	0.02	0.06	0.05	0.001	0.001	0.06	0.08
C.D. (P=0.05)	0.03	0.05	0.18	0.15	0.003	0.004	0.19	0.25
Microbial strains								
S_1 (*Agrobacterium* sp.)	12.74	12.89	11.74	11.79	0.49	0.46	4.17	3.90
S_2 (*Flavobacterium* sp.)	12.68	12.82	11.59	11.75	0.52	0.50	4.49	4.26
S_3 (*Rhizobium* sp.)	12.69	12.85	11.66	11.76	0.51	0.48	4.37	4.08
S_4 (*Trichoderma* sp.)	12.72	12.86	11.70	11.77	0.50	0.47	4.27	3.99
SEm±	0.01	0.01	0.02	0.03	0.001	0.001	0.03	0.04
C.D. (P=0.05)	0.02	0.03	0.06	0.09	0.003	0.003	0.09	0.12

Significant difference in final plant stand was also observed due to different fertility levels at harvest with the higher being observed at 100%NP+75%K (F_3) although it remained at par with 100%NPK (F_4).

Microbial innoculum

A critical analysis of the data clearly indicated that the applications of both bacterial and fungal innoculum improved the initial and final plant stand of baby corn and brought about significant differences at both the stages of crop growth. Among microbial innoculum *Agrobacterium* sp. (S_1) registered the highest plant stand followed by *Trichoderma* sp. during both the years.

Interaction

Interaction between fertility levels and microbial innoculum could not reach the level of significance during any of the years.

Barren plants m^{-2} (no. m^{-2})

Fertilizer Levels

Data presented in table 4.1 indicated that the number of barren plants m^{-2} was significantly affected by fertility levels and microbial innoculum during both the years of experimentation.

The data indicated a decline in number of barren plant m^{-2} with increasing fertility level. Significant reduction in the number of barren plant m^{-2} was found with 100%NP+75%K (F_3) and 100%NPK (F_4) which remained at par with each other. As compared to F_1, on an average of two years data F_3 registered 18.56% lesser number of barren plants than 100%NP+25%K (F_1). Overall it was in the decreasing order of $F_1 > F_2 > F_3 > F_4$.

Microbial innoculum

Significant decline in the number of barren plants m^{-2} was found with *Agrobacterium* sp. (S_1) strain followed by S_4, S_3, S_2. as compared to *Flavobacterium* sp. (S_2) recorded 7.37% lesser barren plants during 2017-18 and 2018-19 put together.

Interaction

Interaction between fertility levels and microbial innoculum could not reach the level of significance during any of the years.

Barrenness (%)

The data on barrenness (%) summarized in Table 4.1 clearly showed that barrenness was markedly influenced by different levels of fertility and microbial innoculum during both the years of study.

Fertilizer Levels

A close examination of the data revealed a significant decrease in barrenness percentage with F_3 and F_4 fertility during both the years of investigation. It was in the order of F_4, $F_3 < F_2 < F_1$.

Microbial innoculum

Further examination of the data indicated that application of microbial innoculum resulted in marked variation in barrenness. Barrenness was reduced significantly by *Agrobacterium* sp. (S_1) and this was followed by *Trichoderma* sp. (S_4), *Rhizobium* sp. (S_3) and *Flavobacterium sp.* (S_2) respectively.

Interaction

None of the interactions could exert significant influence on barrenness in any of the years.

Plant height

The data on plant height (cm) as affected by different levels of fertility and microbial innoculum at 20, 40, 60, 80 DAS and harvest (Table 4.2), revealed that plant height increased as growth progressed from 20 DAS to harvest during both the years irrespective of experimental variables. Plant height remained a little bit higher during second year (2018-19) in comparison to first year at all the stages of plant growth.

Fertilizer Levels

It was apparent from the data (Table 4.2) that with an increase in fertility levels there was a corresponding increase in plant height and significant differences in plant height due to different fertility levels were observed. At 80 DAS, 100%NP+75%K (F_3) recorded 23.99% and 11.52% more height than 100%NP+25%K (F_1) and 100%NP+50%K (F_2) the level where the lowest plant height was observed averaged during both the years. At all the growth stages, 100%NP+75%K (F_3) remained at par with 100%NPK (F_4) and was in the order of F_4, $F_3 > F_2 > F_1$.

Microbial innoculum

Significant differences in plant height were also observed due to the application of microbial innoculum. The tallest plant was recorded with the *Agrobacterium* strain which was significantly superior to S_2 (*Flavobacterium* sp.) and S_3 (*Rhizobium* sp.) but remained at par with S_4 (*Trichoderma* sp.) at all the plant growth stages. *Agrobacterium* sp. was found to produce plant with 15.60% more height than *Flavobacterium sp.* (S_2) at 80 DAS on the basis of two years data.

Table 4.2: Effect of fertility levels and microbial strains on plant height (cm) at different growth stages of baby corn

Treatments	Plant height (cm)									
	20 DAS		40DAS		60 DAS		80DAS		At harvest	
	2017-18	2018-19	2017-18	2018-19	2017-18	2018-19	2017-18	2018-19	2017-18	2018-19
Fertility levels (RDF)										
F_1 (100%NP+25%K)	18.22	19.15	49.12	51.41	98.97	99.63	108.94	112.80	113.28	118.76
F_2 (100%NP+50%K)	19.78	20.24	51.53	52.44	102.48	103.97	119.00	122.86	123.35	126.47
F_3 (100%NP+75%K)	20.88	21.73	53.89	53.56	105.58	107.07	134.92	137.80	133.45	135.35
F_4 (100% NPK)	21.71	22.68	54.64	55.65	107.61	109.89	138.20	139.15	135.28	140.05
SEm±	0.51	0.66	1.04	1.07	1.68	1.79	1.34	1.05	2.15	2.21
C.D. (P=0.05)	1.88	2.43	3.01	3.19	5.12	5.43	4.29	3.37	6.48	6.65
Microbial strains										
S_1 (*Agrobacterium* sp.)	18.27	22.44	49.67	52.49	104.05	114.55	131.79	135.28	130.89	134.37
S_2 (*Flavobacterium* sp.)	15.11	17.40	46.75	48.44	89.67	91.49	114.50	116.53	107.96	115.08
S_3 (*Rhizobium* sp.)	15.89	19.11	39.01	42.99	97.04	99.71	124.04	126.32	124.06	126.96
S_4 (*Trichoderma* sp.)	16.09	21.11	47.02	50.52	101.54	109.69	129.72	132.48	125.89	128.66
SEm±	0.43	0.51	0.98	1.01	1.45	1.68	1.00	1.12	2.01	2.16
C.D.(P=0.05)	1.23	1.46	2.89	3.06	4.62	5.06	2.86	3.21	6.07	6.49

Interaction

Interaction effect between fertility levels and microbial innoculum were found to be significant at 80 DAS only. Perusal of data (Table 4.3) revealed that the combination of 100% NP+75% K (F_3) and *Agrobacterium sp.* (S_1) recorded higher plant height (141.18 and 142.66 cm) but remained at par with 100%NPK (F_4) during first and second year respectively.

Number of green leaves plant^{-1}

It was apparent from the data (Table 4.4) that the different treatments differed significantly in producing the number of green leaves at 20, 40, 60, 80 DAS and at harvest during both the years of experimentation.

Fertilizer Levels

The data exhibited a progressive increase in the number of green leaves plant^{-1} with the advancement of age upto 80 DAS irrespective of the treatments. 100%NP+75%K (F_3) which remained at par with 100%NPK (F_4) produced significantly more number of green leaves than other fertility levels. Overall it remained in the order of F_4, F_3> F_2> F_1 during both the years.

Microbial innoculum

Marked variation in number of green leaves per plant due to different innoculum was also observed. *Agrobacterium* (S_1) produced the highest number of green leaves per plant which remained significantly superior to all other microbial innoculum at 20, 40, 60, 80 DAS and at harvest.

Interaction

Interaction was not found significant in respect to number of green leaves per plant at any of the growth stages of the test crop.

Leaf Area Plant^{-1} (cm^2)

Scanning of the data recorded on leaf area plant^{-1} at all the growth stages (Table 4.5) clearly indicated that leaf area plant^{-1} was significantly affected by various treatments except at 20 DAS in case of microbial innoculum during both the experimental years.

Fertilizer Levels

Increasing fertility levels showed corresponding improvement in the leaf area of baby corn. Fertility level 100%NP+75%K (F_3) and 100%NPK (F_4) which remained statistically at par with each other resulted in significant increase in leaf area of baby corn over all other treatments at all the crop growth stages. Overall, the effect of fertility levels on leaf area was in the order of F_4, F_3> F_2> F_1.

Table 4.3: Interaction effect of fertility levels and microbial strains on plant height at 80 DAS

Treatments	2017-18					2018-19				
	S_1	S_2	S_3	S_4	Mean	S_1	S_2	S_3	S_4	Mean
Fertility levels × microbial strains										
F_1 (100% NP+25%K)	116.66	97.36	106.63	115.11	108.94	120.84	100.93	110.46	118.97	112.80
F_2 (100% NP+50%K)	125.95	108.63	117.50	123.92	119.00	129.88	112.44	121.33	127.78	122.86
F_3 (100% NP+75%K)	141.18	124.44	132.43	138.66	134.93	144.66	124.72	134.16	141.66	137.80
F_4 (100% of NPK)	143.43	128.59	139.61	141.12	138.20	147.73	128.01	139.34	141.51	139.15
Mean	131.79	115.50	124.04	129.72		137.28	116.53	126.32	132.48	
SEm ±			1.83					2.00		
CD (P=0.05) different sub treatment vs same main treatment			5.27					5.72		
SEm ±			2.19					2.21		
CD (P=0.05) different sub treatment for different main treatment			5.90					6.12		

S_1 - *Agrobacterium* sp., S_2 - *Flavobacterium* sp., S_3 - *Rhizobium* sp., S_4 - *Trichoderma* sp.

Table 4.4: Effect of fertility levels and microbial strains on number of green leaves plant^{-1} at different growth stages of baby corn

Treatments	Number of green leaves plant $^{-1}$									
	20 DAS		40 DAS		60 DAS		80 DAS		At harvest	
	2017-18	2018-19	2017-18	2018-19	2017-18	2018-19	2017-18	2018-19	2017-18	2018-19
Fertility levels (RDF)										
F_1 (100%NP+25%K)	5.29	6.10	9.02	9.85	10.25	10.29	11.89	11.92	11.58	11.71
F_2 (100%NP+50%K)	5.41	6.21	9.86	9.99	10.63	10.47	12.29	12.31	11.94	12.08
F_3 (100%NP+75%K)	5.66	6.39	9.94	10.02	10.85	10.79	13.08	12.99	13.23	13.12
F_4 (100% NPK)	6.12	6.70	10.13	10.30	11.21	11.25	13.87	13.90	13.66	13.75
SEm±	0.15	0.16	0.07	0.09	0.13	0.19	0.29	0.31	0.32	0.34
C.D. (P=0.05)	0.47	0.32	0.21	0.28	0.38	0.47	0.87	0.94	0.97	1.05
Microbial strains										
S_1 (*Agrobacterium* sp.)	6.04	6.15	10.19	10.26	11.18	11.40	13.51	13.59	13.09	13.45
S_2 (*Flavobacterium* sp.)	5.27	5.31	8.63	9.48	9.74	10.62	12.10	12.15	11.16	11.82
S_3 (*Rhizobium* sp.)	5.59	5.65	9.65	9.65	10.13	10.87	12.24	12.27	12.05	12.48
S_4 (*Trichoderma* sp.)	5.81	5.86	9.92	9.95	10.81	11.01	13.10	13.14	12.54	12.72
SEm±	0.05	0.09	0.08	0.10	0.12	0.13	0.11	0.12	0.25	0.29
C.D.(P=0.05)	0.15	0.29	0.26	0.30	0.36	0.37	0.33	0.36	0.76	0.90

Table 4.5: Effect of fertility levels and microbial strains on leaf area (cm^2) per plant at different growth stages of baby corn

Treatments	Leaf area (cm^2)									
	20 DAS		40DAS		60 DAS		80DAS		At harvest	
	2017-18	2018-19	2017-18	2018-19	2017-18	2018-19	2017-18	2018-19	2017-18	2018-19
Fertility levels (RDF)										
F_1 (100%NP+25%K)	83.70	87.40	859.00	989.90	1820.30	2168.20	3171.30	3204.90	2820.50	3050.50
F_2 (100%NP+50%K)	107.10	114.30	949.90	1004.00	2542.50	2804.80	4050.10	4129.40	3820.60	3956.30
F_3 (100%NP+75%K)	133.41	140.77	1278.44	1372.41	3469.80	3638.70	4938.30	5006.80	4879.00	4956.60
F_4 (100% NPK)	144.20	151.50	1415.90	1535.20	3999.50	4163.60	5419.40	5496.90	5299.00	5334.20
SEm±	3.40	3.90	44.10	49.60	171.10	173.50	151.20	152.20	141.10	144.90
C.D. (P=0.05)	10.88	11.76	147.50	163.90	531.90	533.20	482.50	495.50	449.80	450.90
Microbial strains										
S_1 (*Agrobacterium* sp.)	96.60	103.70	1401.92	1521.22	968.10	1028.10	2193.40	2399.60	4014.00	4338.90
S_2 (*Flavobacterium* sp.)	94.08	100.69	845.02	975.92	801.90	807.00	1387.50	1467.14	3095.00	3379.10
S_3 (*Rhizobium* sp.)	94.20	101.80	935.92	990.02	816.80	851.65	1526.70	1625.80	3336.60	3617.40
S_4 (*Trichoderma* sp.)	96.00	102.20	1224.42	1300.02	842.40	893.58	1750.54	1911.40	3552.10	3854.25
SEm±	1.51	1.92	37.89	43.82	139.99	143.44	147.97	149.53	129.59	131.79
C.D. (P=0.05)	NS	NS	115.22	133.96	441.96	471.12	451.19	469.61	396.77	405.40

Microbial innoculum

Significant differences in leaf area due to microbial innoculum were recorded at all the stages of growth except at 20 DAS. *Agrobacterium* recorded the highest leaf area than other innoculum followed by *Trichoderma* sp. at all the growth stages of baby corn.

Interaction

None of the interactions between fertility levels and microbial innoculum could reach the level of significance during any of the years.

Leaf Area Index (LAI)

The leaf area index as affected by various treatments at different growth stages (20, 40, 60 and 80 DAS and at harvest) are presented in Table 4.6.

Fertilizer Levels

Fertility level 100%NP+75%K (F_3) which remained at par with 100%NPK (F_4) showed maximum leaf area index in baby corn at 20, 40, 60 and 80 DAS of crop growth during 2017-18 and 2018-19. The lowest LAI was recorded with 100%NP+25%K (F_1) and it was in the order of F_4, F_3> F_2> F_1.

Microbial innoculum

Significant improvement in leaf area index of baby corn was recorded with *Agrobacterium* sp. (S_1) at all the crop growth stages and this was followed by *Trichoderma* sp. (S_4), during both the years.

Interaction

Interaction failed to reach the level of significance during any of the years of investigation.

Chlorophyll Content of Leaf (SPAD)

The data on chlorophyll content of leaf (SPAD value) as affected by different levels of fertilizers and microbial innoculum recorded at 20, 40, 60, 80 DAS and at harvest are presented in table 4.7.

Fertilizer Levels

The data revealed that leaf chlorophyll content (SPAD value) recorded at 20, 40, 60, 80 DAS and at harvest differed significantly due to different fertility levels. The chlorophyll content increased significantly with fertility levels upto 100% NP+75%K (F_3) and 100%NPK (F_4) at all the growth stages but they remained statistically at par with each other, while the lowest was found with F_1 (100%NP+25%K) at all growth stages during both the years of experimentation.

Table 4.6: Effect of fertility levels and microbial strains on leaf area index (LAI) at different growth stages of baby corn

Treatments	Leaf area Index (LAI)									
	20 DAS		40 DAS		60 DAS		80 DAS		At harvest	
	2017-18	2018-19	2017-18	2018-19	2017-18	2018-19	2017-18	2018-19	2017-18	2018-19
Fertility levels (RDF)										
F_1 (100%NP+25%K)	0.10	0.11	1.05	1.21	2.23	2.65	3.88	3.92	3.45	3.73
F_2 (100%NP+50%K)	0.13	0.14	1.16	1.23	3.11	3.43	4.95	5.05	4.67	4.84
F_3 (100%NP+75%K)	0.16	0.17	1.61	1.68	4.24	4.45	6.04	6.12	5.97	6.05
F_4 (100% NPK)	0.18	0.19	1.73	1.88	4.89	5.09	6.63	6.72	6.48	6.52
SEm±	0.01	0.01	0.05	0.09	0.24	0.32	0.27	0.31	0.28	0.31
C.D. (P=0.05)	0.03	0.03	0.15	0.27	0.73	1.01	0.81	0.95	0.86	0.95
Microbial strains										
S_1 (*Agrobacterium* sp.)	0.12	0.13	1.18	1.26	2.68	2.93	4.91	5.31	4.45	4.71
S_2 (*Flavobacterium* sp.)	0.11	0.12	0.98	0.99	1.70	1.79	3.79	4.13	3.43	3.77
S_3 (*Rhizobium* sp.)	0.12	0.12	1.00	1.04	1.87	1.99	4.08	4.42	3.73	3.92
S_4 (*Trichoderma* sp.)	0.12	0.13	1.03	1.09	2.14	2.34	4.34	4.71	3.97	4.21
SEm ±	0.001	0.002	0.05	0.07	0.14	0.27	0.19	0.22	0.21	0.23
C.D.(P=0.05)	NS	NS	0.14	0.22	0.41	0.83	0.56	0.66	0.64	0.70

Table 4.7: Effect of fertility levels and microbial strains on chlorophyll content of leaves (SPAD value) at different growth stages of baby corn

Treatments	Chlorophyll content (SPAD value)									
	20 DAS		40 DAS		60 DAS		80 DAS		At harvest	
	2017-18	2018-19	2017-18	2018-19	2017-18	2018-19	2017-18	2018-19	2017-18	2018-19
Fertility levels (RDF)										
F_1 (100%NP+25%K)	19.21	22.42	24.91	28.02	36.04	37.20	41.31	43.35	37.42	38.44
F_2 (100%NP+50%K)	20.11	23.36	26.13	29.91	38.40	39.15	44.79	44.81	40.89	40.90
F_3 (100%NP+75%K)	20.98	23.97	29.25	31.56	40.64	42.51	46.06	46.74	43.41	44.55
F_4 (100% NPK)	21.54	24.85	29.54	32.47	41.72	43.97	48.41	49.39	43.64	44.83
SEm±	0.21	0.32	0.25	0.33	0.35	0.51	0.89	0.91	0.89	0.92
C.D. (P=0.05)	0.63	0.96	0.76	0.99	1.09	1.54	2.39	2.69	2.69	2.76
Microbial strains										
S_1 (*Agrobacterium* sp.)	20.11	20.17	28.46	29.78	43.16	43.93	47.58	48.01	39.28	41.17
S_2 (*Flavobacterium* sp.)	19.25	19.41	26.25	26.69	35.57	36.77	41.22	42.27	36.67	37.13
S_3 (*Rhizobium* sp.)	19.94	19.98	28.00	27.15	39.32	40.02	43.65	44.01	37.52	38.03
S_4 (*Trichoderma* sp.)	20.01	20.10	27.73	27.93	40.93	41.44	45.03	45.39	38.05	40.73
SEm±	0.02	0.04	0.21	0.26	0.31	0.35	0.61	0.77	0.85	0.87
C.D.(P=0.05)	0.07	0.13	0.63	0.8	0.95	1.08	1.83	2.32	2.58	2.61

Microbial innoculum

Significant differences were observed at all the growth stages of the crop in respect of chlorophyll content (SPAD value) due to microbial innoculum. *Agrobacterium* sp. (S_1) exhibited the highest chlorophyll content followed by *Trichoderma* sp. (S_4) during both the years. It was in order of $S_1 > S_4 > S_3 > S_2$.

Interaction

Interaction between fertility levels and microbial innoculum could not reach the level of significance during any of the years of investigation.

Fresh wt. plant^{-1} (g) (excluding underground root system)

The data of fresh wt. plant^{-1} (g) excluding its underground root system were recorded and presented in table 4.8.

Fertilizer Levels

The data revealed that fresh wt. plant^{-1} (g) at 20, 40, 60, 80 DAS and at harvest differed significantly due to different fertility levels. It was found higher with 100% NP+75%K (F_3) and 100%NPK (F_4) which remained at par at all the stages of growth.

The fresh wt. at 100% NP+75%K (F_3) registered 21.19% increase at 60 DAS, 18.52% at 80 DAS and 9.58 % at harvest over F_1 (100%NP+25%K) where the lowest fresh wt. was recorded during both the years of experimentation. Finally it was in the order of F_4, $F_3 > F_2 > F_1$.

Microbial innoculum

The variation in fresh wt. per plant due to microbial innoculum was found to be significant at all the growth stages of crop during both the years of experimentation. *Agrobacterium* sp. (S_1) produced higher fresh weight followed by *Trichoderma* sp. (S_4) and this was found to be statistically significant at all the growth stages of baby corn. On an average *Agrobacterium* sp. (S_1) registered 25.75%, 14.16% and 14.48% more fresh wt. at 60, 80 DAS and at harvest than *Flavobacterium* sp. (S_2)-the lowest fresh wt. producer.

Interaction

Interaction between fertility levels and microbial innoculum could not reach the level of significance during any of the years of investigation.

Dry matter production plant^{-1} (g)

The data pertaining to dry matter production per plant as affected by different fertility levels and microbial innoculum have been summarized in table 4.9. Perusal of data revealed significant variation on dry matter production due to various treatments at all the growth stages during both the years of experimentation.

Table 4.8: Effect of fertility levels and microbial strains on fresh wt. plant^{-1} (g) (excluding underground root system) at different growth stages of baby corn

Treatments	Fresh wt. plant^{-1} (g)									
	20 DAS		40 DAS		60 DAS		80 DAS		At harvest	
	2017-18	2018-19	2017-18	2018-19	2017-18	2018-19	2017-18	2018-19	2017-18	2018-19
Fertility levels (RDF)										
F_1 (100%NP+25%K)	9.66	10.33	73.20	76.45	300.72	315.21	406.53	421.55	545.10	547.38
F_2 (100%NP+50%K)	11.62	11.81	82.20	85.42	334.96	341.47	430.03	461.33	556.49	560.26
F_3 (100%NP+75%K)	13.67	14.31	90.52	93.84	367.12	379.31	484.50	496.95	597.25	599.88
F_4 (100% NPK)	14.27	14.95	94.21	97.44	375.13	387.69	491.56	501.00	605.04	607.01
SEm±	0.69	0.72	1.31	1.33	3.24	3.29	3.31	3.35	3.16	3.19
C.D. (P=0.05)	2.11	2.19	3.95	3.99	9.74	9.88	9.95	10.05	9.51	9.65
Microbial strains										
S_1 (*Agrobacterium* sp.)	12.70	13.61	88.58	95.98	342.71	353.39	446.54	464.49	580.84	592.77
S_2 (*Flavobacterium* sp.)	10.50	11.08	67.44	77.86	265.46	288.08	384.17	413.83	502.32	522.86
S_3 (*Rhizobium* sp.)	11.26	11.65	73.84	86.46	273.03	307.45	401.96	434.60	522.72	535.31
S_4 (*Trichoderma* sp.)	11.62	12.64	79.34	90.51	307.64	316.47	416.22	449.50	565.44	577.08
SEm±	0.21	0.27	1.22	1.26	3.11	3.12	2.79	2.81	2.69	2.71
C.D.(P=0.05)	0.65	0.83	3.71	3.81	9.23	9.21	8.39	8.45	8.07	8.13

Table 4.9: Effect of fertility levels and microbial strains on dry wt. plant^{-1} (g) (excluding underground root system) at different growth stages of baby corn

Treatments	Dry matter plant^{-1} (g)									
	20 DAS		40 DAS		60 DAS		80 DAS		At harvest	
	2017-18	2018-19	2017-18	2018-19	2017-18	2018-19	2017-18	2018-19	2017-18	2018-19
Fertility levels (RDF)										
F_1 (100%NP+25%K)	3.21	3.42	24.16	25.23	97.32	101.68	134.13	141.64	185.60	189.75
F_2 (100%NP+50%K)	3.86	3.91	27.13	27.99	108.40	110.15	142.85	152.37	190.89	194.90
F_3 (100%NP+75%K)	4.58	4.67	29.27	29.69	117.86	120.52	162.91	164.70	213.62	214.92
F_4 (100% NPK)	4.74	4.95	31.09	32.16	121.40	125.06	164.60	167.49	218.60	220.13
SEm±	0.13	0.19	1.29	1.34	1.71	1.75	1.44	1.58	1.96	1.98
C.D. (P=0.05)	0.39	0.58	3.81	4.05	5.27	6.17	4.62	5.05	5.94	6.01
Microbial strains										
S_1 (*Agrobacterium* sp.)	4.22	4.52	29.33	31.78	110.91	113.63	157.65	163.63	199.6	205.11
S_2 (*Flavobacterium* sp.)	3.49	3.68	22.33	25.78	85.91	92.63	142.47	140.84	172.62	180.92
S_3 (*Rhizobium* sp.)	3.74	3.87	24.45	28.63	88.36	98.86	150.00	153.77	179.63	185.23
S_4 (*Trichoderma* sp.)	3.86	4.20	26.27	29.97	99.56	101.76	152.37	160.96	193.31	198.00
SEm±	0.11	0.12	1.18	1.21	1.34	1.41	1.06	1.21	2.01	2.03
C.D.(P=0.05)	0.33	0.37	3.56	3.65	4.06	4.26	3.05	3.48	6.08	6.10

Fertilizer Levels

The result showed significant variation in dry matter production due to different fertility levels at all the growth stages. Application of 100% NP+75%K (F_3) and 100%NPK (F_4) which remained statistically at par produced the higher dry matter as compared to other doses and remained significantly superior to other treatments. Finally 100% NP+75%K (F_3) registered an average dry matter increase of 19.79% at 60 DAS, 15.90% at 80 DAS and 14.17% at harvest over 100%NP+25%K (F_1).

Overall the effect of fertility levels on dry matter production was in the order of F_4, F_3> F_2> F_1.

Microbial innoculum

The variation in dry matter production due to different microbial innoculum was found significant at all the growth stages. *Agrobacterium* sp. produced the highest dry matter of baby corn followed by *Trichoderma* sp. and finally at harvest it registered an increase of 25.76% at 60 DAS, 13.40% at 80 DAS and 14.47% dry matter at harvest over *Flavobacterium* sp. (S_2). The dry matter yield was in the order of S_1> S_4> S_3> S_2.

Interaction

Fertility levels were found to interact significantly with microbial innoculum in increasing the dry matter yield of the plant at 80 DAS during both the years (Table 4.10). Higher dry matter production at 100% NP+75% K (F_3) with *Agrobacterium sp.* (S_1) was recorded (167.50 and 170.01g during 1st and 2nd year) although it remained at par with 100%NPK (F_4).

Yield attributes

Data on yield attributes *i.e.* days to cob initiation, length and girth of baby corn (without husk) (cm), number of cobs plant^{-1}, baby corn (with and without husk) weight (g) and baby corn (without husk): baby corn (with husk) ratio have been presented in Table 4.11. and depicted in figure 4.1 and 4.2.

Days to Initiation of Cob

The data on days to initiation of cob as affected by different fertility levels and microbial innoculum are furnished in Table 4.11.

Fertilizer Levels

The fertility levels markedly reduced the days to initiation of cob in both the years. Fertilizer application @ 100%NP+ 75%K (F_3) and 100%NPK (F_4) remaining at par with each other resulted in the latest cob initiation whereas 100%NP+ 25%K (F_1) took minimum time. Overall it was in the order of F_4, F_3> F_2> F_1.

Table 4.10: Interaction effect of fertility levels and microbial strains on dry matter plant^{-1} at 80 DAS

Treatments	2017-18					2018-19				
	S_1	S_2	S_3	S_4	Mean	S_1	S_2	S_3	S_4	Mean
Fertility levels × microbial strains										
F_1 (100% NP+25%K)	139.92	125.01	134.54	137.05	134.13	149.75	129.81	139.12	147.88	141.64
F_2 (100% NP+50%K)	150.18	134.74	145.07	141.39	142.85	161.58	134.39	153.53	159.98	152.37
F_3 (100% NP+75%K)	169.50	153.45	159.65	163.05	162.91	170.01	145.77	159.37	164.64	164.70
F_4 (100% of NPK)	173.02	156.68	160.73	167.98	164.60	174.20	158.39	163.05	171.34	167.49
Mean	159.65	142.47	150.00	152.37		164.63	142.84	153.77	160.96	
SEm ±			1.90					1.92		
CD (P=0.05) different sub treatment vs same main treatment			5.44					5.49		
SEm ±			2.38					2.42		
CD (P=0.05) different sub treatment for different main treatment			6.22					6.38		

S_1 - *Agrobacterium* sp., S_2 - *Flavobacterium* sp., S_3 - *Rhizobium* sp., S_4 - *Trichoderma* sp.

Table 4.11: Effect of fertility levels and microbial strains on yield attributes of baby corn

Treatments	Days to baby cob initiation		Baby corn length (without husk) (cm)		Baby corn girth (without husk) (cm)		Baby corn weight (without husk) (g/cob)		Baby corn weight (with husk) (g/cob)		No. of cobs plant^{-1}		Baby corn (with husk) : baby corn (without husk)	
	2017-18	2018-19	2017-18	2018-19	2017-18	2018-19	2017-18	2018-19	2017-18	2018-19	2017-18	2018-19	2017-18	2018-19
Fertility levels (RDF)														
F_1 (100%NP+25%K)	61.79	61.65	7.75	8.12	3.10	3.11	5.52	6.07	26.22	28.95	1.97	2.04	4.75	4.77
F_2 (100%NP+50%K)	62.30	62.69	8.38	8.74	3.32	3.38	5.91	6.5	28.83	32.78	2.21	2.45	4.88	5.04
F_3 (100%NP+75%K)	65.59	65.14	9.31	9.76	3.64	3.65	6.52	6.99	32.87	37.51	2.35	2.61	5.04	5.37
F_4 (100% NPK)	69.35	69.01	9.73	10.21	3.83	3.89	6.79	7.39	34.42	39.92	2.47	2.77	5.07	5.40
SEm ±	0.91	0.86	0.17	0.19	0.07	0.09	0.12	0.14	0.63	0.71	0.04	0.06	0.05	0.06
C.D. (P=0.05)	2.83	2.64	0.58	0.61	0.22	0.26	0.38	0.43	2.05	2.24	0.13	0.18	0.16	0.18
Microbial strains														
S_1 (*Agrobacterium* sp.)	71.83	69.6	9.42	10.08	3.61	3.74	6.58	7.14	31.89	34.78	2.42	2.61	4.85	4.87
S_2 (*Flavobacterium* sp.)	62.28	62.13	7.69	8.01	2.93	3.14	5.45	6.25	25.08	28.79	2.07	2.22	4.60	4.61
S_3 (*Rhizobium* sp.)	64.11	64.01	8.09	8.71	3.12	3.29	5.84	6.32	27.62	29.95	2.19	2.35	4.73	4.74
S_4 (*Trichoderma* sp.)	67.51	66.06	8.88	9.57	3.41	3.47	6.45	6.68	30.86	32.05	2.25	2.44	4.78	4.80
SEm ±	1.03	0.90	0.16	0.15	0.06	0.09	0.10	0.11	0.31	0.49	0.05	0.06	0.03	0.04
C.D.(P=0.05)	3.01	2.71	0.51	0.49	0.19	0.25	0.31	0.32	0.99	1.39	0.14	0.17	0.09	0.11

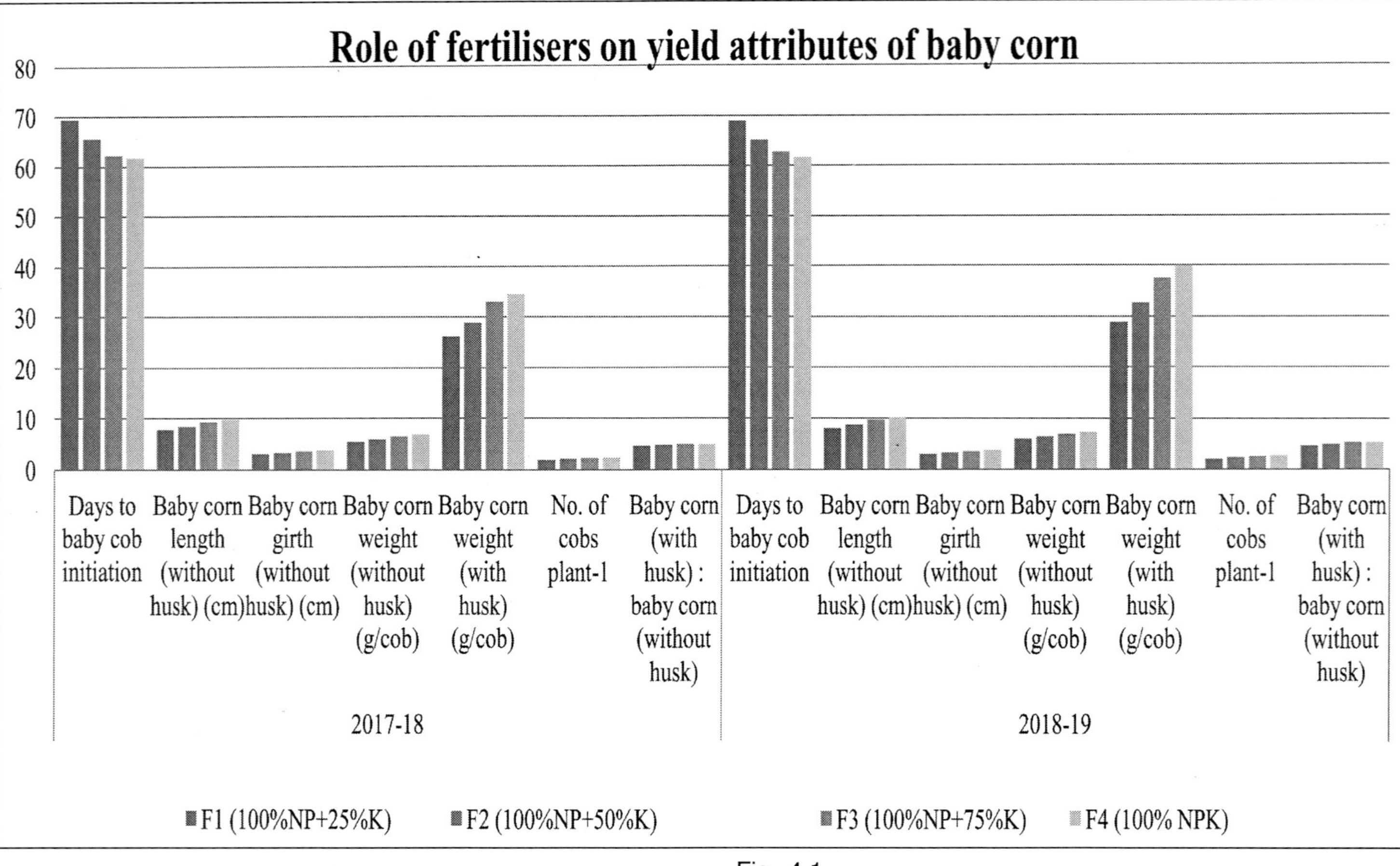
Role of fertilisers on yield attributes of baby corn
80
70
60
50
40
30
20
10
0
Days to baby cob initiation
Baby corn length (without husk) (cm)
Baby corn girth (without husk) (cm)
Baby corn weight (without husk) (g/cob)
Baby corn weight (with husk) (g/cob)
No. of cobs plant-1
Baby corn (with husk) : baby corn (without husk)
2017-18
Days to baby cob initiation
Baby corn length (without husk) (cm)
Baby corn girth (without husk) (cm)
Baby corn weight (without husk) (g/cob)
Baby corn weight (with husk) (g/cob)
No. of cobs plant-1
Baby corn (with husk) : baby corn (without husk)
2018-19
F1 (100%NP+25%K)
F2 (100%NP+50%K)
F3 (100%NP+75%K)
F4 (100% NPK)

Fig. 4.1

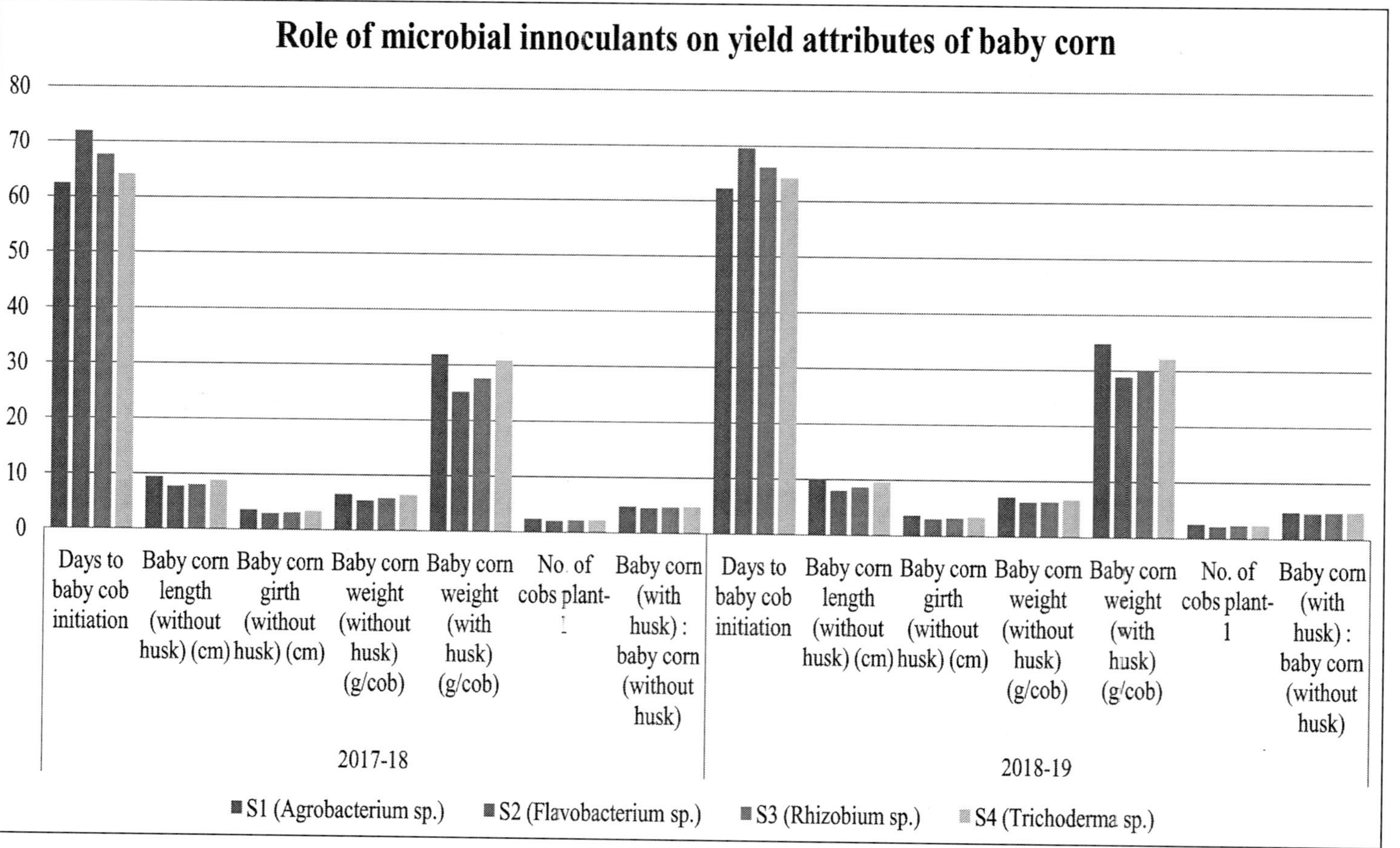

Role of microbial innoculants on yield attributes of baby corn
0
10
20
30
40
50
60
70
80
Days to baby cob initiation
Baby corn length (without husk) (cm)
Baby corn girth (without husk) (cm)
Baby corn weight (without husk) (g/cob)
Baby corn weight (with husk) (g/cob)
No. of cobs plant-1
Baby corn (with husk) : baby corn (without husk)
2017-18
2018-19
S1 (Agrobacterium sp.)
S2 (Flavobacterium sp.)
S3 (Rhizobium sp.)
S4 (Trichoderma sp.)

Fig. 4.2

Microbial innoculum

Number of days required for initiation of cob differed significantly due to microbial innoculum at all the growth stages during both the years of experimentation. *Agrobacterium* sp. (S_1) took maximum no. of days for initiation of cob followed by *Trichoderma* sp. (S_4) and it was in the order of S_1>S_4>S_3>S_2.

Interaction

However, none of the interactions was found significant in any of the years.

Length of Baby corn (without husk) (cm)

The data pertaining to length of baby corn (without husk) as affected by different fertility levels and microbial innoculum are presented in table 4.11.

Fertilizer Levels

Perusal of the data showed marked difference in baby corn length due to different fertility levels. The fertility level at 100%NP+ 75%K (F_3) produced the corn the length of which was 20.16% more than the corn produced at the level of 100% NP+25%K (F_1) on the basis of mean value of two years and F_3 remained at par with F_4. Further baby corn length was found higher during second year (2017-18) than in first year (2018-19) and length of baby corn was in the order of F_4, F_3> F_2> F_1.

Microbial innoculum

The data further revealed that the application of microbial innoculum also significantly influenced the baby corn length. *Agrobacterium* sp. (S_1) recorded the highest baby corn length among all the innoculum and it was 24.20% (on the basis of mean of two years data) more than *Flavobacterium* sp. (S_4) which produced the shortest baby corn.

Interaction

None of the interactions could reach the level of significance during any of the years.

Baby corn girth (without husk) (cm)

Data pertaining to this parameter presented in table 4.11 indicated that application of different fertility levels and microbial innoculum had significant influence on baby corn (without husk) girth during both the years of investigation.

Fertilizer Levels

Among the fertility levels, 100%NP+ 75%K (F_3) and 100% NPK (F_4) registered greater baby corn girth (3.86 and 3.65 cm on average of two years) and it remained significantly superior to all other levels. The response of baby corn girth to different fertility levels was in the order of F_4, F_3> F_2> F_1.

Microbial innoculum

Perusal of the data clearly indicated that microbial innoculum of *Agrobacterium* sp. (S_1) recorded significantly higher baby corn girth with a value of 3.61cm and 3.74 cm and this was followed by *Trichoderma* sp. (S_4) during 2017-18 and 2018-19 respectively.

Interaction

None of the interactions between fertility levels and microbial innoculum was found significant in any of the years.

Baby corn weight (without husk) (g/cob)

Data on baby corn (without husk) weight as affected by different levels of fertility and microbial innoculum are furnished in table 4.11.

Fertilizer Levels

It was clear from the Table 4.11 that fertility levels resulted in significant variation in individual cob weight. On an average, 100%NP+ 75%K (F_3) registered 16.57% more weight than 100%NP+25%K (F_1) during both the years. The response of baby corn (without husk) weight to different fertility levels was in the order of F_4, F_3> F_2> F_1.

Microbial innoculum

Agrobacterium sp. (S_1) exhibited maximum positive influence on baby corn weight (6.58 and 7.14 g) and this was followed by *Trichoderma* sp. (S_4) (6.25 and 6.80 g) during both the years. Overall it was in the order of S_1> S_4> S_3> S_2 and on an average the extent of increase in cob weight by *Agrobacterium* sp. (S_1) over *Flavobacterium* sp. (S_2) was 17.26%.

Interaction

None of the interactions was found significant in respect of baby corn weight during any of the years.

Baby corn (with husk) weight (g/cob)

Data presented in table 4.11 indicates the effect of fertility levels and microbial innoculum on baby corn weight with husk.

Fertilizer Levels

It was apparent from the data (Table 4.11) that baby corn weight increased significantly due to different fertility levels during both the years. Higher weight was recorded at 100%NP+ 75%K (F_3) and 100%NPK (F_4), which remained significantly superior to all other treatments but at par with each other. Baby corn weight remained higher during second year (2018-19) than first year (2017-18). On an average F_3 registered 27.57% increase over 100%NP+ 25%K (F_1) in baby corn weight.

Microbial innoculum

The weight of baby corn differed significantly due to different microbial innoculum. On the basis of two years mean *Agrobacterium* sp. (S_1) recorded 23.76% higher weight than *Flavobacterium* sp. (S_2). Overall the performance of microbial strain was in the order of $S_1>S_4>S_3>S_2$.

Interaction

No interaction between fertility levels and microbial innoculum was found significant with respect to baby corn weight in any of the years.

No. of Cobs Plant^{-1}

Data associated with number of cobs plant^{-1} as affected by fertility levels and microbial innoculum during both the years of trial are presented in table 4.11.

Fertilizer Levels

Perusal of data (Table 4.11) revealed significant variation in number of cobs plant^{-1} due to the levels of fertility. Higher number of cobs plant^{-1} was observed with the application of 100%NP+75%K (F_3) and 100%NPK (F_4) which remained statistically at par with each other. On an average F_3 registered 23.69% increase in the number of cobs plant^{-1} over F_1.

Microbial innoculum

An inspection of the data revealed that microbial innoculum also significantly influenced the number of cobs plant^{-1}. Among all the microbial innoculum, *Agrobacterium* sp. (S_1) produced maximum number of cobs plant^{-1} with 17.25% increase over *Flavobacterium* sp. (S_2) followed by *Trichoderma* sp. (S_4) and it remained significantly superior to all the innoculum during both the years.

Interaction

No interaction between fertility levels and microbial innoculum could exert significant influence on number of cobs plant^{-1} in any of the years.

Baby Corn (with Husk): Baby Corn (without Husk) Ratio

A glance of data on baby corn (with husk): baby corn (without husk) ratio as influenced by different levels of fertility and microbial innoculum are presented in table 4.11.

Fertilizer Levels

Fertility levels exerted significant influence on baby corn (with husk): baby corn (without husk) ratio. Higher ratio was recorded with 100%NP+75%K (F_3) (5.04 and 5.37 average of two years) but it remained at par with 100%NPK (F_4). The response of baby corn (with husk): baby corn (without husk) ratio to different fertility levels was in the order of F_4, $F_3> F_2> F_1$.

Microbial innoculum

Significant variation in the ratio was also observed due to various innoculum. While the maximum ratio was found with *Agrobacterium* sp. (S_1), the minimum was recorded with *Flavobacterium* sp. (S_2).

Interaction

None of the interactions between fertility levels and microbial innoculum could exert any significant effect on the ratio of with husk and without husk in any of the years.

No. of cobs ha^{-1} (plucking wise)

Data presented in table 4.12 clearly indicated significant effect of different levels of fertilizers and microbial innoculum on the number of cobs ha^{-1} in each plucking during both the years.

Fertilizer Levels

It was evident from the data (Table 4.12) that there was significant variation in number of cobs ha^{-1} due to different levels of fertilizers. Higher number of cobs ha^{-1} (plucking wise) was observed with the application of 100%NP+75%K (F_3) and 100%NPK (F_4) which remained statistically at par with each other at all the individual harvests. The increases by F_3 on an average were 35.53% at 1st, 41.47% at 2nd, 51.78% at 3rd, 37.80% at 4th and 29.81% at 5th harvest over 100% NP +25%K (F_1). Out of all the harvests, the maximum number of cobs was found at 3rd plucking.

Microbial innoculum

An examination of the data (Table 4.12) revealed that microbial innoculum also brought about significant differences among themselves in number of cobs ha^{-1} at all the plucking stages. *Agrobacterium* sp. (S_1) produced maximum number of cobs ha^{-1}. The average increases were 39.29% at 1st, 27.91% at 2nd, 28.08% at 3rd, 20.06% at 4th and 44.34% at 5th plucking over *Flavobacterium* sp. (S_2) with the highest being observed at 3rd plucking.

Interaction

None of the interactions between fertility levels and microbial innoculum could exert significant influence on number of cobs ha^{-1} during any of the years.

Baby corn yield

Baby corn yield (without husk) (q ha^{-1})

The data on baby corn (without husk) yield as influenced by fertility levels and microbial innoculum are presented in table 4.13 and illustrated graphically in figure 4.3 and figure 4.4.

Table 4.12: Effect of fertility levels and microbial strains on number of cobs /ha at 1st, 2nd, 3rd, 4th and 5th plucking of baby corn

Treatments	No. of cobs at 1st plucking (cobs/ha)		No. of cobs at 2nd plucking (cobs/ha)		No. of cobs at 3rd plucking (cobs /ha)		No. of cobs at 4th plucking (cobs/ha)		No. of cobs at 5th (final) plucking (cobs /ha)	
	2017-18	2018-19	2017-18	2017-18	2017-18	2018-19	2017-18	2018-19	2017-18	2018-19
Fertility levels (RDF)										
F_1 (100%NP+25%K)	10480.79	12647.64	17196.85	20559.45	29636.56	32246.36	25376.44	29465.00	17693.36	18676.29
F_2 (100%NP+50%K)	12136.08	13924.02	23454.18	24467.33	34848.40	36679.96	30053.27	32229.24	18092.99	20814.06
F_3 (100%NP+75%K)	14606.85	16739.45	26339.30	27073.28	46327.91	47595.86	37352.84	38216.21	22612.27	24598.59
F_4 (100% NPK)	17231.89	19782.35	29312.31	30414.74	49222.40	50257.54	40244.20	41729.90	25793.17	27863.75
SEm±	876.89	1021.58	989.33	1114.89	1263.22	1369.11	989.36	1206.14	1067.29	1141.29
C.D. (P=0.05)	2638.63	3060.78	2980.25	3346.67	3809.89	4107.52	2968.59	3619.81	3221.87	3423.87
Microbial strains										
S_1 (*Agrobacterium* sp.)	15394.94	15594.44	26355.42	27697.71	45469.96	46494.90	40549.76	41711.66	20075.70	21686.33
S_2 (*Flavobacterium* sp.)	11017.16	11231.64	19333.90	22925.79	35125.85	36679.08	33647.46	34870.31	14303.65	14628.84
S_3 (*Rhizobium* sp.)	11419.48	11537.79	21374.26	23321.08	37669.63	38671.94	35521.99	36525.41	15300.04	16168.17
S_4 (*Trichoderma* sp.)	12475.99	12571.79	23760.75	25162.42	41734.18	42587.04	37575.22	38383.56	17190.84	18694.60
SEm±	792.57	998.69	804.68	838.12	1098.23	1178.58	952.25	1175.05	945.36	989.95
C.D.(P=0.05)	2387.89	2996.70	2424.04	2514.36	3182.09	3439.79	2866.75	3298.95	2845.80	2971.89

Table 4.13 Effect of fertility levels and microbial strains on yield of baby corn

Treatments	Baby corn yield (q/ha) (without husk)		Baby corn yield (q/ha) (with husk)		Stover yield (q/ha)	
	2017-18	2018-19	2017-18	2018-19	2017-18	2018-19
Fertility levels (RDF)						
F_1 (100%NP+25%K)	10.94	11.01	58.37	60.01	177.40	180.22
F_2 (100%NP+50%K)	11.00	12.00	65.08	69.23	224.20	229.47
F_3 (100%NP+75%K)	14.78	15.26	70.99	77.33	246.76	251.73
F_4 (100% NPK)	15.03	15.69	73.81	79.96	248.07	253.39
SEm±	0.34	0.36	1.03	1.14	1.82	1.96
C.D. (P=0.05)	1.09	1.15	3.28	3.66	5.45	5.87
Microbial strains						
S_1 (*Agrobacterium* sp.)	13.82	14.48	72.92	78.82	227.94	230.85
S_2 (*Flavobacterium* sp.)	12.25	12.80	59.98	62.41	220.26	226.52
S_3 (*Rhizobium* sp.)	12.48	13.12	65.42	69.76	222.71	228.28
S_4 (*Trichoderma* sp.)	13.20	13.57	69.92	75.55	225.50	229.15
SEm±	0.16	0.19	0.59	0.60	1.06	1.02
C.D.(P=0.05)	0.50	0.55	1.68	1.72	3.19	3.03

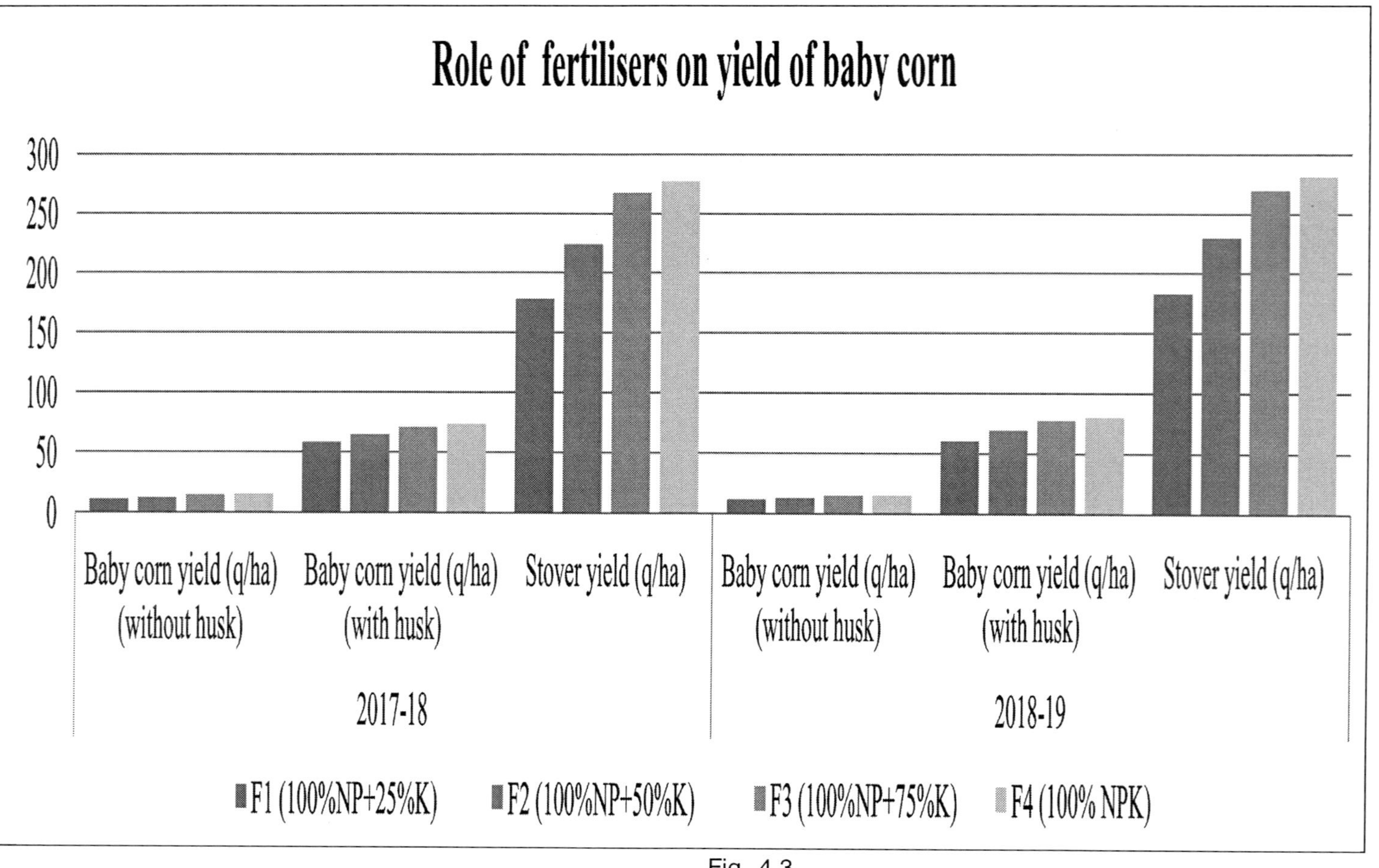
Role of fertilisers on yield of baby corn
300
250
200
150
100
50
0
Baby corn yield (q/ha) (without husk)
Baby corn yield (q/ha) (with husk)
Stover yield (q/ha)
2017-18
Baby corn yield (q/ha) (without husk)
Baby corn yield (q/ha) (with husk)
Stover yield (q/ha)
2018-19
F1 (100%NP+25%K)
F2 (100%NP+50%K)
F3 (100%NP+75%K)
F4 (100% NPK)

Fig. 4.3

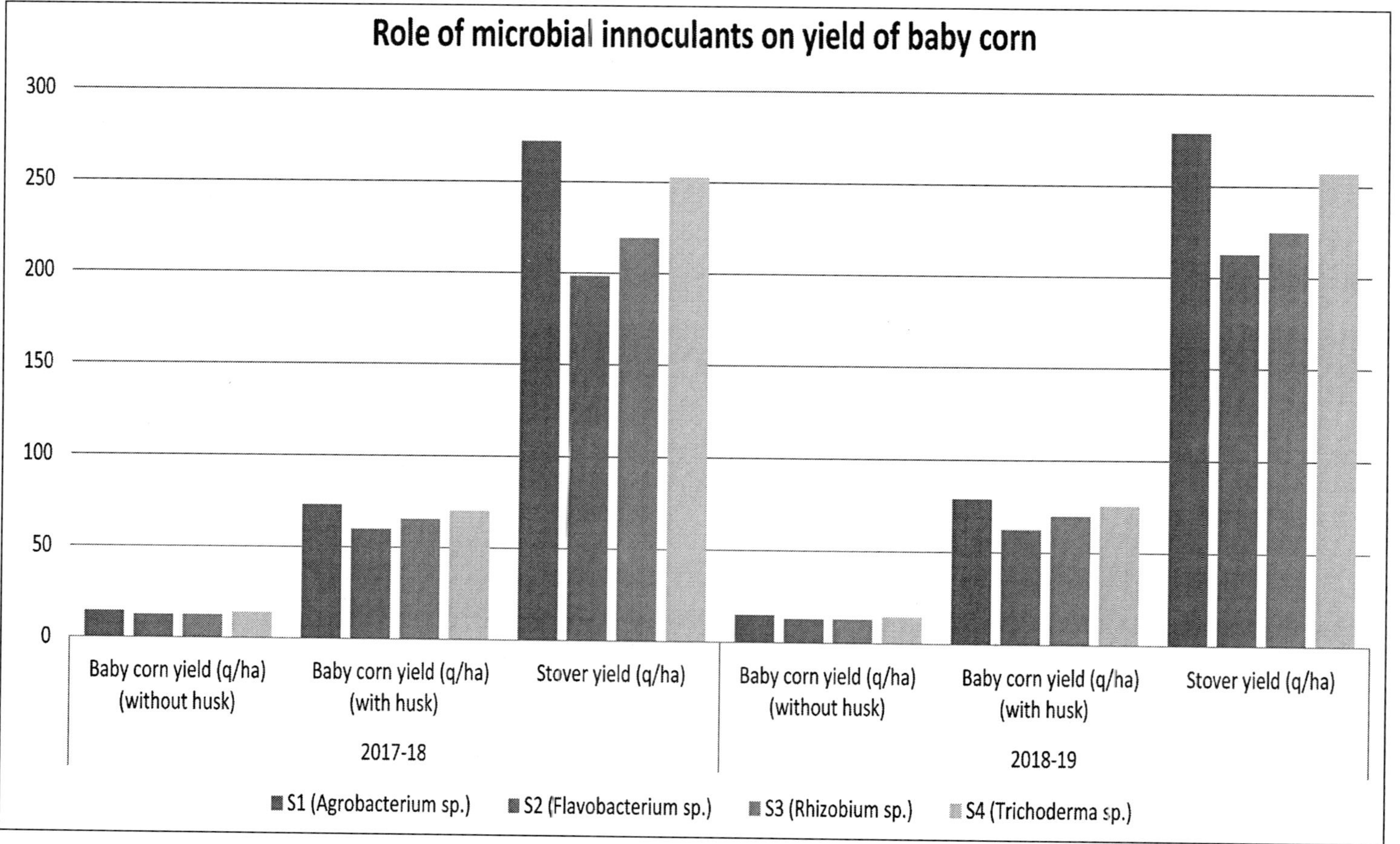
Role of microbial innoculants on yield of baby corn
300
250
200
150
100
50
0
Baby corn yield (q/ha) (without husk)
Baby corn yield (q/ha) (with husk)
Stover yield (q/ha)
2017-18
Baby corn yield (q/ha) (without husk)
Baby corn yield (q/ha) (with husk)
Stover yield (q/ha)
2018-19
S1 (Agrobacterium sp.)
S2 (Flavobacterium sp.)
S3 (Rhizobium sp.)
S4 (Trichoderma sp.)

Fig. 4.4

Fertilizer Levels

An examination of the data (Table 4.13) revealed that the higher baby corn yield (without husk) was obtained by the application of 100%NP+75%K (F_3) and 100%NPK (F_4) which remained statistically at par with each other. On an average F_3 recorded 36.86% increase over F_1 (100%NP+25%K) and 30.61% increase over F_2 (100%NP+50%K) in yield. Overall the effect of fertility levels on baby corn yield (without husk) was in the order of F_4, F_3> F_2> F_1.

Microbial innoculum

It was further evident from the data presented in table 4.13 that microbial innoculum brought about significant effect on the baby corn yield. On the basis of means of two years data *Agrobacterium* sp. (S_1) recorded 12.97% increase over S_2 (*Flavobacterium* sp.), 10.55% increase over S_3 (*Rhizobium* sp.) and 5.72% increase over S_4 (*Trichoderma* sp.) in baby corn yield. Overall the yields obtained from different microbial innoculum were in the order of S_1> S_4> S_3> S_2.

Interaction

As regards interactions (Table 4.14), fertility levels and microbial innoculum interacted significantly to increase the baby corn yield. 100% NP+75%K (F_3) and *Agrobacterium* sp. (S_1) recorded higher baby corn yield (16.25 and 16.29 q/ha) but remained at par with 100%NPK (F_4) during both the years and exhibited distinct superiority over other combinations.

Baby corn yield (with husk) (q ha^{-1})

The data on baby corn yield (with husk) as influenced by different fertility levels and microbial innoculum is presented in table 4.13 and depicted graphically in figure 4.3 and figure 4.4.

Fertilizer Levels

It was evident from the data that higher baby corn yield was obtained from 100%NP+75%K (F_3) and 100%NPK (F_4) which were found statistically at par with each other. On an average F_3 registered an increase in yield of 25.29% over F_1 (100%NP+25%K) and 10.43% over F_2 (100%NP+50%K). Overall the effect of fertility levels on baby corn yield (with husk) was in the order of F_4, F_3> F_2> F_1.

Microbial innoculum

A close examination of the data presented in table 4.13 further revealed that microbial innoculum brought about significant differences in baby corn yield (with husk). On an average *Agrobacterium* sp. (S_1) registered 23.98% increase in yield over S_2 (*Flavobacterium* sp.), 12.25% over S_3 (*Rhizobium* sp.) and 4.31% over S_4 (*Trichoderma* sp.) Overall the yields obtained from different microbial innoculum were in the order of S_1> S_4> S_3> S_2.

Table 4.14: Interaction effect of fertility levels and microbial strains on baby corn yield (q ha^{-1}) (without husk)

Treatments	2017-18					2018-19				
	S_1	S_2	S_3	S_4	Mean	S_1	S_2	S_3	S_4	Mean
Fertility levels × microbial strains										
F_1 (100% NP+25%K)	11.24	10.75	10.87	10.90	10.94	11.03	10.90	11.00	11.13	11.01
F_2 (100% NP+50%K)	11.25	10.78	10.95	11.00	11.00	13.12	11.14	11.62	12.12	12.00
F_3 (100% NP+75%K)	16.25	13.63	14.14	15.11	14.78	16.29	14.44	15.03	15.29	15.26
F_4 (100% of NPK)	16.52	13.85	13.97	15.77	15.03	17.50	14.71	14.83	15.74	15.69
Mean	13.82	12.25	12.48	13.20		14.48	12.80	13.12	13.57	
SEm±			0.37					0.38		
CD (P=0.05) different sub treatment vs same main treatment			1.07					1.09		
SEm±			0.41					0.51		
CD (P=0.05) different sub treatment for different main treatment			1.14					1.31		

S_1 - *Agrobacterium* sp., S_2 - *Flavobacterium* sp., S_3 - *Rhizobium* sp., S_4 - *Trichoderma* sp.

Interaction

As regards interaction effect (Table 4.15), fertility levels and microbial innoculum interacted significantly in increasing the baby corn yield (with husk). 100%NP+75%K (F_3) and *Agrobacterium sp.* (S_1) recorded the higher baby corn yield (77.90 and 85.60 q/ha) but remained at par with 100%NPK (F_4) during both the years. These two combinations exhibited distinct superiority over others in producing more yield.

Stover yield (q ha^{-1})

The data on stover yield as influenced by levels of fertility and different microbial innoculum are summarized and presented in table 4.13 and illustrated graphically in figure 4.3 and figure 4.4.

Fertilizer Levels

It was evident from the data that the higher stover yield was registered by 100%NP+75%K (F_3) and 100%NPK (F_4) which remained statistically at par with each other. On the basis of two years average F_3 (100%NP+75%K) fertility level was found to produce 39.39% more stover yield than F_1 (100%NP+25%K) and 9.88% more than F_2 (100%NP+50%K). Overall the effect of fertility levels on stover yields was in the order of F_4, F_3> F_2> F_1.

Microbial innoculum

Similarly in case of microbial innoculum also *Agrobacterium* (S_1) proved its superiority over others in increasing the stover yield. On an average *Agrobacterium* (S_1) registered an increase of 2.69% over S_2 (*Flavobacterium*), 1.73% over S_3 (*Rhizobium*) and 0.91% over S_4 (*Trichoderma*) in stover yield. Overall the stover yield obtained from different microbial innoculum were in the order of S_1> S_4> S_3> S_2.

Interaction

The interaction between fertility levels and microbial innoculum pertaining to this parameter was not found to be significant in any of the years.

Quality Parameters

The data related to protein, carbohydrate, sugar and starch contents of baby corn as influenced by fertility levels and microbial innoculum are presented in table 4.16.

Protein content in baby corn (%)

Data pertaining to protein content in baby corn indicated that both fertility levels and microbial innoculum had significant influence on this parameter during both the years of investigation.

Table 4.15: Interaction effect of fertility levels and microbial strains on baby corn yield (q ha^{-1}) (with husk)

Treatments	2017-18					2018-19				
	S_1	S_2	S_3	S_4	Mean	S_1	S_2	S_3	S_4	Mean
Fertility levels × microbial strains										
F_1 (100% NP+25%K)	65.03	50.48	54.75	63.23	58.37	66.67	52.12	56.39	64.87	60.01
F_2 (100% NP+50%K)	69.84	56.52	65.89	68.06	65.08	75.76	58.50	68.87	73.79	69.23
F_3 (100% NP+75%K)	77.90	65.41	67.51	73.13	70.99	85.60	68.51	74.75	80.48	77.33
F_4 (100% of NPK)	78.93	67.52	73.54	75.26	73.81	87.27	70.51	79.03	83.05	79.96
Mean	72.92	59.98	65.42	69.92		78.82	62.41	69.76	75.55	
SEm±			1.17					1.20		
CD (P=0.05) different sub treatment vs same main treatment			3.36					3.44		
SEm ±			1.44					1.54		
CD (P=0.05) different sub treatment for different main treatment			3.79					4.01		

S_1 - *Agrobacterium* sp., S_2 - *Flavobacterium* sp., S_3 - *Rhizobium* sp., S_4 - *Trichoderma* sp.

Table 4.16: Effect of fertility levels and microbial strains on quality attributes of baby corn (on dry weight basis)

Treatments	Protein content in baby corn (%)		Protein content in stover (%)		Carbohydrate content (%)		Starch content (%)		Sugar (%)	
	2017-18	2018-19	2017-18	2018-19	2017-18	2018-19	2017-18	2018-19	2017-18	2018-19
F_1 (100%NP+25%K)	10.19	10.75	4.88	5.19	70.66	71.47	64.46	64.98	1.59	1.62
F_2 (100%NP+50%K)	11.38	12.25	5.50	5.63	72.96	73.39	66.68	67.07	1.66	1.69
F_3 (100%NP+75%K)	13.25	14.00	7.50	7.56	75.59	77.16	67.09	68.59	1.79	1.85
F_4 (100% NPK)	13.38	14.06	7.63	7.75	77.07	78.66	69.22	70.77	1.82	1.89
SEm±	0.11	0.13	0.09	0.08	0.77	0.79	0.69	0.72	0.04	0.05
C.D. (P=0.05)	0.33	0.39	0.28	0.25	2.32	2.39	2.19	2.31	0.12	0.16
S_1 (*Agrobacterium* sp.)	12.19	13.19	6.69	6.94	75.14	76.89	65.54	66.03	1.71	1.73
S_2 (*Flavobacterium* sp.)	11.31	11.94	5.56	5.69	69.36	70.76	60.34	60.82	1.55	1.59
S_3 (*Rhizobium* sp.)	11.69	12.25	5.88	6.06	71.07	72.28	62.86	62.11	1.61	1.66
S_4 (*Trichoderma* sp.)	11.94	12.75	6.25	6.50	72.95	73.39	63.53	63.84	1.67	1.69
SEm±	0.08	0.09	0.05	0.07	0.68	0.71	0.65	0.70	0.02	0.03
C.D.(P=0.05)	0.25	0.27	0.14	0.21	2.06	2.14	1.95	2.17	0.06	0.09

S_1 - *Agrobacterium* sp., S_2 - *Flavobacterium* sp., S_3 - *Rhizobium* sp., S_4 - *Trichoderma* sp.

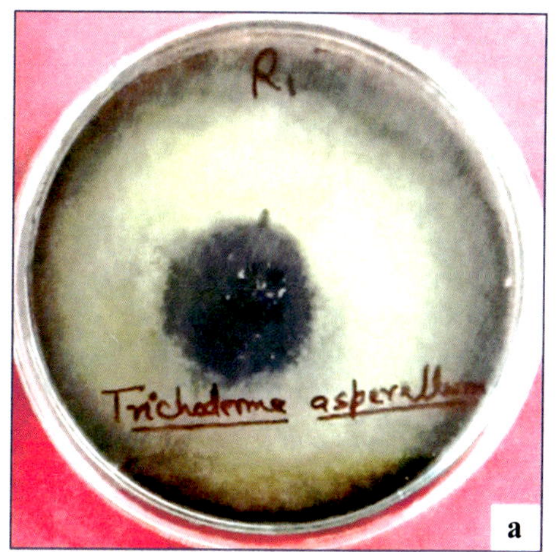

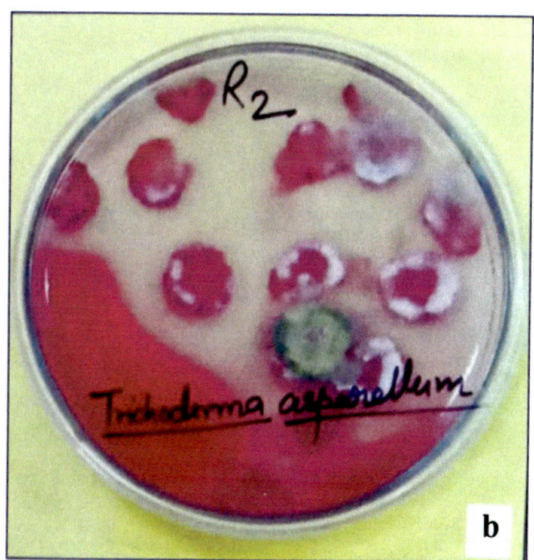

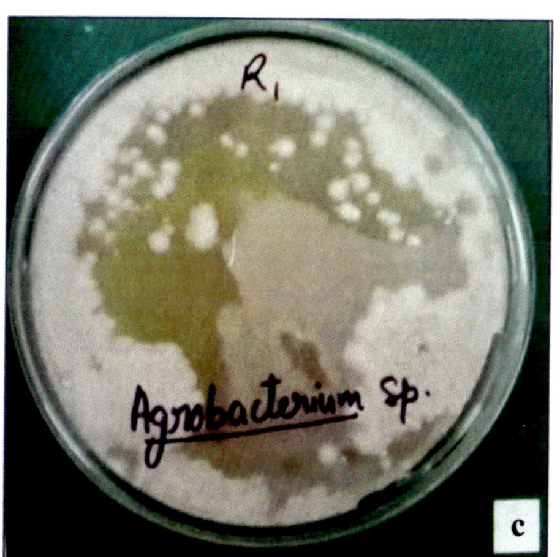

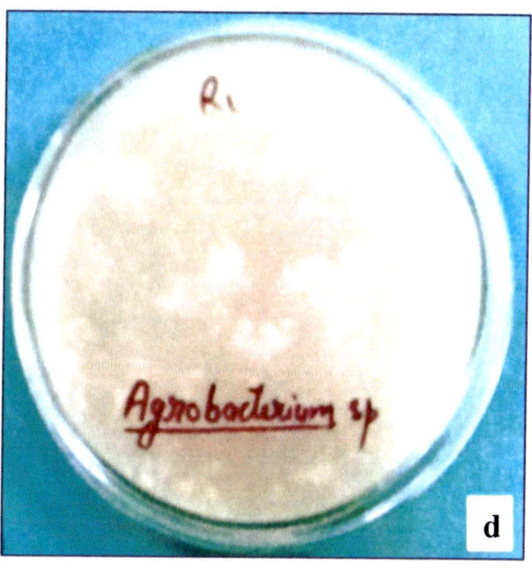

Plate Showing a: *Trichoderma* sp. Showing full colony on culture plate,
b: *Trichoderma* sp. Showing lesser colony on culture plate,
c: *Agrobacterium* sp. Showing lesser colony on culture plate,
d: *Agrobacterium* sp. Showing full colony on culture plate

Plate a and b showing different growth stages of baby corn

Plate showing chopped biomass (stover) added uniformly in the same plot

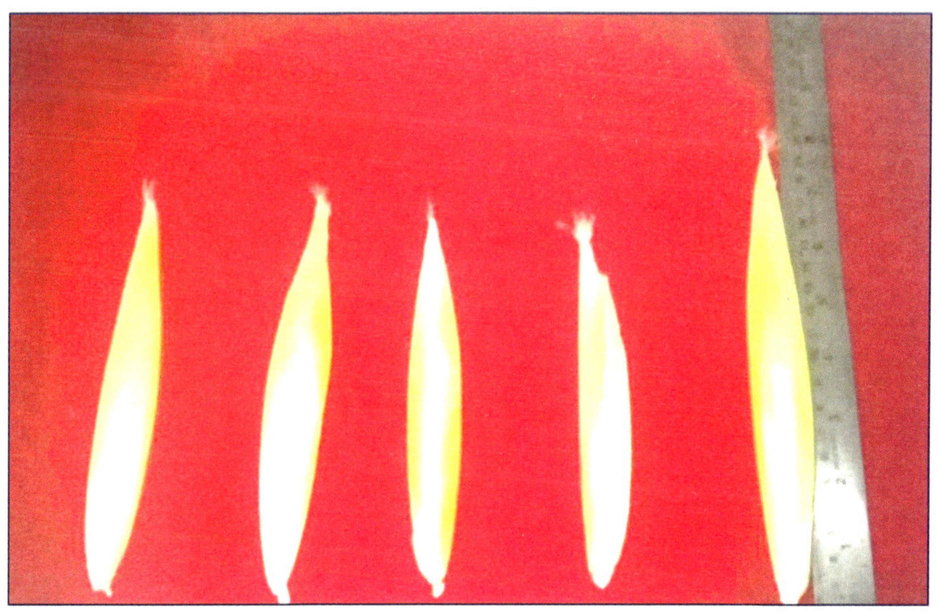

Plate showing length of baby corn at 2-3 days of silk emergence

Plate c and d showing different growth stages of baby corn

Fertilizer Levels

Fertility levels influenced significantly the protein content of baby corn and registered higher protein content at 100%NP+75%K (F_3) and 100%NPK (F_4) which remained at par with each other. F_3 fertility level on an average of two years data recorded 30.13% increase in protein content over 100%NP+25%K (F_1). The response in terms of protein content (%) to different fertility levels was in the order of F_4, F_3> F_2> F_1 during both the years of investigation.

Microbial innoculum

It was evident from the data (Table 4.16) that protein content increased markedly with the application of *Agrobacterium* sp. (S_1). *Agrobacterium* (S_1) recorded 9.16% more protein content than S_2 (*Flavobacterium*) which incidentally registered the lowest protein content among all the microbial innoculum. The response of protein content (%) to different microbial innoculum was in the order of S_1> S_4> S_3> S_2 during both the years.

Interaction

Fertility levels and microbial innoculum failed to interact significantly in increasing the protein content in baby corn during both the years.

Protein content in stover (%)

A critical analysis of data summarized in table 4.16 revealed that protein content of stover was positively affected by fertility levels and microbial innoculum during both the years.

Fertilizer Levels

Fertility levels had a profound influence on protein content of stover during the present study. 100%NP+75%K (F_3) exhibited 49.55% more protein content than 100%NP+25%K (F_1) on the basis of average of two years data and F_3 was found to be at par with 100%NPK (F_4). The response of the protein content in stover (%) to different fertility levels was in the order of F_4, F_3> F_2> F_1.

Microbial innoculum

Microbial innoculum also exhibited a significant effect on protein content (%) in stover. *Agrobacterium* sp. (S_1) - the highest protein producer registered 21.16% increase in protein content over S_2 (*Flavobacterium* sp.) and was found to be in the order of S_1> S_4> S_3> S_2 during both the year of experimentation.

Interaction

Interaction between fertility levels and microbial innoculum could not evince any significant influence on protein content in any of the years.

Carbohydrate content (%)

It was clear from the data (Table 4.16) that carbohydrate content (%) in baby corn was significantly affected by fertility levels and microbial innoculum during both the years.

Fertilizer Levels

There was an increase in carbohydrate content (%) with an increase in fertility level where 100%NP+75%K (F_3) and 100%NPK (F_4) remaining at par with each other exhibited higher carbohydrate content (%) than other fertility levels. Application of 100%NP+75%K (F_3) on an average recorded 8.50% increase over 100%NP+25%K (F_1) – the lowest carbohydrate yielder.

Microbial innoculum

Perusal of the data manifested significant effect of microbial innoculum on this attribute. The microbial innoculum of *Agrobacterium* sp. (S_1) on an average showed 7.83% increase over *Flavobacterium* sp. (S_2) in carbohydrate content of baby corn. Overall it was in the order of $S_1 > S_4 > S_3 > S_2$.

Interaction

Interaction between fertility levels and microbial innoculum could not exert any significant influence on this attribute in any of the years of trial.

Starch Content in Baby Corn (%)

Data pertaining to starch content (%) in baby corn as influenced by different fertility levels and microbial innoculum are presented in table 4.16.

Fertilizer Levels

An examination of the data revealed that the fertility levels brought about significant improvement in starch content (%) in baby corn during both the years. On an average higher starch content in baby corn was found with 100%NP+75%K (F_3) and 100%NPK (F_4) which remained statistically at par with each other. 100%NP+75%K (F_3) recorded 4.82% increase over 100%NP+25%K (F_1) in starch content of the baby corn.

Microbial innoculum

Innoculum also brought about marked changes in starch content of grain during both the years of investigation. *Agrobacterium* sp. (S_1) showed the highest starch content with an average 8.59% increase over *Flavobacterium* sp. (S_2) – the lowest starch producer.

Interaction

Interactions between fertility levels and microbial innoculum could not exert any significant effect on starch content during any of the years.

Sugar Content in Baby Corn (%)

It was clear from the data (Table 4.16) that sugar content in baby corn (%) was significantly affected by fertility levels and microbial innoculum during both the years.

Fertilizer Levels

It was clear from the data that 100%NP+75%K (F_3) and 100%NPK (F_4) exhibited significant superiority in sugar content over other treatments and remained at par with each other. On an average sugar content in baby corn with 100%NP+75%K (F_3) recorded 13.40% increase over 100%NP+25%K (F_1). The response of sugar content (%) in baby corn to different fertility levels was in the order of F_4, F_3> F_2> F_1.

Microbial innoculum

Significant differences in sugar content of baby corn due to different microbial innoculum were also observed during both the years and *Agrobacterium* sp. (S_1) recorded on an average 9.55% more sugar than *Flavobacterium* sp. (S_2), which showed the minimum sugar content. Overall it was in the order of S_1> S_4> S_3> S_2.

Interaction

Interactions between fertility levels and microbial innoculum were not found significant in any of the years.

Nutrient content (%)

Nitrogen content in baby corn (without husk) and stover (%)

The data pertaining to N content (%) in baby corn (without husk) and stover as affected by the fertility levels and microbial innoculum are presented in (Table 4.17).

Fertilizer Levels

Perusal of the data indicated that fertility level at 100%NP+75%K (F_3) and 100%NPK (F_4) remaining at par with each other increased nitrogen content in both baby corn and stover significantly. On an average of two years of investigation F_3 was found with 30.15% and 49.69% more N content than 100%NP+25%K (F_1) in baby corn and stover respectively and it remained significantly higher than all other treatments.

Microbial innoculum

The scanning of data (Table 4.17) indicated that nitrogen content in baby corn (without husk) and stover was significantly influenced by various microbial innoculum. *Agrobacterium* sp. (S_1) registered an average of 9.14% and 21.11% more nitrogen content than *Flavobacterium* sp. (S_2) in baby corn and stover respectively. Overall it was in the order of S_1> S_4> S_3> S_2.

Table 4.17: Effect of fertility levels and microbial strains on N content (%) and removal of N by baby corn (on dry weight basis)

Treatments	N content in baby corn (%)		N content in stover (%)		N removal by baby corn (kg ha^{-1})		N removal by stover (kg ha^{-1})		Total N removal (kg ha^{-1})	
	2017-18	2018-19	2017-18	2018-19	2017-18	2018-19	2017-18	2018-19	2017-18	2018-19
Fertility levels (RDF)										
F_1 (100%NP+25%K)	1.63	1.72	0.78	0.83	3.57	3.91	56.66	58.86	60.23	62.77
F_2 (100%NP+50%K)	1.82	1.96	0.88	0.90	4.14	4.38	61.97	64.85	66.11	69.23
F_3 (100%NP+75%K)	2.12	2.24	1.20	1.21	5.44	5.40	69.87	72.11	75.31	77.51
F_4 (100% NPK)	2.14	2.25	1.22	1.24	5.47	5.45	74.41	76.58	79.88	82.03
SEm±	0.08	0.09	0.05	0.06	0.23	0.24	1.50	1.65	1.47	1.59
C.D. (P=0.05)	0.26	0.28	0.15	0.18	0.70	0.73	4.52	4.74	4.71	5.12
Microbial strains										
S_1 (*Agrobacterium* sp.)	1.95	2.11	1.07	1.11	4.64	4.81	69.29	70.81	73.93	75.62
S_2 (*Flavobacterium* sp.)	1.81	1.91	0.89	0.91	4.43	4.57	59.57	63.50	64.00	68.07
S_3 (*Rhizobium* sp.)	1.87	1.96	0.94	0.97	4.50	4.68	63.51	65.95	68.01	70.63
S_4 (*Trichoderma* sp.)	1.91	2.04	1.00	1.04	4.59	4.77	64.85	66.79	69.44	71.56
SEm±	0.06	0.07	0.01	0.02	0.02	0.04	1.19	1.25	1.38	1.50
C.D. (P=0.05)	0.19	0.21	0.03	0.07	0.06	0.11	3.59	3.99	3.97	4.90

Interaction

The combination between fertility levels and microbial innoculum could not evince any marked effect on this attribute in any of the years.

Nitrogen removal (kg ha^{-1})

It was clear from the data table 4.17 and figure 4.7 and 4.8 that N removal by baby corn, stover and consequent total removal were significantly affected by fertility levels and microbial innoculum during both the years of investigation.

Fertilizer Levels

An insight into the data (Table 4.17) clearly highlighted marked effect of fertility levels on N removal. Amount of nitrogen removal by baby corn was increased by an increase in fertility levels and on an average 100%NP+75%K (F_3) recorded 44.92% and 22.91% more removal than F_1 by corn and stover. Consequently total N removal at F_3 was also found to be 24.24% higher than F_1. However, in all these parameters F_3 remained statistically at par with F_4 level of fertility.

Microbial innoculum

Application of microbial innoculum caused significant effect in N removal by baby corn, stover and consequent total removal. Maximum N removal was found by *Agrobacterium* sp. (S_1) and on an average it recorded 5.00%, 13.84% and 13.24% more removal than *Flavobacterium* sp. (S_2). Overall the removal was in the order of $S_1 > S_4 > S_3 > S_2$.

Interaction

The interaction of the experimental variables, however, could not evince any marked effect on this attribute in any of the years.

Phosphorus content in baby corn (without husk) and stover (%)

The data on total phosphorus content (%) in baby corn (without husk) and stover as influenced by different fertility levels and microbial innoculum are presented in table 4.18.

Fertilizer Levels

A close analysis of the data revealed that fertility levels had a marked effect on phosphorus content of baby corn and its stover. 100%NP+75%K (F_3) registered an average increase in P content by 55.36% and 60.00% over 100%NP+25%K (F_1) while F_3 and 100%NPK (F_4) remained at par with each other. F_3 and F_4 proved their distinct superiority over all other treatments during both the years of experimentation in enriching the baby corn with P content.

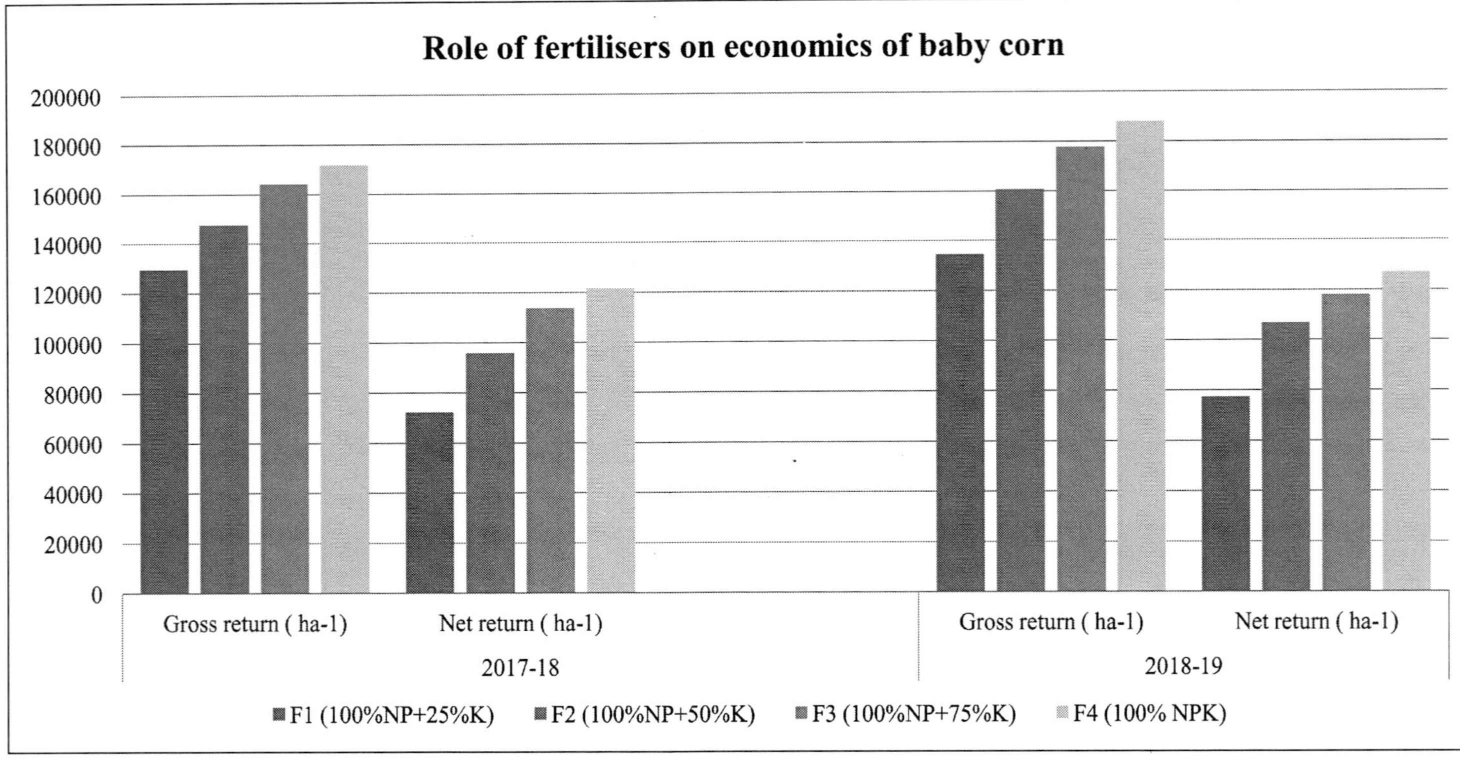

Role of fertilisers on economics of baby corn
200000
180000
160000
140000
120000
100000
80000
60000
40000
20000
0
Gross return (ha-1)
Net return (ha-1)
2017-18
Gross return (ha-1)
Net return (ha-1)
2018-19
F1 (100%NP+25%K)
F2 (100%NP+50%K)
F3 (100%NP+75%K)
F4 (100% NPK)

Fig. 4.5

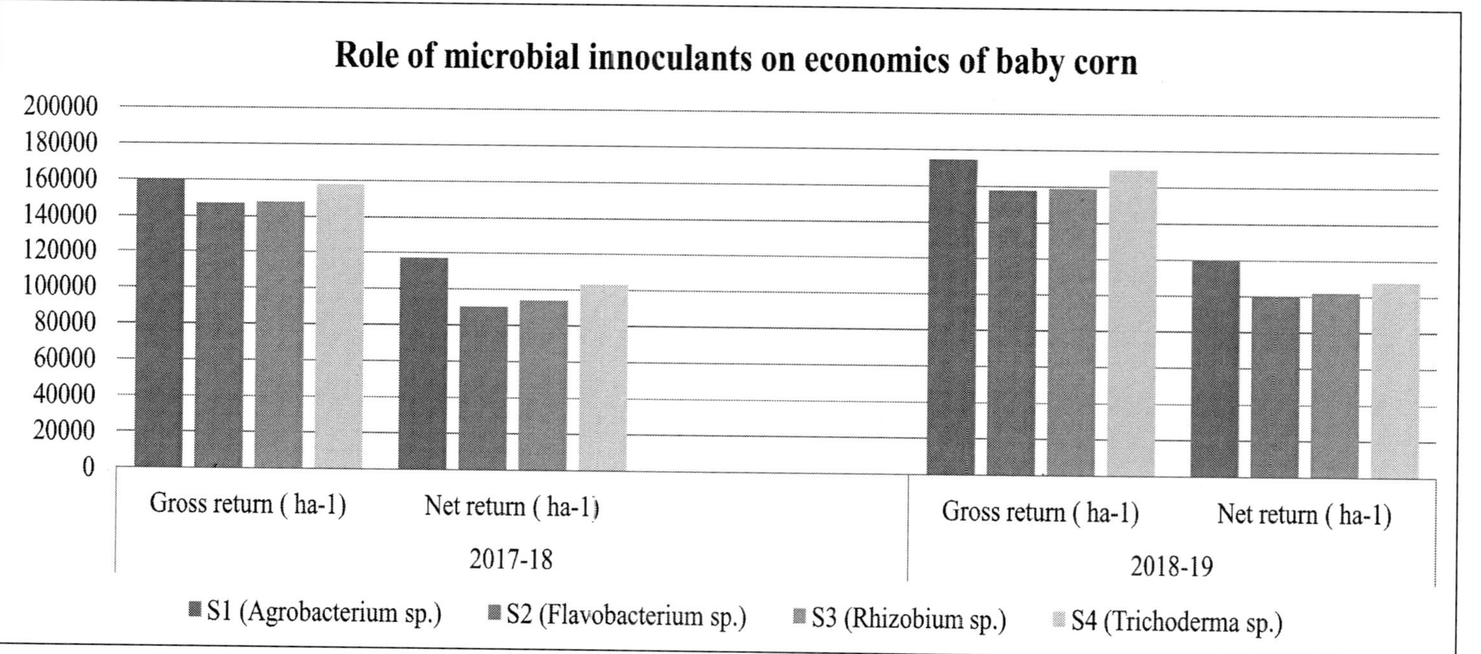
Role of microbial innoculants on economics of baby corn
200000
180000
160000
140000
120000
100000
80000
60000
40000
20000
0
Gross return (ha-1)
Net return (ha-1)
2017-18
Gross return (ha-1)
Net return (ha-1)
2018-19
S1 (Agrobacterium sp.)
S2 (Flavobacterium sp.)
S3 (Rhizobium sp.)
S4 (Trichoderma sp.)

Fig. 4.6

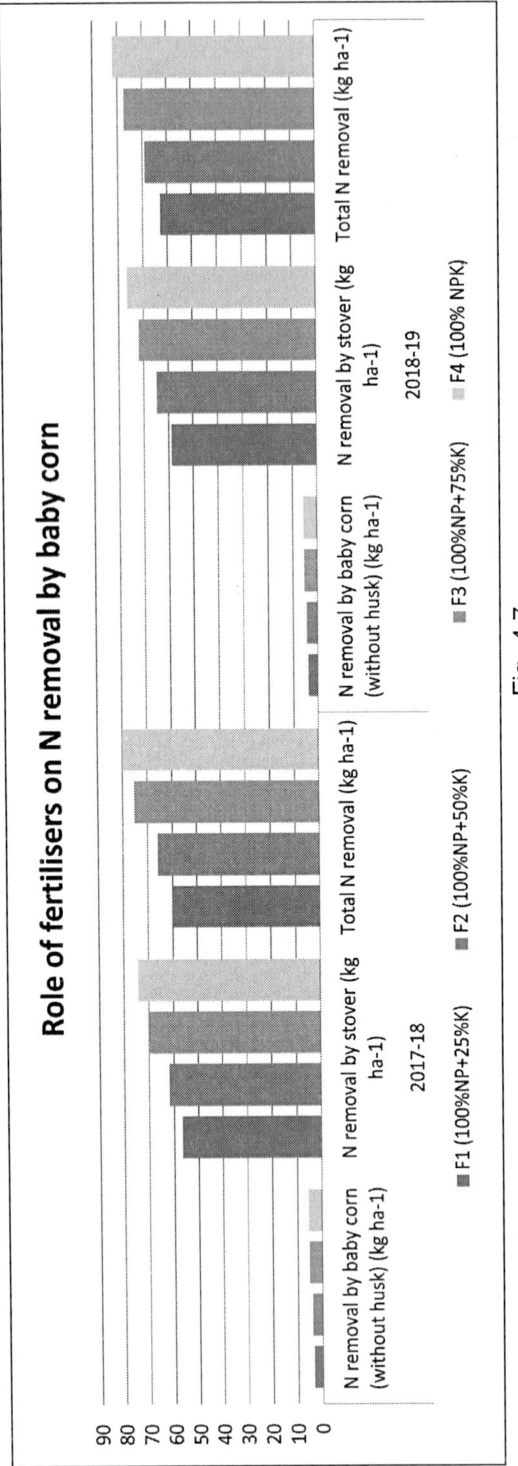
Role of fertilisers on N removal by baby corn
90
80
70
60
50
40
30
20
10
0
N removal by baby corn (without husk) (kg ha-1)
N removal by stover (kg ha-1)
Total N removal (kg ha-1)
2017-18
N removal by baby corn (without husk) (kg ha-1)
N removal by stover (kg ha-1)
Total N removal (kg ha-1)
2018-19
F1 (100%NP+25%K)
F2 (100%NP+50%K)
F3 (100%NP+75%K)
F4 (100% NPK)

Fig. 4.7

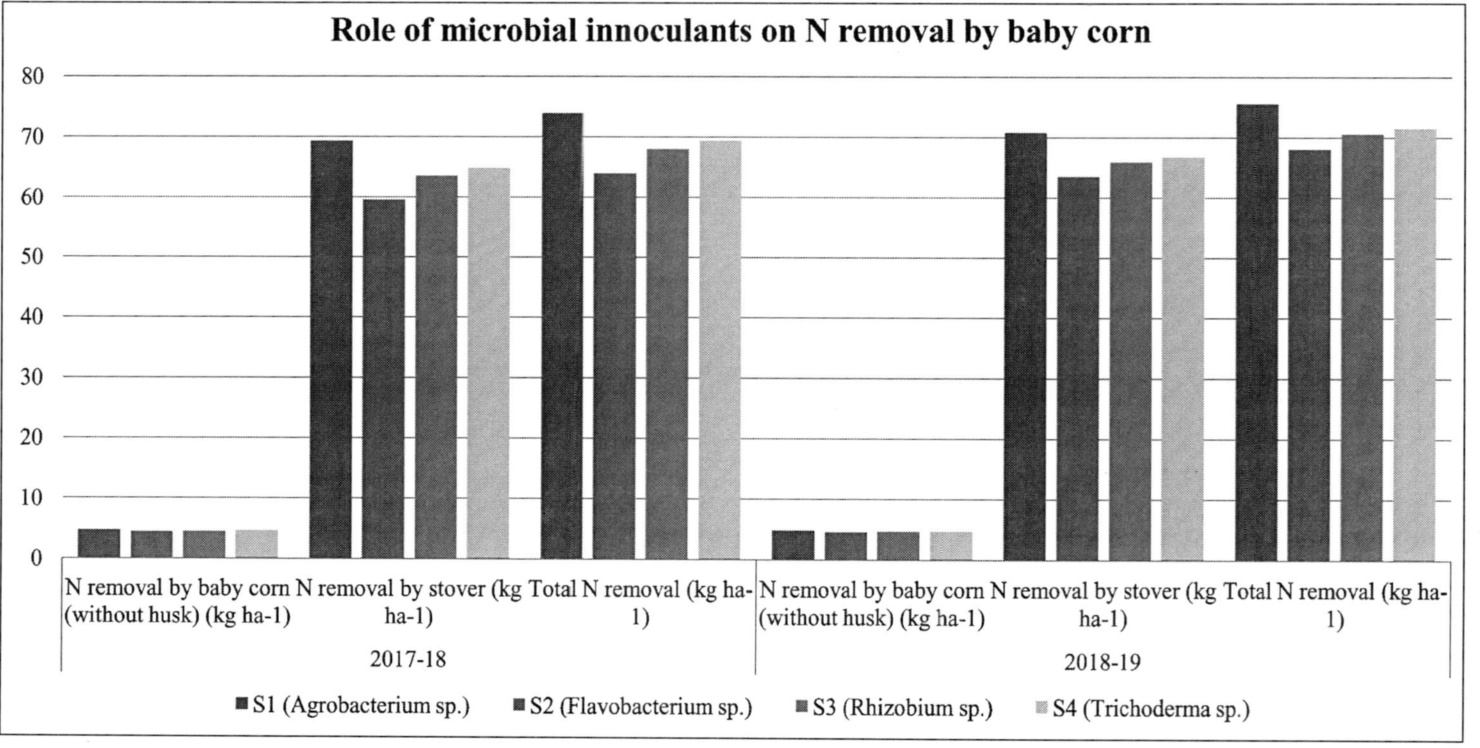
Role of microbial innoculants on N removal by baby corn
80
70
60
50
40
30
20
10
0
N removal by baby corn (without husk) (kg ha-1)
N removal by stover (kg ha-1)
Total N removal (kg ha-1)
2017-18
N removal by baby corn (without husk) (kg ha-1)
N removal by stover (kg ha-1)
Total N removal (kg ha-1)
2018-19
S1 (Agrobacterium sp.)
S2 (Flavobacterium sp.)
S3 (Rhizobium sp.)
S4 (Trichoderma sp.)

Fig. 4.8

Table 4.18: Effect of fertility levels and microbial strains on P content (%), removal of P by baby corn (on dry weight basis)

Treatments	P content in baby corn (%)		P content in stover (%)		P removal by baby corn (kg ha^{-1})		P removal by stover (kg ha^{-1})		Total P removal (kg ha^{-1})	
	2017-18	2018-19	2017-18	2018-19	2017-18	2018-19	2017-18	2018-19	2017-18	2018-19
Fertility levels (RDF)										
F_1 (100%NP+25%K)	0.27	0.29	0.12	0.13	0.74	0.85	8.60	9.68	9.34	10.53
F_2 (100%NP+50%K)	0.31	0.34	0.14	0.15	0.98	1.12	10.27	11.22	11.25	12.34
F_3 (100%NP+75%K)	0.42	0.45	0.19	0.21	1.20	1.23	12.51	13.65	13.71	14.88
F_4 (100% NPK)	0.45	0.48	0.20	0.22	1.24	1.29	14.58	15.40	15.82	16.69
SEm±	0.02	0.02	0.002	0.002	0.08	0.06	0.66	0.74	0.74	0.75
C.D. (P=0.05)	0.06	0.07	0.006	0.007	0.24	0.15	2.10	2.31	2.25	2.30
Microbial strains										
S_1 (*Agrobacterium* sp.)	0.42	0.45	0.18	0.20	1.18	1.23	13.6	14.42	14.78	15.66
S_2 (*Flavobacterium* sp.)	0.27	0.29	0.12	0.13	0.71	0.77	7.62	8.70	8.33	9.48
S_3 (*Rhizobium* sp.)	0.33	0.35	0.14	0.15	0.94	0.99	9.29	10.24	10.23	11.23
S_4 (*Trichoderma* sp.)	0.37	0.39	0.16	0.18	1.02	1.09	11.63	12.14	12.65	13.24
SEm±	0.01	0.01	0.001	0.001	0.02	0.03	0.57	0.63	0.71	0.73
C.D.(P=0.05)	0.02	0.03	0.003	0.003	0.06	0.09	1.35	1.86	2.16	2.22

Microbial innoculum

A critical analysis of the data indicated that *Agrobacterium* sp. (S_1) caused higher phosphorus content in baby corn and stover and this was followed by *Trichoderma* sp. (S_4). On an average P content due to *Agrobacterium* sp. (S_1) was found to increase by 55.36% and 52.00% in baby corn and stover over *Flavobacterium* sp. (S_2) respectively.

Interaction

The interaction between fertility levels and microbial innoculum was not found significant in respect to phosphorus content.

Phosphorus removal (kg ha^{-1})

The data on removal of phosphorus by baby corn, stover as well as total P as affected by different levels of fertility and microbial innoculum are summarized in table 4.18 and illustrated graphically in figure 4.9 and 4.10.

Fertilizer Levels

A close analysis of the data (Table 4.18) revealed that application of different levels of fertilizers caused marked effect in P removal by baby corn and stover. 100%NP+75%K (F_3) and 100%NPK (F_4) which remained at par with each other proved their distinct superiority in P removal over all other treatments during both the years. On an average fertilizer up to the level of F_3 was found to enhance P removal by 52.83%, 43.11% and 43.89% by baby corn, stover and total P over 100%NP+25%K (F_1).

Microbial innoculum

Significant differences were recorded due to microbial innoculum in respect of phosphorous removal by baby corn. On an average *Agrobacterium* sp. (S_1) registered higher P removal by 62.84%, 71.69% and 70.92% by baby corn, stover and total P over *Flavobacterium* sp. (S_2) and it was found in the order of $S_{1>}$ $S_{4>}$ $S_{3>}$ S_2.

Interaction

None of the interactions was found significant in respect of phosphorous removal by baby corn in any of the experimental years.

Potassium content in baby corn (without husk) and stover (%)

It was clear from the data presented in table 4.19 that potassium content in baby corn (without husk) and stover was markedly influenced by different levels of fertility and microbial innoculum during both the years.

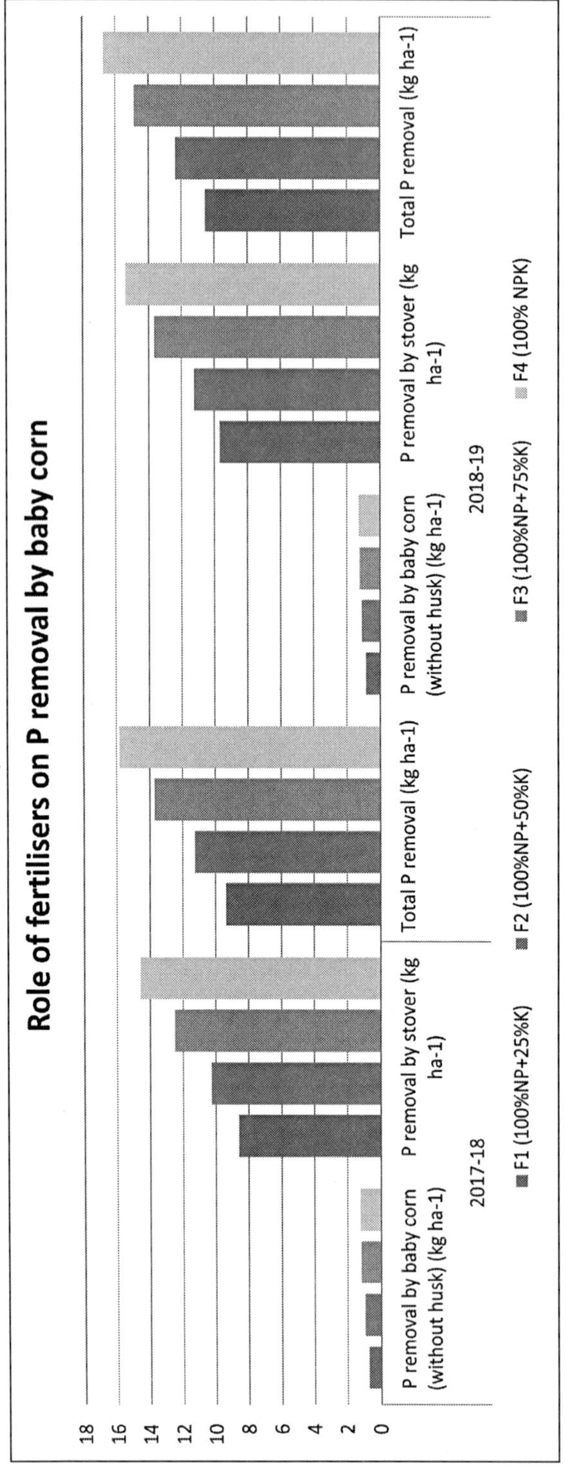

Role of fertilisers on P removal by baby corn
18
16
14
12
10
8
6
4
2
0
P removal by baby corn (without husk) (kg ha-1)
P removal by stover (kg ha-1)
Total P removal (kg ha-1)
P removal by baby corn (without husk) (kg ha-1)
P removal by stover (kg ha-1)
Total P removal (kg ha-1)
2017-18
2018-19
F1 (100%NP+25%K)
F2 (100%NP+50%K)
F3 (100%NP+75%K)
F4 (100% NPK)

Fig. 4.9

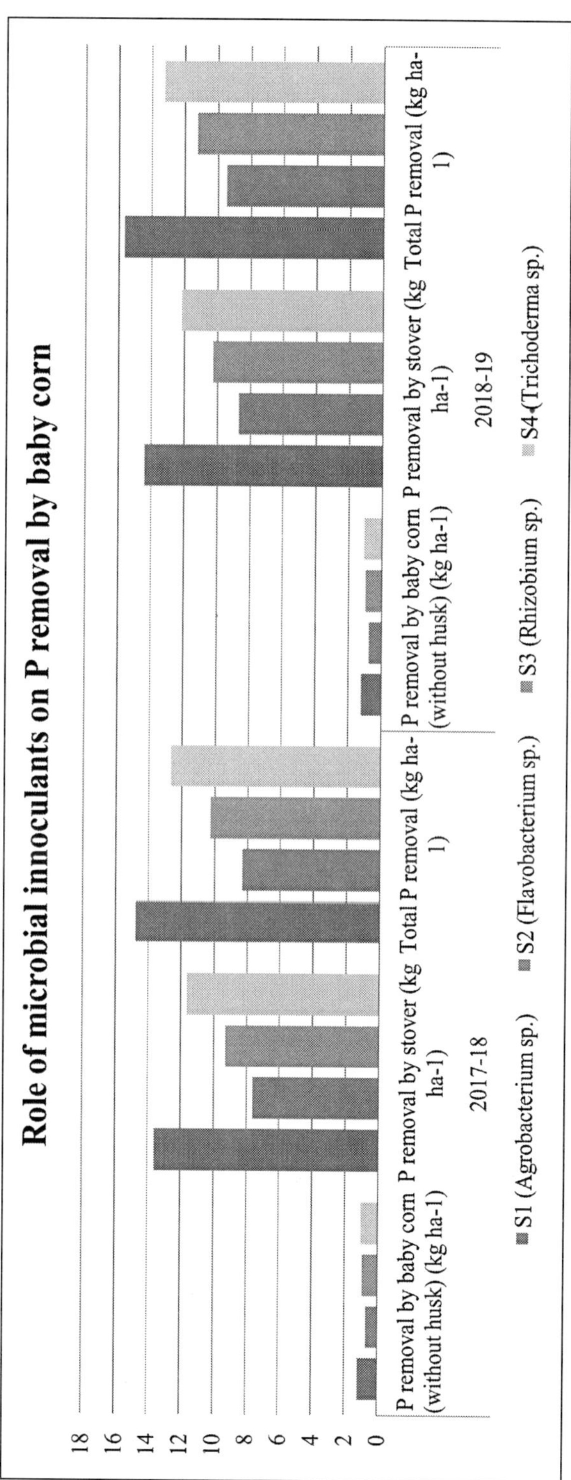
Role of microbial innoculants on P removal by baby corn
18
16
14
12
10
8
6
4
2
0
P removal by baby corn (without husk) (kg ha-1)
P removal by stover (kg ha-1)
Total P removal (kg ha-1)
2017-18
2018-19
S1 (Agrobacterium sp.)
S2 (Flavobacterium sp.)
S3 (Rhizobium sp.)
S4 (Trichoderma sp.)

Fig. 4.10

Table 4.19: Effect of fertility levels and microbial strains on K content (%), removal of K by baby corn (on dry weight basis)

Treatments	K content in baby corn (%)		K content in stover (%)		K removal by baby corn (kg ha^{-1})		K removal by stover (kg ha^{-1})		Total K removal (kg ha^{-1})	
	2017-18	2018-19	2017-18	2018-19	2017-18	2018-19	2017-18	2018-19	2017-18	2018-19
Fertility levels (RDF)										
F_1 (100%NP+25%K)	0.81	0.88	0.99	1.02	1.75	1.91	61.21	63.02	62.95	64.93
F_2 (100%NP+50%K)	0.89	0.91	1.03	1.05	1.89	2.06	64.53	69.04	66.42	71.11
F_3 (100%NP+75%K)	1.19	1.20	1.16	1.17	2.61	2.72	78.27	79.97	80.88	82.69
F_4 (100% NPK)	1.21	1.23	1.19	1.21	2.73	2.85	82.51	85.32	85.24	88.17
SEm±	0.02	0.02	0.01	0.01	0.09	0.10	1.64	2.33	2.19	2.21
C.D. (P=0.05)	0.06	0.07	0.03	0.04	0.28	0.31	5.25	7.45	6.57	6.63
Microbial strains										
S_1 (*Agrobacterium* sp.)	1.10	1.15	1.14	1.17	2.28	2.45	77.50	79.32	79.78	81.77
S_2 (*Flavobacterium* sp.)	0.92	0.97	0.98	1.01	1.91	2.08	66.56	68.13	68.47	70.21
S_3 (*Rhizobium* sp.)	0.99	1.02	1.05	1.09	1.98	2.15	69.13	70.07	71.11	72.22
S_4 (*Trichoderma* sp.)	1.04	1.09	1.09	1.12	2.13	2.29	71.93	72.96	74.06	75.25
SEm±	0.01	0.01	0.01	0.01	0.05	0.07	1.56	2.14	1.89	1.91
C.D.(P=0.05)	0.03	0.03	0.03	0.04	0.15	0.22	4.67	6.44	5.67	5.73

Fertilizer Levels

Application of 100%NP+75%K (F_3) while remaining at par with 100%NPK (F_4) produced baby corn and stover with higher K content. On an average the potassium content in baby corn by F_3 was recorded 41.42% and 15.92% higher than 100%NP+25%K (F_1) level of fertility. Overall the effect of fertility levels on potassium content in baby corn (without husk) and stover was in the order of F_4, F_3> F_2> F_1.

Microbial innoculum

Perusal of data revealed significant variation in potassium content in baby corn and stover due to different microbial innoculum. *Agrobacterium* sp. (S_1) exhibited on an average 19.05% and 16.08% more potassium content in baby corn and stover than *Flavobacterium* sp. (S_2). Over all it was in the order of S_1> S_4> S_3> S_2.

Interaction

All the variables were independent in their effect on K content resulting in no significant interaction.

Potassium removal (kg ha^{-1})

The data recorded on potassium removal by baby corn, stover as well as total K as affected by different fertility levels and microbial innoculum have been presented in table 4.19 and illustrated graphically in figure 4.11 and 4.12.

Fertilizer Levels

Fertility levels manifested a profound effect on removal of potassium by baby corn during both the years of study. Application of 100%NP+75%K (F_3) and 100%NPK (F_4) was found to be statistically at par with each other in K removal. F_3 recorded 45.63%, 27.38% and 27.91% more removal by baby corn, stover and total K than 100%NP+25%K (F_1) during both the years and it was found in the order of F_4, F_3> F_2> F_1.

Microbial innoculum

The effect of microbial innoculum on potassium removal was found to be significant during experimentation. *Agrobacterium* sp. (S_1) recorded 18.55%, 16.43% and 16.49% more removal of potassium by baby corn, stover and consequent total removal over *Flavobacterium* sp. (S_2) in which the minimum was observed. Overall it was in the order of S_1> S_4 >S_3> S_2.

Interaction

The interaction of the experimental variables could not evince any marked effect on this attribute in any of the years.

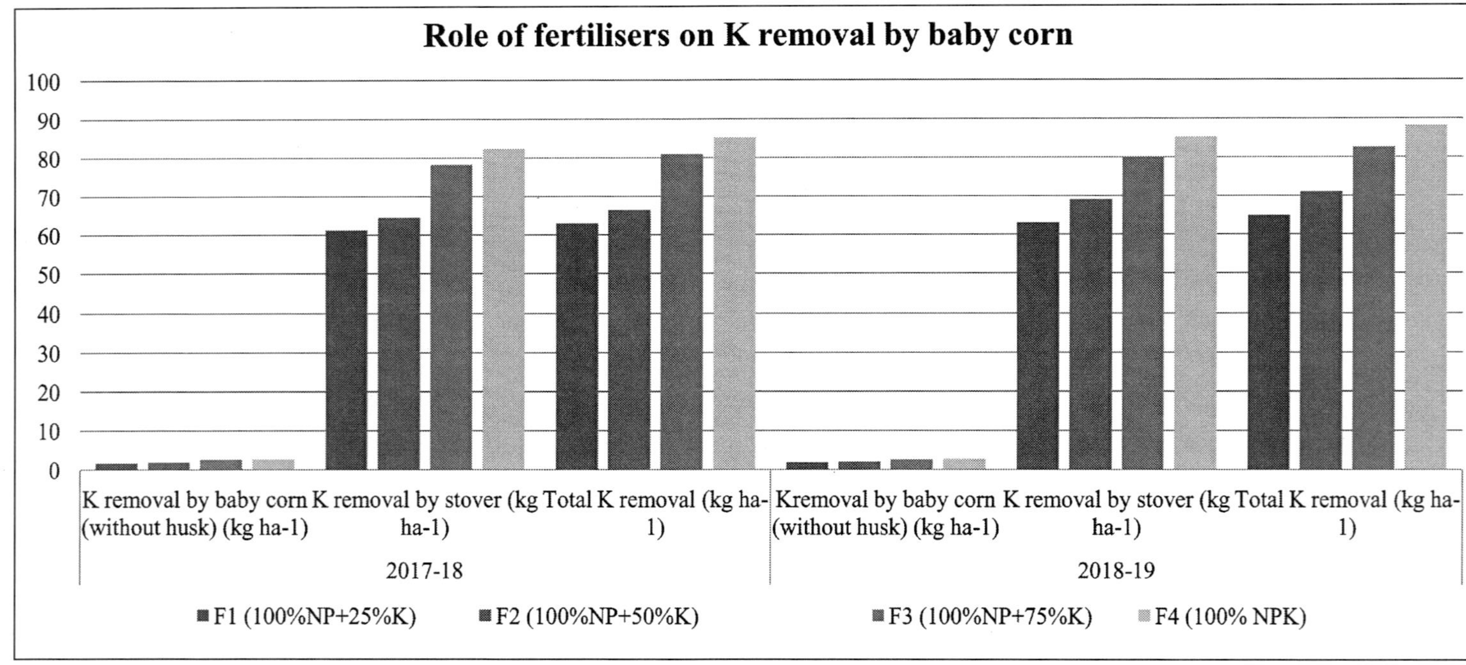
Role of fertilisers on K removal by baby corn
100
90
80
70
60
50
40
30
20
10
0
K removal by baby corn (without husk) (kg ha-1)
K removal by stover (kg ha-1)
Total K removal (kg ha-1)
2017-18
Kremoval by baby corn (without husk) (kg ha-1)
K removal by stover (kg ha-1)
Total K removal (kg ha-1)
2018-19
F1 (100%NP+25%K)
F2 (100%NP+50%K)
F3 (100%NP+75%K)
F4 (100% NPK)

Fig. 4.11

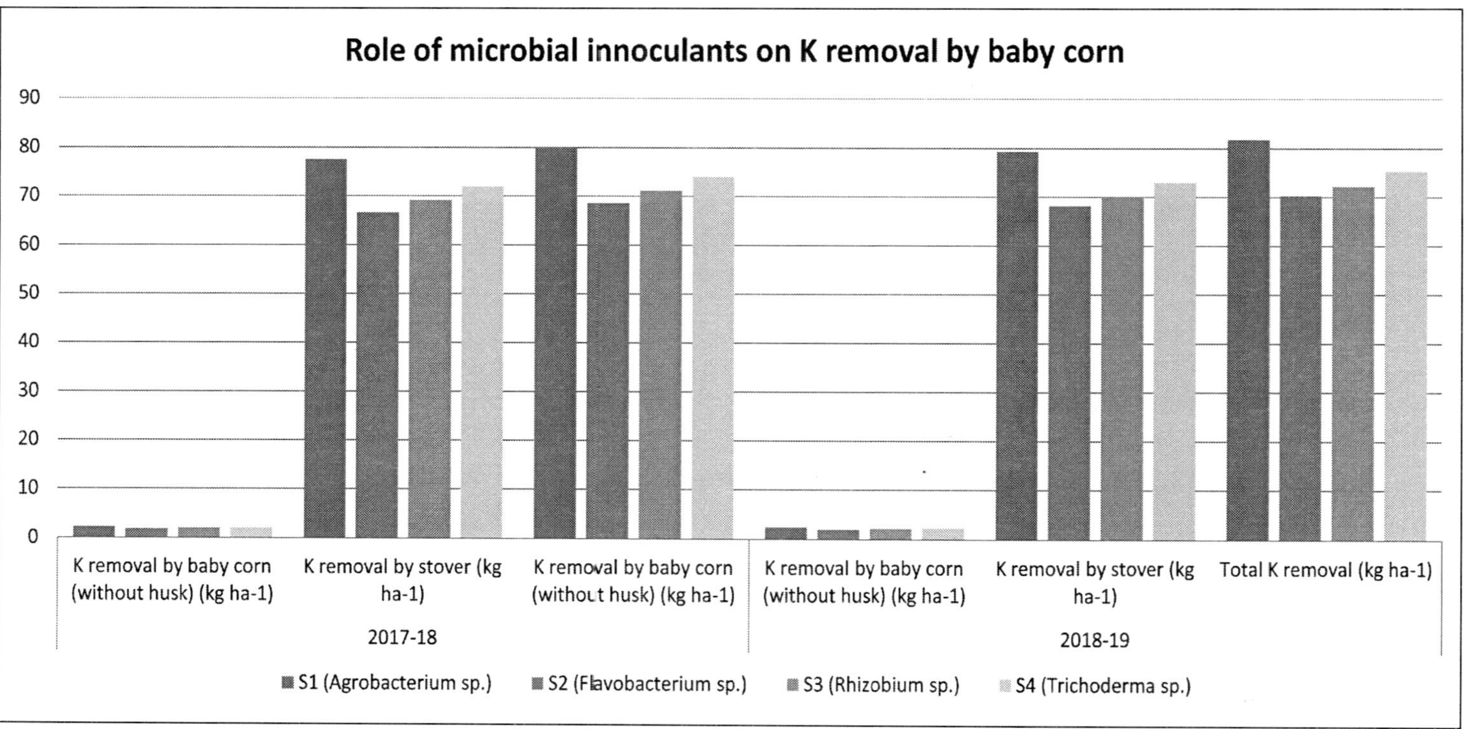
Role of microbial innoculants on K removal by baby corn
90
80
70
60
50
40
30
20
10
0
K removal by baby corn (without husk) (kg ha-1)
K removal by stover (kg ha-1)
K removal by baby corn (without husk) (kg ha-1)
2017-18
K removal by baby corn (without husk) (kg ha-1)
K removal by stover (kg ha-1)
Total K removal (kg ha-1)
2018-19
S1 (Agrobacterium sp.)
S2 (Flavobacterium sp.)
S3 (Rhizobium sp.)
S4 (Trichoderma sp.)

Fig. 4.12

Soil Microbial Population

The data pertaining to soil microbial population (bacterial, actinomycetes and fungal) as influenced by levels of fertility and application of microbial innoculum have been summarized in tables 4.20, 4.21 and 4.22. It was observed that the fertility status of the soil improved in the second year and the population was more in 2018-19 than the previous year 2017-18.

Bacterial Population (cfu g^{-1} of soil).

Fertilizer Levels

It was evident from the data that greater number of colonies of bacteria was observed at 100%NP+75%K (F_3) and 100%NPK (F_4) level which remained statistically at par with each other. The fertility level of F_3 on the basis of average of two year data exhibited 18.49% more bacterial colonies than 100%NP+25%K (F_1) at 60 DAS. No. of bacterial colonies increased upto 60 DAS at 10^{-6} dilutions of cfu/g of soil after which there was a decrease in the number at harvest of baby corn. The response of bacterial population to different fertility levels was in the order of F_4, F_3> F_2> F_1.

Microbial innoculum

It was clear from the data (Table 4.20) that microbial innoculum played a significant role in maintaining fertility. *Agrobacterium* sp. produced maximum no. of bacterial colonies which was on an average 19.07% more than *Flavobacterium* sp. (S_2) at 60 DAS. Higher no. of colonies was found at 60 DAS of the crop growth after which there was a decrease.

Interaction

Interaction between fertility levels and microbial innoculum on number of bacterial colonies failed to produce any significant results.

Actinomycetes population (cfu g^{-1} of soil)

Fertilizer Levels

It was evident from the data (Table 4.21) that actinomycetes showed higher population at 100%NP+75%K (F_3) and 100%NPK (F_4) which remained statistically at par with each other at all the stages of growth. The fertility level at F_3 on an average exhibited 9.43% more population than 100%NP+25%K (F_1) at 60 DAS.

Microbial innoculum

Further examination of the data (Table 4.21) revealed that the maximum actinomycetes population was observed at 60 DAS of baby corn growth. On an average *Agrobacterium* sp. (S_1) produced 18.36% more colonies than *Flavobacterium* sp. (S_2) – the least effective strain in increasing actinomycetes population. The overall effect of innoculum on the population was found to be in the order of S_1> S_4> S_3> S_2.

Table 4.20: Effect of fertility levels and microbial strains on bacterial population (colony forming unit) cfu/g of soil

Treatments	Bacterial population					
	Before sowing		60 DAS		After harvesting of baby corn	
	cfu/gx10^6 dilutions		cfu/gx10^6 dilutions		cfu/gx10^6 dilutions	
	2017-18	2018-19	2017-18	2018-19	2017-18	2018-19
Fertility levels (RDF)						
F_1 (100%NP+25%K)	92.52	95.61	117.45	126.55	99.51	101.74
F_2 (100%NP+50%K)	95.85	99.14	128.56	132.74	108.12	112.56
F_3 (100%NP+75%K)	98.18	109.42	142.65	146.46	126.42	132.41
F_4 (100% NPK)	101.47	112.74	146.78	151.41	129.51	135.89
SEm±	1.16	1.12	1.50	1.63	1.22	1.26
C.D. (P=0.05)	3.42	3.71	4.61	5.39	3.42	3.66
Microbial strains						
S_1 (*Agrobacterium* sp.)	97.14	100.87	138.47	141.12	118.65	121.54
S_2 (*Flavobacterium* sp.)	89.12	91.29	115.98	118.84	98.15	100.41
S_3 (*Rhizobium* sp.)	93.42	95.56	119.89	123.54	104.77	106.87
S_4 (*Trichoderma* sp.)	93.55	97.39	125.17	130.52	109.85	112.54
SEm±	1.14	1.15	1.47	1.58	1.31	1.20
C.D.(P=0.05)	3.55	3.4	4.46	5.22	3.94	3.57

Table 4.21: Effect of fertility levels and microbial strains on actinomycetes population (colony forming unit) cfu/g of soil

Treatments	Actinomycetes population					
	Before sowing		60DAS		After harvesting of baby corn	
	cfu/gx10^5 dilutions		cfu/gx10^5 dilutions		cfu/gx10^5 dilutions	
	2017-18	2018-19	2017-18	2018-19	2017-18	2018-19
Fertility levels (RDF)						
F_1 (100%NP+25%K)	39.99	41.87	44.24	46.49	41.23	43.85
F_2 (100%NP+50%K)	42.68	44.23	46.74	48.87	43.84	45.77
F_3 (100%NP+75%K)	45.95	48.45	48.91	50.38	45.19	47.51
F_4 (100% NPK)	47.69	50.55	52.65	55.14	48.87	50.29
SEm±.	0.62	0.73	1.51	1.59	1.21	0.98
C.D. (P=0.05)	1.94	2.25	4.65	4.86	3.74	2.88
Microbial strains						
S_1 (*Agrobacterium* sp.)	44.85	48.58	52.21	53.25	47.14	48.85
S_2 (*Flavobacterium* sp.)	38.84	40.10	43.98	45.12	42.54	42.91
S_3 (*Rhizobium* sp.)	40.1	42.69	45.82	47.68	44.19	44.83
S_4 (*Trichoderma* sp.)	42.75	44.99	47.07	48.91	46.15	46.34
SEm±	0.59	0.69	1.48	1.42	1.15	0.82
C.D.(P=0.05)	1.81	2.11	2.25	4.31	3.48	2.49

Table 4.22: Effect of fertility levels and microbial strains on fungal population (colony forming unit) cfu/g of soil

Treatments	Fungal population					
	Before sowing		60 DAS		After harvesting of baby corn	
	cfu/gx10^4 dilutions		cfu/gx10^4 dilutions		cfu/gx10^4 dilutions	
	2017-18	2018-19	2017-18	2018-19	2017-18	2018-19
Fertility levels (RDF)						
F_1 (100%NP+25%K)	20.12	21.74	32.59	33.19	28.45	29.05
F_2 (100%NP+50%K)	24.52	26.23	35.77	36.55	31.63	32.41
F_3 (100%NP+75%K)	27.64	29.32	39.83	40.59	36.89	39.55
F_4 (100% NPK)	30.41	32.29	43.61	45.50	39.47	42.36
SEm±	0.92	1.06	1.23	1.61	0.88	0.91
C.D. (P=0.05)	2.97	3.41	3.84	4.99	2.71	2.86
Microbial strains						
S_1 (*Agrobacterium* sp.)	27.14	29 87	40.59	42.25	36.45	38.11
S_2 (*Flavobacterium* sp.)	20.35	21.56	32.68	33.08	28.54	30.94
S_3 (*Rhizobium* sp.)	22.47	23.95	35.09	36.68	31.05	32.54
S_4 (*Trichoderma* sp.)	24.86	26.12	36.92	38.03	33.72	35.79
SEm±	0.42	0.85	1.19	1.12	0.84	0.54
C.D.(P=0.05)	1.34	2.71	3.63	3.42	2.67	1.71

Interaction

Interaction between fertility levels and microbial innoculum was not found to be significant during any of the years.

Fungal Population (cfu $g^{-1}$of soil)

In comparison to total bacterial and actinomycetes count, fungal population was found to be the least.

Fertilizer Levels

Perusal of the data (Table 4.22) revealed that the fertility level at 100%NP+75%K (F_3) while remaining at par with 100%NPK (F_4) exhibited higher no. of colonies at 10^{-4} dilution and remained statistically superior to other treatments. On an average F_3 registered 22.26% more fungal population than 100%NP+25%K (F_1) at 60 DAS of the crop growth.

Microbial innoculum

A critical analysis of the data revealed that the maximum fungal population was observed with *Agrobacterium* sp. (S_1) colonies at 60 DAS which was statistically significant over other treatments. It registered 25.97% more population than *Flavobacterium* sp. (S_2). Over all the effect was found in the order of S_1> S_4> S_3> S_2.

Interaction

Interaction between fertility levels and microbial innoculum was not found to be significant in any of the years.

Soil Microbial Biomass Carbon (SMBC)

The data pertaining to soil microbial biomass carbon (µg C g^{-1} soil) obtained through decomposition of microorganism releasing C (as a source of nutrients to plants) and as influenced by levels of fertilizers and application of microbial innoculum have been summarized in table 4.23. The data established the fact that SMBC of the soil was higher in the second year as compared to the first year.

Fertilizer Levels

It was evident from the data that soil microbial biomass carbon was higher at 100%NP+75%K (F_3) and 100%NPK (F_4) which remained statistically at par to each other. On an average biomass carbon at F_3 was 17.86% higher than the 100%NP+25%K (F_1). Higher biomass carbon was observed at 60 DAS of crop growth and was in the order F_4, F_3> F_2> F_1.

Microbial innoculum

It was apparent from the data (Table 4.23) that SMBC was highest with *Agrobacterium* sp. (S_1) and this was followed by *Trichoderma* sp. (S_4) at all the stages of observation during both the years. On an average the biomass carbon by S_1 was 31.34% higher than the *Flavobacterium* sp. (S_2).

Table 4.23: Effect of fertility levels and microbial strains on soil microbial biomass carbon

Treatments	SMBC (μg C g^{-1} soil)					
	Before sowing of baby corn		60 DAS		After harvesting of baby corn	
	2017-18	2018-19	2017-18	2018-19	2017-18	2018-19
Fertility levels (RDF)						
F_1 (100%NP+25%K)	73.39	76.52	98.65	99.12	90.85	92.36
F_2 (100%NP+50%K)	79.36	82.36	102.63	103.41	94.21	96.77
F_3 (100%NP+75% K)	92.74	96.32	119.86	120.92	98.32	99.47
F_4 (100% NPK)	94.23	100.15	124.85	126.11	102.12	103.88
SEm±	0.52	1.23	1.65	2.09	1.42	1.79
C.D. (P=0.05)	1.74	4.15	5.32	6.95	4.24	5.25
Microbial strains						
S_1 (*Agrobacterium* sp.)	92.63	94.36	120.87	122.65	100.65	101.41
S_2 (*Flavobacterium* sp.)	70.56	72.44	91.86	93.55	84.01	85.21
S_3 (*Rhizobium* sp.)	79.21	83.65	98.93	101.11	88.05	90.33
S_4 (*Trichoderma* sp.)	85.36	90.31	105.66	107.31	94.12	95.88
SEm±	0.56	1.16	0.99	1.76	0.62	1.78
C.D.(P=0.05)	1.74	3.59	3.19	5.63	1.98	5.41

Interaction

Interaction between fertility levels and microbial innoculum was not found to be significant at any of the years.

Economics of Baby Corn

Data pertaining to economics of baby corn cultivation have been presented in table 4.24. It was clear from the data that irrespective of the treatments, gross return, net return and benefit:cost ratio were comparatively higher during second year than that of first year of experimentation.

Gross return (₹/ha)

Data in relation to gross return as affected by fertility levels and microbial innoculum during both the years of experimentation are presented in table 4.24 and illustrated graphically in figure 4.5 and figure 4.6.

Fertilizer Levels

Perusal of the data indicated that 100%NP+75%K (F_3) and 100%NPK (F_4) recorded higher gross return and remained statistically at par with each other. On an average of two years data 100%NP+75%K (F_3) showed an increased gross return of 37.39% and 25.67% over 100%NP+25%K (F_1) and 100%NP+50%K (F_2) respectively and was in the order F_4, F_3> F_2> F_1.

Microbial innoculum

The data revealed marked variation in gross return due to different microbial innoculum during both the years of experimentation. On an average *Agrobacterium* sp. (S_1) recorded 10.68% higher gross return than *Flavobacterium* sp. (S_2). The gross return of different innoculum was in the order S_1>S_4>S_3>S_2.

Interaction

Interaction between fertility levels and microbial innoculum recorded significant effect in gross return (Table 4.25). The combination between 100%NP+75%K (F_3) and *Agrobacterium* sp. (S_1) resulted in the higher gross return of (₹ 253345.56 and ₹ 254190.00) during 1st and 2nd year but remained at par with100%NPK (F_4) during both the years of experimentation.

Net returns (₹/ha)

Analysis of the data on net return as influenced by different levels of fertilizers and microbial innoculum during both the years are presented in table 4.24 and depicted graphically in figures 4.5 and 4.6.

Table 4.24: Effect of fertility levels and microbial strains on economics of baby corn

Treatments	Economics							
	Cost of cultivation(₹ ha^{-1})		Gross return(₹ ha^{-1})		Net return(₹ ha^{-1})		Benefit : Cost ratio	
	1st year	2nd year	1st year	2nd year	1st year	2nd year	1st year	2nd year
Fertility levels (RDF)								
F_1 (100%NP+25%K)	60633.34	61683.34	172221.34	173699.40	111588.00	112016.06	1.84	1.82
F_2 (100%NP+50%K)	61286.81	62336.81	182284.96	195893.64	120998.15	133556.83	1.97	2.14
F_3 (100%NP+75%K)	61940.08	62990.08	234143.71	241119.01	172203.63	178128.93	2.78	2.83
F_4 (100% NPK)	62593.34	63643.34	237477.74	246858.44	174884.40	183215.10	2.79	2.88
SE m±	-	-	2689.06	4280.57	2689.06	4280.57	0.04	0.07
C.D. (P=0.05)	-	-	8601.48	13692.22	8601.48	13692.22	0.14	0.22
Microbial strains								
S_1 (*Agrobacterium* sp.)	61634.89	62684.89	218276.29	227209.50	156641.40	164524.61	2.54	2.62
S_2 (*Flavobacterium* sp.)	61634.89	62684.89	197224.22	205288.69	135589.33	142603.80	2.20	2.27
S_3 (*Rhizobium* sp.)	61634.89	62684.89	200589.44	209648.73	138954.55	146963.84	2.25	2.34
S_4 (*Trichoderma* sp.)	61548.89	62598.89	210037.79	215423.56	148488.90	152824.67	2.41	2.44
SE m±	-	-	2386.82	2020.06	2386.82	2020.06	0.04	0.03
C.D. (P=0.05)	-	-	6844.75	5792.99	6844.75	5792.99	0.11	0.09

Table 4.25: Interaction effect of fertility levels and microbial strains on economics (gross return) of baby corn

Treatments	2017-18					2018-19				
	S_1	S_2	S_3	S_4	Mean	S_1	S_2	S_3	S_4	Mean
Fertility levels × microbial strains										
F_1 (100% NP+25%K)	176663.35	169260.05	171119.49	171842.48	172221.34	174571.10	171699.05	173308.49	175218.98	173699.40
F_2 (100% NP+50%K)	185979.16	179081.56	181573.85	182505.26	182284.96	210376.91	184635.56	191002.85	197559.26	195893.64
F_3 (100% NP+75%K)	253345.56	218782.50	225820.00	238626.79	234143.71	254190.00	230363.91	238308.60	241613.52	241119.01
F_4 (100% of NPK)	257117.11	221772.77	223844.44	247176.62	237477.74	264700.00	234456.25	240975.00	247302.50	246858.44
Mean	218276.29	197224.22	200589.44	210037.79		227209.50	205288.69	209648.73	215423.56	
SEm ±			4773.65					4040.13		
CD (P=0.05) different sub treatment vs same main treatment			13689.51					11585.98		
SEm ±			4931.72					5528.59		
CD (P=0.05) different sub treatment for different main treatment			13499.41					14187.31		

S_1 - *Agrobacterium* sp., S_2 - *Flavobacterium* sp., S_3 - *Rhizobium* sp., S_4 - *Trichoderma* sp.

RDF: 150, 80, 80 kg/ha of N, P and K.

Fertilizer Levels

An insight into the data clearly highlighted marked effect of all the variables on net returns of the crop. 100%NP+75%K (F_3) and 100%NPK (F_4) which remained statistically at par with each other showed higher net return and was significantly superior to other treatments. On an average F_3 registered 56.68% and 37.63% more net returns than 100%NP+25%K (F_1) and 100%NP+50%K (F_2). The response of the crop in its net return to different fertility levels was in the order of F_4, F_3> F_2> F_1.

Microbial innoculum

Similarly *Agrobacterium* sp. (S_1) registered the maximum net return among all the innoculum and on an average it led to 15.45% more net return than *Flavobacterium* sp. (S_2). The net return from different innoculum was in the order S_1>S_4>S_3>S_2 during both the years.

Interaction

The interaction between fertility levels and microbial innoculum (Table 4.26) registered significant effect in respect of net return. 100%NP+75%K (F_3) and *Agrobacterium* sp. (S_1) registered a net return of (191383.98 and 192178.42) but remained at par with 100%NPK (F_4) during both the years of experimentation.

Benefit: Cost Ratio

Data on benefit: cost ratio as affected by different variables like levels of fertility and microbial innoculum during both the years of study are presented in table 4.24.

Fertilizer Levels

A keen examination of the data (Table 4.24) revealed that benefit: cost ratio increased with increasing levels of fertilizers during both the years of study. In general, 100%NP+75%K (F_3) and 100%NPK (F_4) registered the higher benefit: cost ratio and remained statistically at par with each other. It was higher in the first year than the second year. On an average of two years, F_3 registered 53.28% and 36.50% more benefit: cost ratio than 100%NP+25%K (F_1) and 100%NP+50%K (F_2).

Microbial innoculum

Higher benefit cost ratio was noted with *Agrobacterium* sp. (S_1) with 15.44% increase over *Flavobacterium* sp. followed by *Trichoderma* sp. (S_4). Overall it was in the order S_1>S_4>S_3>S_2.

Interaction

Significant interaction was observed between the levels of fertility and microbial strain in respect of benefit cost ratio (Table 4.27). 100%NP+75%K (F_3) with *Agrobacterium* sp. (S_1) registered the benefit cost ratio of (₹ 3.09 and ₹ 3.05) during first and second year respectively but it remained at par with 100%NPK (F_4).

Table 4.26: Interaction effect of fertility levels and microbial strains on economics (net return) of baby corn

Treatments	2017-18					2018-19				
	S_1	S_2	S_3	S_4	Mean	S_1	S_2	S_3	S_4	Mean
Fertility levels × microbial strains										
F_1 (100% NP+25%K)	116008.51	108605.21	110464.65	111273.64	111588.00	112866.26	109994.21	111603.65	113600.14	112016.06
F_2 (100% NP+50%K)	124670.85	117773.25	120265.54	121282.95	120998.15	148018.60	122277.25	128644.54	135286.95	133556.83
F_3 (100% NP+75%K)	191383.98	156820.92	163858.42	176751.21	172203.63	192178.42	167352.33	176297.02	178687.94	178128.93
F_4 (100% of NPK)	194502.27	159157.93	161229.60	184647.78	174884.40	199035.16	170791.41	179310.16	183723.66	183215.10
Mean	156641.40	135589.33	138954.55	148488.90		164524.61	142603.80	146963.84	152824.67	
SEm±			4773.65					4040.13		
CD (P=0.05) different sub treatment vs same main treatment			13689.51					11585.98		
SEm±			4931.72					5528.59		
CD (P=0.05) different sub treatment for different main treatment			13499.41					14187.31		

S_1 - *Agrobacterium* sp., S_2 - *Flavobacterium* sp., S_3 - *Rhizobium* sp., S_4 - *Trichoderma* sp.

RDF: 150, 80, 80 kg/ha of N, P and K.

Table 4.27: Interaction effect of fertility levels and microbial strains on economics (B:C ratio) of baby corn

Treatments	2017-18					2018-19				
	S_1	S_2	S_3	S_4	Mean	S_1	S_2	S_3	S_4	Mean
Fertility levels × microbial strains										
F_1 (100% NP+25%K)	1.91	1.79	1.82	1.84	1.84	1.83	1.78	1.81	1.84	1.82
F_2 (100% NP+50%K)	2.03	1.92	1.96	1.98	1.97	2.37	1.96	2.06	2.17	2.14
F_3 (100% NP+75%K)	3.09	2.53	2.64	2.86	2.78	3.05	2.66	2.78	2.82	2.83
F_4 (100% of NPK)	3.11	2.54	2.57	2.95	2.79	3.15	2.68	2.81	2.89	2.88
Mean	1.89	1.65	1.69	1.80		2.62	2.27	2.34	2.44	
SEm±			0.08					0.08		
CD (P=0.05) different sub treatment vs same main treatment			0.19					0.22		
SEm±			0.08					0.09		
CD (P=0.05) different sub treatment for different main treatment			0.22					0.23		

S_1 - *Agrobacterium* sp., S_2 - *Flavobacterium* sp., S_3 - *Rhizobium* sp., S_4 - *Trichoderma* sp.
RDF: 150, 80, 80 kg/ha of N, P and K.

Soil health after Harvesting of Baby Corn

Fertilizer Levels

Data on physico-chemical properties of soil after harvesting of baby corn as influenced by fertility levels and various microbial innoculum as seed treatment into the soil are presented in table 4.28. It was evident from the data that soil pH, electrical conductivity (EC) and organic carbon (OC) of soil could not differ significantly due to various fertility levels during both of the years.

Microbial innoculum

Electrical conductivity (EC), organic carbon (OC) and pH in soil after harvest of baby corn did not differ significantly due to microbial innoculum throughout the present study. They all remained statistically non-significant during both the years.

Interaction

None of the interactions could exert significant influence on pH, electrical conductivity (EC) and organic carbon (OC) in soil after harvest of baby corn in any of the years.

Available Nitrogen in Soil (kg ha^{-1})

The data related to residual available N in soil after crop harvest as affected by fertility levels and different microbial innoculum are presented in table 4.28.

Fertilizer Levels

Perusal of the data indicated that available nitrogen in soil after harvesting of baby corn increased with the increasing fertility level. 100%NP+75%K (F_3) and 100%NPK (F_4) were found statistically at par with each other and registered higher available N. On an average F_3 recorded 10.93% and 8.06% more available N than 100% NP+25%K (F_1) and 100% NP+50%K (F_2) in soil respectively.

Microbial innoculum

It was further evident from the data that among all the innoculum *Agrobacterium* sp. (S_1) left maximum available N in soil after harvest of baby corn and on an average it was found to be 10.89% more than *Flavobacterium* sp. (S_2). Overall the effect was in the order of $S_1>S_4>S_3>S_2$.

Interaction

None of the interactions could exert significant influence on available nitrogen (kg/ha) in soil after harvesting of baby corn.

Table 4.28: Effect of fertility levels and microbial strains on soil health after harvesting of baby corn

Treatments	pH		EC (dsm^{-1})		OC (%)		Available N (kg ha^{-1})		Available P (kg ha^{-1})	
	2017-18	2018-19	2017-18	2018-19	2017-18	2018-19	2017-18	2018-19	2017-18	2018-19
Fertility levels (RDF)										
F_1 (100%NP+25%K)	7.36	7.37	0.33	0.34	0.37	0.38	191.01	193.08	16.83	17.32
F_2 (100%NP+50%K)	7.38	7.39	0.34	0.35	0.39	0.41	195.79	198.53	17.16	18.76
F_3 (100%NP+75%K)	7.34	7.36	0.34	0.36	0.41	0.42	211.55	214.54	20.83	22.09
F_4 (100% NPK)	7.39	7.40	0.35	0.37	0.43	0.44	217.50	220.37	21.32	22.92
SEm±	0.09	0.11	0.01	0.01	0.01	0.01	2.64	2.69	0.29	0.31
C.D. (P=0.05)	NS	NS	NS	NS	NS	NS	7.81	8.01	0.85	0.92
Microbial strains										
S_1 (*Agrobacterium* sp.)	7.38	7.39	0.35	0.38	0.40	0.42	210.98	213.84	19.27	20.87
S_2 (*Flavobacterium* sp.)	7.35	7.36	0.33	0.36	0.38	0.40	189.15	193.95	15.93	16.59
S_3 (*Rhizobium* sp.)	7.36	7.37	0.34	0.37	0.39	0.41	196.83	198.94	17.01	17.99
S_4 (*Trichoderma* sp.)	7.38	7.39	0.35	0.38	0.40	0.42	200.32	204.19	18.30	18.90
SEm±	0.11	0.13	0.01	0.01	0.01	0.02	2.51	2.49	0.27	0.29
C.D.(P=0.05)	NS	NS	NS	NS	NS	NS	7.55	7.47	0.82	0.85

Available Phosphorus in Soil (kg ha^{-1})

The data related to available P in soil after harvesting of baby corn as affected by fertility levels and various microbial innoculum are presented in table 4.28.

Fertilizer Levels

The data revealed that available phosphorus in soil after harvesting of baby corn increased with increasing fertility levels during both the years of study. P content in soil through 100%NP+75%K (F_3) and 100%NPK (F_4) was statistically at par and higher than other treatments. On an average F_3 registered an increase of 25.68% and 19.49% available phosphorus over 100% NP+25%K (F_1) and 100% NP+50%K (F_2) respectively. Over all it was in the order of F_4, F_3> F_2> F_1.

Microbial innoculum

Available phosphorus content in soil through *Agrobacterium* sp. (S_1) was statistically superior to other treatments and recorded 23.43% more than *Flavobacterium* sp. (S_2) while *Trichoderma* sp. registered 7.90% more available P in soil than *Flavobacterium* sp. (S_2).

Interaction

The interaction between fertility levels and microbial innoculum could not exert any significant influence on available phosphorus (kg ha^{-1}) in soil after harvest of baby corn during any of the years.

Available potassium in soil (kg ha^{-1})

Data pertaining to available potassium in soil at all the stages of crop growth as affected by fertility levels and microbial innoculum are presented in table 4.29. As baby corn is a heavy feeder of K, it depletes higher amount of K from soil from beginning to end. It was observed that K status in soil after plant removal was higher in the second year of experiment.

Fertilizer Levels

Perusal of the data indicated that available potassium in soil at all the growth stages of baby corn increased with an increasing fertility level. 100%NP+75%K (F_3) and 100%NPK (F_4) registered higher available potassium but remained statistically at par with each other and superior to other treatments. On an average F_3 registered 17.70% and 8.13% more available K in soil than 100%NP+25%K (F_1) and 100% NP+50%K (F_2) respectively at harvest.

Microbial innoculum

Available potassium in soil after harvesting of baby corn was significantly influenced due to various microbial innoculum. On an average *Agrobacterium* sp. (S_1) recorded significantly highest available potassium in soil and was found to be 15.58% more than *Flavobacterium* sp. (S_2) at harvest. This was followed by *Trichoderma* sp. (S_4) during both the years of study.

Table 4.29: Effect of fertility levels and microbial strains on K availability (kg ha^{-1}) in soil at different growth stages of baby corn

Treatments	20 DAS		40 DAS		60 DAS		80 DAS		At harvest	
	2017-18	2018-19	2017-18	2018-19	2017-18	2018-19	2017-18	2018-19	2017-18	2018-19
Fertility levels (RDF)										
F_1 (100%NP+25%K)	207.69	210.47	201.42	203.86	195.63	197.79	189.29	191.86	183.58	187.47
F_2 (100%NP+50%K)	216.45	219.25	208.84	210.49	199.12	202.58	192.11	194.65	200.93	202.97
F_3 (100%NP+75%K)	232.88	234.55	229.93	232.41	223.88	226.97	220.69	223.45	218.25	220.48
F_4 (100% NPK)	238.11	240.21	235.81	237.82	231.19	233.42	226.42	229.86	228.99	230.89
SEm±	2.10	2.15	2.22	2.25	2.94	3.01	2.28	2.31	5.92	6.06
C.D. (P=0.05)	6.25	6.41	6.60	6.69	8.48	8.79	6.71	6.89	18.92	19.39
Microbial strains										
S_1 (*Agrobacterium* sp.)	232.49	235.66	230.47	233.89	228.95	231.77	224.45	227.81	225.00	226.54
S_2 (*Flavobacterium* sp.)	209.40	212.79	202.41	205.65	196.89	198.14	184.99	186.89	194.43	196.25
S_3 (*Rhizobium* sp.)	218.63	221.65	210.84	214.62	200.19	205.86	192.84	195.21	199.96	203.03
S_4 (*Trichoderma* sp.)	227.42	230.38	223.68	226.35	219.81	221.45	206.43	209.12	211.36	214.99
SEm ±	1.66	1.74	2.10	2.16	2.81	2.89	2.23	2.27	3.45	3.33
C.D. (P=0.05)	4.91	5.19	6.19	6.23	8.37	8.57	6.59	6.63	9.90	9.56

Interaction

Interaction effect on the available K (Table 4.30) was found to be significant at harvest only. 100%NP+75%K (F_3) and *Agrobacterium* sp. (S_1) recorded 240.36 and 241.48 kg ha^{-1} available potassium in soil during 1st and 2nd year respectively although it remained at par with 100%NPK (F_4).

Moong

Yield Attribute

No. of Pods plant^{-1}

Data on the no. of pods plant^{-1} in moong as influenced by various treatments imposed on the previous crop are presented in table 4.31. The data indicated that the number of pods plant^{-1} were comparatively higher in 2018-19 than 2017-18.

Residual Fertility Levels

Residual fertility levels favorably influenced no. of pods plant^{-1} in moong during both the years. The residual fertility level at 100%NP+75%K (F_3) and 100%NPK (F_4) applied to the previous crop resulted in marked increase on no. of pods plant^{-1} of moong. F_3 and F_4 remained at par with each other and on an average F_3 registered 27.34% and 15.56% more pods plant^{-1} than 100%NP+25%K (F_1) and 100%NP+50%K (F_2) respectively.

Effect of Microbial innoculum

Agrobacterium sp. (S_1) recorded the highest no. of pods plant^{-1} in moong which was on an average 29.71% more than *Flavobacterium* sp. (S_2). Overall the effect was S_1>S_4>S_3>S_2.

Interaction

None of the interactions could make any significant influence on the number of pods plant^{-1} in moong during any of the years.

Number of Seeds per pod and Test Weight

Data pertaining to number of seeds per pod and test weight as influenced by various treatments are presented in table 4.31.

Residual Fertility Levels

Inspection of the data revealed that residual fertility levels could not significantly influence the number of seeds per pod and test weight during any of the years.

Effect of Microbial innoculum

Similar non significant effect due to microbial treatment to the previous crop was also observed in number of seeds per pod and its test weight.

Table 4.30: Interaction effect of fertility levels and microbial strains on K availability (kg ha^{-1}) in soil at harvest

Treatments	2017-18					2018-19				
	S_1	S_2	S_3	S_4	Mean	S_1	S_2	S_3	S_4	Mean
Fertility levels × microbial strains										
F_1 (100% NP+25%K)	187.82	175.82	184.34	186.34	183.58	189.75	177.87	186.39	195.89	187.47
F_2 (100% NP+50%K)	221.10	184.30	193.98	204.35	200.93	223.15	186.29	196.03	206.40	202.97
F_3 (100% NP+75%K)	240.36	204.86	200.68	223.12	218.25	241.48	205.92	206.05	224.49	220.48
F_4 (100% of NPK)	250.72	212.75	220.86	231.65	228.99	251.77	214.92	223.66	233.20	230.89
Mean	225.00	194.43	199.96	211.36		226.54	196.25	203.03	214.99	
SEm±			6.66					6.90		
CD (P=0.05) different sub treatment vs same main treatment			19.12					19.79		
SEm±			8.37					8.40		
CD (P=0.05) different sub treatment for different main treatment			21.87					22.12		

S_1 - *Agrobacterium* sp., S_2 - *Flavobacterium* sp., S_3 - *Rhizobium* sp., S_4 - *Trichoderma* sp.
RDF: 150, 80, 80 kg/ha of N, P and K.

Table 4.31: Effect of fertility levels and microbial strains on yield attributes of moong

Treatments	No. of pods plant^{-1}		No. of seeds pod^{-1}		Test weight (g)		Grain yield (q ha^{-1})		Stover yield (kg ha^{-1})		Biological yield (kg ha^{-1})		Harvest index (%)	
	2017-18	2018-19	2017-18	2018-19	2017-18	2018-19	2017-18	2018-19	2017-18	2018-19	2017-18	2018-19	2017-18	2018-19
Fertility levels (RDF)														
F_1 (100%NP+25%K)	18.41	20.73	7.99	8.01	43.99	44.12	9.40	10.22	15.85	18.86	25.25	29.08	0.37	0.35
F_2 (100%NP+50%K)	20.53	22.6	8.02	8.06	44.12	44.47	10.95	11.41	23.07	26.09	34.02	37.5	0.32	0.30
F_3 (100%NP+75%K)	23.52	26.32	8.10	8.15	44.24	44.39	12.03	12.44	34.69	37.71	46.72	50.15	0.26	0.25
F_4 (100% NPK)	24.42	27.46	8.13	8.18	44.85	44.99	12.04	12.49	34.75	37.77	46.79	50.26	0.26	0.25
SEm±	0.41	0.46	0.12	0.13	0.06	0.08	0.05	0.08	0.16	0.18	0.36	0.42	0.02	0.03
C.D. (P=0.05)	1.28	1.37	NS	NS	NS	NS	0.16	0.25	0.51	0.55	1.17	1.41	NS	NS
Microbial strains														
S_1 (*Agrobacterium* sp.)	22.12	24.99	8.03	8.05	44.45	44.51	11.26	11.80	27.41	30.43	38.67	42.23	0.29	0.28
S_2 (*Flavobacterium* sp.)	17.43	18.89	7.98	7.99	43.98	44.03	10.94	11.44	26.78	29.80	37.72	41.24	0.29	0.28
S_3 (*Rhizobium* sp.)	18.61	20.71	7.99	8.01	43.69	43.71	11.05	11.59	26.96	29.98	38.01	41.57	0.29	0.28
S_4 (*Trichoderma* sp.)	20.45	22.99	8.02	8.03	44.12	44.29	11.17	11.72	27.19	30.21	38.36	41.93	0.29	0.28
SEm±	0.19	0.29	0.09	0.10	0.05	0.06	0.06	0.07	0.11	0.12	0.29	0.34	0.01	0.01
C.D.(P=0.05)	0.60	0.89	NS	NS	NS	NS	0.19	0.20	0.34	0.35	0.91	1.05	NS	NS

Interaction

None of the interactions between fertility levels and microbial innoculum could reach the level of significance on number of seeds per pod and its test weight in any of the years.

Moong yield

Moong grain yield (kg ha^{-1})

Moong grain yield (kg ha^{-1}) as influenced by various treatments is presented in table 4.31.

Residual Fertility Levels

The data indicated that residual fertility levels caused significant variation in moong grain yield. Higher grain yield was recorded with residual fertilizer 100%NP+75%K (F_3) and 100%NPK (F_4) which remained statistically at par with each other but significantly superior to other treatments. On an average of two years F_3 fertility level recorded 24.72% more yield than F_1 (100%NP+25%K) and 9.44% more yield than F_2 (100%NP+50%K). Overall the effect of fertility levels on moong yield was in the order of F_4, F_3> F_2> $F_{1.}$

Effect of microbial innoculum

Perusal of data presented in table 4.31 further revealed that microbial innoculum also caused significant variation in moong yield. On the basis of 2 years mean data *Agrobacterium* (S_1) recorded 3.04% increase over S_2 (*Flavobacterium*), 1.86% increase over S_3 (*Rhizobium*) and 0.74% increase over S_4 (*Trichoderma*) in grain yield. Overall the yield obtained from different microbial innoculum was in the order of S_1> S_4> S_3> $S_{2.}$

Interaction

None of the variables could interact with each other in enhancing yield of moong in any of the years.

Moong stover yield (q ha^{-1})

Data related to moong stover yield as influenced by various treatments are presented in table 4.31.

Residual Fertility Levels

It was evident from the data that the increasing fertility level registered progressive improvement in moong stover yield. The higher stover yield was recorded with residual fertilizer 100%NP+75%K (F_3) which remained at par with 100%NPK (F_4). Overall the effect of fertility levels on stover yield was in the order of F_4, F_3> F_2> $F_{1.}$ F_3 fertility level registered 108.59% increase over F_1 (100%NP+25%K) and 47.27% increase in stover yield over F_2 (100%NP+50%K).

Microbial innoculum

Microbial innoculum also exerted significant effect on moong stover yield. On an average *Agrobacterium* sp. (S_1) recorded 2.23% more yield than S_2 (*Flavobacterium*), 1.58% more than S_3 (*Rhizobium*) and 0.77% more than S_4 (*Trichoderma*). Overall the yield obtained from different microbial innoculum was in the order of $S_1 > S_4 > S_3 > S_2$.

Interaction

None of the interactions between fertility levels and microbial innoculum was found significant in any of the years.

Biological yield and Harvest Index

Data pertaining to biological yield and harvest index as influenced by various treatments are presented in table 4.31.

Residual Fertility Levels

Inspection of the data revealed that 100%NP+75%K (F_3) and 100%NPK (F_4) were at par with each other and registered higher biological yield than other treatments. On an average F_3 registered 78.30% and 35.44% more biological yield of moong than 100%NP+25%K (F_1) and 100%NP+50%K (F_2) respectively. Harvest index could not be significantly influenced during any of the years.

Effect of microbial innoculum

Agrobacterium sp. (S_1) recorded the highest biological yield of moong and was on an average 2.46% more than *Flavobacterium* sp. (S_2). Overall the effect was $S_1 > S_4 > S_3 > S_2$. However, non significant effect due to microbial treatment to the previous crop was observed in harvest index of moong.

Interaction

None of the interactions between fertility levels and microbial innoculum could reach the level of significance in biological yield and harvest index in any of the years.

Nutrient Content and Removal

N, P and K content in grain and stover (%)

Data pertaining to nutrients (N, P and K) content in grain (%) as affected by residual fertility levels and microbial innoculum are presented in table 4.32, table 4.33 and table 4.34.

Table 4.32: Effect of fertility levels and microbial strains on N content (%) and its removal (kg ha^{-1}) by moong

Treatments	N content in moong (%)		N content in stover (%)		N removal by moong (kg ha^{-1})		N removal by stover (kg ha^{-1})		Total N removal (kg ha^{-1})	
	2017-18	2018-19	2017-18	2018-19	2017-18	2018-19	2017-18	2018-19	2017-18	2018-19
Fertility levels (RDF)										
F_1 (100%NP+25%K)	1.03	1.19	0.45	0.51	18.24	25.73	14.12	18.36	32.36	46.48
F_2 (100%NP+50%K)	1.27	1.38	0.54	0.61	29.31	34.77	21.26	27.77	50.57	71.83
F_3 (100%NP+75%K)	1.49	1.64	0.61	0.70	41.50	45.91	29.81	39.42	71.31	103.26
F_4 (100% NPK)	1.51	1.66	0.62	0.71	43.59	47.90	32.30	42.20	75.89	108.19
SEm±	0.03	0.04	0.01	0.02	0.70	0.79	0.86	0.99	1.78	1.55
C.D. (P=0.05)	0.09	0.12	0.02	0.03	2.11	2.38	2.61	2.97	5.64	5.23
Microbial strains										
S_1 (*Agrobacterium* sp.)	1.32	1.46	0.55	0.63	33.04	38.45	23.75	31.61	56.79	70.06
S_2 (*Flavobacterium* sp.)	1.31	1.45	0.51	0.59	31.72	37.08	22.96	30.44	54.68	67.55
S_3 (*Rhizobium* sp.)	1.31	1.45	0.54	0.63	31.94	37.49	23.15	30.78	55.09	68.27
S_4 (*Trichoderma* sp.)	1.32	1.46	0.55	0.63	32.81	38.04	23.56	31.27	56.37	69.31
SEm±	0.01	0.01	0.02	0.03	0.62	0.65	0.29	0.31	0.85	1.06
C.D. (P=0.05)	NS	NS	NS	NS	NS	NS	NS	NS	NS	NS

Table 4.33: Effect of fertility levels and microbial strains on P content (%) and its removal (kg ha^{-1}) of P by moong

Treatments	P content in moong (%)		P content in stover (%)		P removal by moong (kg ha^{-1})		P removal by stover (kg ha^{-1})		Total P removal (kg ha^{-1})	
	2017-18	2018-19	2017-18	2018-19	2017-18	2018-19	2017-18	2018-19	2017-18	2018-19
Fertility levels (RDF)										
F_1 (100%NP+25%K)	0.20	0.24	0.16	0.18	2.61	4.13	3.40	4.78	6.01	9.41
F_2 (100%NP+50%K)	0.24	0.27	0.20	0.21	4.35	5.33	6.27	7.86	10.62	16.89
F_3 (100%NP+75%K)	0.34	0.35	0.23	0.23	8.24	8.64	9.59	11.65	17.83	27.42
F_4 (100% NPK)	0.35	0.36	0.24	0.25	8.51	8.98	10.60	12.57	19.11	29.71
SEm±	0.01	0.01	0.00	0.01	0.09	0.11	0.33	0.31	1.23	1.26
C.D. (P=0.05)	0.02	0.03	0.01	0.02	0.29	0.35	1.02	0.97	3.69	3.79
Microbial strains										
S_1 (*Agrobacterium* sp.)	0.26	0.29	0.20	0.21	5.57	6.48	7.35	8.94	12.92	15.42
S_2 (*Flavobacterium* sp.)	0.26	0.29	0.20	0.21	5.39	6.25	7.20	8.67	12.61	14.98
S_3 (*Rhizobium* sp.)	0.26	0.29	0.20	0.21	5.41	6.32	7.21	8.75	12.62	15.07
S_4 (*Trichoderma* sp.)	0.26	0.29	0.20	0.21	5.56	6.42	7.34	8.87	12.90	15.29
SEm±	0.001	0.001	0.001	0.001	0.10	0.11	0.12	0.13	0.16	0.19
C.D.(P=0.05)	NS	NS	NS	NS	NS	NS	NS	NS	NS	NS

Table 4.34: Effect of fertility levels and microbial strains on K content (%) and its removal (kg ha^{-1}) of K by moong

Treatments	K content in moong (%)		K content in stover (%)		K removal by moong (kg ha^{-1})		K removal by stover (kg ha^{-1})		Total K removal (kg ha^{-1})	
	2017-18	2018-19	2017-18	2018-19	2017-18	2018-19	2017-18	2018-19	2017-18	2018-19
Fertility levels (RDF)										
F_1 (100%NP+25%K)	0.94	0.99	1.04	1.06	1.78	1.92	50.17	52.42	51.95	54.34
F_2 (100%NP+50%K)	1.09	1.16	1.20	1.16	2.23	2.41	62.58	71.47	64.81	73.88
F_3 (100%NP+75%K)	1.31	1.32	1.45	1.31	2.89	2.93	89.16	99.59	92.05	103.52
F_4 (100% NPK)	1.34	1.35	1.48	1.35	3.03	3.18	92.92	105.48	95.95	108.66
SEm±	0.01	0.02	0.03	0.03	0.06	0.07	1.69	2.03	1.72	2.10
C.D. (P=0.05)	0.03	0.05	0.09	0.11	0.18	0.21	3.85	5.95	5.60	6.19
Microbial strains										
S_1 (*Agrobacterium* sp.)	1.11	1.15	1.23	1.30	2.53	2.69	76.34	85.93	78.87	88.62
S_2 (*Flavobacterium* sp.)	1.04	1.06	1.17	1.19	2.18	2.31	66.42	74.14	68.60	76.45
S_3 (*Rhizobium* sp.)	1.06	1.09	1.18	1.22	2.26	2.40	69.06	76.97	71.32	79.37
S_4 (*Trichoderma* sp.)	1.07	1.11	1.19	1.25	2.44	2.60	71.85	79.77	74.29	82.37
SEm±	0.01	0.01	0.01	0.01	0.05	0.07	1.56	2.14	1.19	1.21
C.D.(P=0.05)	0.03	0.03	0.03	0.04	0.15	0.22	4.47	6.14	4.56	4.63

Residual Fertility Levels

Beneficial effect of residual fertility levels (applied to baby corn) on nutrient (N, P and K) content in grain and stover of succeeding moong was reflected very well during both the years of investigation. The highest N, P and K content in grain was recorded with residual 100%NP+75%K (F_3) and 100% of NPK (F_4) which remained at par with each other but significantly superior to other treatments during both the years. Overall it was in the order of F_4, F_3> F_2> F_1.

Microbial innoculum

No significant effect on N and P contents in grain and stover of moong due to different microbial innoculum was observed in any of the years of experimentation.

However, in case of K, its contents in grain and stover were both significantly influenced by different microbial innoculum. Like that of other characters *Agrobacterium* sp. (S_1) applied to the previous crop exhibited maximum content of K in moong and it remained statistically superior to all other innoculum. Overall the effect was in the order of S_1>S_4>S_3>S_2 respectively.

Interaction

None of the interactions could exert significant influence on nutrients (N, P and K) content in grain and stover during any of the years.

N, P and K individual removal and total removal by grain and stover (kg ha^{-1})

Data pertaining to individual and total nutrients (N, P and K) removal by grain and stover (kg ha^{-1}) as affected by residual fertility levels and microbial innoculum were presented in table 4.32, table 4.33 and table 4.34.

Residual Fertilizer Levels

It was evident from the data that residual fertility levels caused significant variation in nutrients (N, P and K) removal by both grain and stover and consequent total removal. Higher values in this regard were recorded with residual 100%NP+75%K (F_3) and 100 % of NPK (F_4) which were found to be at par with each other but significantly superior to other treatments during both the years of study. Overall the removal were in the order of F_4, F_3> F_2> F_1.

Microbial innoculum

Like that of nutrient content, removal and total removal of N and P were not significantly influenced by microbial innoculum in any of the years. However, in case of K, its removal by grain and stover and consequent total removal were significantly affected by the microbial innoculum. Among all the innoculum *Agrobacterium* sp. (S_1) resulted in maximum increase in K removal from soil by the crop. Again the overall effect was in the order of S_1>S_4>S_3>S_2 respectively.

Interaction

None of the variables could exert any significant interactive influence on nutrients (N, P and K) removal by grain and stover and its total removal (kg ha^{-1}) in any of the years.

Soil health after harvest of moong (pH, EC and OC)

Fertilizer Levels

It was evident from the data (Table 4.35) that soil pH, electrical conductivity (EC) and OC after harvest of moong could not differ significantly due to different fertility levels during any of the years.

Microbial innoculum

Microbial innoculum also failed to bring about any significant change in soil pH, electrical conductivity (EC) and organic carbon (OC) content in soil after harvest of moong in any of the years of study and the effect remained non-significant in nature.

Interaction

Interaction effect was not found to be significant in any of the years.

Available nitrogen in soil (kg ha^{-1})

The data related to residual available N in soil after harvest of moong as affected by fertility levels and different microbial innoculum are presented in table 4.35.

Fertilizer Levels

Perusal of the data indicated that fertility levels significantly affected the available nitrogen in soil after harvest of moong during both the years. With an increasing fertility level, available N in soil increased significantly with F_3 and F_4 levels which remained at par with each other. On an average 100%NP+75%K (F_3) registered 16.75% and 11.77% more available N in soil than 100%NP+25%K (F_1) and 100%NP+50%K (F_2) respectively.

Microbial innoculum

It was evident from the data that application of microbial innoculum to the previous crop had a positive effect on the N content of the soil after harvest of moong. Among the innoculum *Agrobacterium* sp. (S_1) showed 18.10% more available N than *Flavobacterium* sp. (S_2). Overall the effect was in the order of S_1>S_4>S_3>S_2.

Table 4.35 Effect of fertility levels and microbial strains of preceding baby corn on soil health after harvesting of moong

Treatments	pH		EC (dsm^{-1})		OC (%)		N (kg ha^{-1})		P (kg ha^{-1})		K (kg ha^{-1})	
	2017-18	2018-19	2017-18	2018-19	2017-18	2018-19	2017-18	2018-19	2017-18	2018-19	2017-18	2018-19
Fertility levels (RDF)												
F_1 (100%NP+25%K)	7.15	7.20	0.30	0.32	0.40	0.41	181.01	183.08	15.83	16.52	179.99	181.24
F_2 (100%NP+50%K)	7.18	7.23	0.31	0.34	0.41	0.42	188.79	191.53	17.16	18.76	184.38	186.75
F_3 (100%NP+75%K)	7.19	7.22	0.32	0.34	0.42	0.43	210.55	214.54	20.51	22.09	193.89	195.23
F_4 (100% NPK)	7.20	7.27	0.33	0.35	0.43	0.44	217.50	220.37	21.32	22.92	199.19	201.36
SEm±	0.05	0.07	0.03	0.04	0.03	0.04	2.64	2.69	0.29	0.31	2.13	2.18
C.D. (P=0.05)	NS	NS	NS	NS	NS	NS	7.81	8.01	0.85	0.92	6.40	6.55
Microbial strains												
S_1 (*Agrobacterium* sp.)	7.19	7.21	0.34	0.35	0.41	0.43	212.98	215.84	19.27	20.87	196.52	198.28
S_2 (*Flavobacterium* sp.)	7.17	7.18	0.32	0.33	0.39	0.41	179.15	183.95	13.93	14.59	187.89	188.63
S_3 (*Rhizobium* sp.)	7.17	7.19	0.33	0.34	0.39	0.41	186.83	188.94	15.01	16.99	190.45	191.59
S_4 (*Trichoderma* sp.)	7.18	7.20	0.33	0.34	0.40	0.42	200.32	204.19	17.30	18.90	191.02	192.71
SEm±	0.03	0.04	0.01	0.01	0.02	0.03	2.51	2.40	0.27	0.32	1.81	1.86
C.D.(P=0.05)	NS	NS	NS	NS	NS	NS	7.49	7.22	0.92	0.99	5.42	5.51

Interaction

Both the variables failed to interact significantly with each other in enhancing the available N content in the soil post moong cultivation.

Available phosphorus in soil (kg ha^{-1})

The data related to available P in soil after harvest of moong as affected by fertility levels and varied microbial innoculum are presented in table 4.35.

Fertilizer Levels

A keen examination of the data revealed that available phosphorus in soil after harvest of moong increased with increasing fertility levels during both the years of study. 100%NP+75%K (F_3) and 100 % of NPK (F_4) remained at par with each other but were significantly superior to other treatments during both the years of study. F_3 registered on an average 31.68% and 18.60% more available phosphorus in soil than 100%NP+25%K (F_1) and 100%NP+50%K (F_2) respectively and was in the order of F_4, F_3> F_2> F_1.

Microbial innoculum

Agrobacterium sp. (S_1) recorded an average higher available P level in soil of 40.74% more than *Flavobacterium* sp. (S_2) after harvest of moong. Overall the sequence was S_1>S_4>S_3>S_2.

Interaction

The interaction between fertility levels and microbial innoculum could not evince any significant influence on available phosphorus (kg/ha) content in soil after harvest of moong.

Available potassium in soil (kg ha^{-1})

Data pertaining to available potassium in soil after harvest of moong as affected by fertility levels and microbial innoculum are presented in table 4.35. K status in soil was found to be more in the second year of experiment than first year.

Fertilizer Levels

Perusal of data indicated that available potassium in soil after harvest of moong increased progressively with the increasing level of fertility. 100%NP+75%K (F_3) and 100 % NPK (F_4) remained at par with each other but significantly superior to other treatments during both the years of study. On an average F_3 registered the 7.72% and 4.85% more available potassium in soil. Overall the available potassium in soil after harvest of moong was in the order of F_4, F_3> F_2> F_1.

Microbial innoculum

Available potassium in soil after harvesting of moong was significantly influenced due to application of various microbial innoculum to the previous crop. Among them *Agrobacterium* sp. (S_1) recorded the highest available potassium which was 4.85% more than *Flavobacterium* sp. (S_2) after harvesting of moong.

Interaction

Interaction was not found to be significant in affecting any change in the available potassium content in soil during any of the years of investigation.

Economics of moong

Data pertaining to economics of moong have been presented in table 4.36 and illustrated graphically in figure 4.13 and figure 4.14.

Gross return (₹/ha)

Data on gross return as affected by different fertility levels and microbial innoculum during two years of study are presented in table 4.36 and depicted graphically in figure 4.13 and figure 4.14.

Fertilizer Levels

An analysis of the data revealed marked variation in gross return due to different fertility levels applied to baby corn during both the years of experimentation. 100%NP+75%K (F_3) and 100%NPK (F_4) recorded higher gross return and remained statistically at par with each other. The response of gross return to different fertility levels was in the order of F_4, F_3> F_2> F_1 Further, on an average F_3 was found to generate 25.98% and 10.14% more gross return than 100%NP+25%K (F_1) and 100%NP+50%K (F_2) respectively.

Microbial innoculum

An insight into the data highlighted marked variation in gross return due to different microbial innoculum. On an average *Agrobacterium* sp. (S_1) recorded 2.99% higher gross return than *Flavobacterium* sp. (S_2) and it was found to be in the order of S_1> S_4> S_3> S_2.

Interaction

The interaction between fertility levels and microbial innoculum failed to produce any significant effect with respect to gross return.

Net return (₹/ha)

Data on net return as affected by different fertility levels and microbial innoculum during two years of study are presented in table 4.36 and depicted graphically in figure 4.13 and figure 4.14.

Table 4.36: Effect of fertility levels and microbial strains on economics of moong

Treatments	Economics							
	Cost of cultivation (₹ ha^{-1})		Gross return (₹ ha^{-1})		Net return (₹ ha^{-1})		Benefit : Cost ratio	
	1st year	2nd year	1st year	2nd year	1st year	2nd year	1st year	2nd year
Fertility levels (RDF)								
F_1 (100%NP+25%K)	10270.00	11015.00	53428.39	58185.39	43158.39	47170.39	4.20	4.28
F_2 (100%NP+50%K)	10270.00	11015.00	62483.91	65175.91	52213.91	54160.91	5.08	4.92
F_3 (100%NP+75%K)	10270.00	11015.00	69088.29	71521.29	58818.29	60506.29	5.72	5.49
F_4 (100% NPK)	10270.00	11015.00	69164.89	71849.89	58894.89	60834.89	5.73	5.52
SE m±	-	-	42.93	104.85	42.93	104.85	0.01	0.01
C.D. (P=0.05)	-	-	137.32	335.39	137.32	335.39	0.03	0.03
Microbial strains								
S_1 (*Agrobacterium* sp.)	10270.00	11015.00	64419.60	67619.10	54149.60	56604.10	5.27	5.14
S_2 (*Flavobacterium* sp.)	10270.00	11015.00	62620.59	65578.59	52350.59	54563.59	5.10	4.95
S_3 (*Rhizobium* sp.)	10270.00	11015.00	63210.30	66399.30	52940.30	55384.30	5.16	5.04
S_4 (*Trichoderma* sp.)	10270.00	11015.00	63914.98	67135.48	53644.98	56120.48	5.22	5.09
SE m±	-	-	94.59	83.71	94.59	83.71	0.01	0.01
C.D. (P=0.05)	-	-	271.26	240.06	271.26	240.06	0.03	0.02

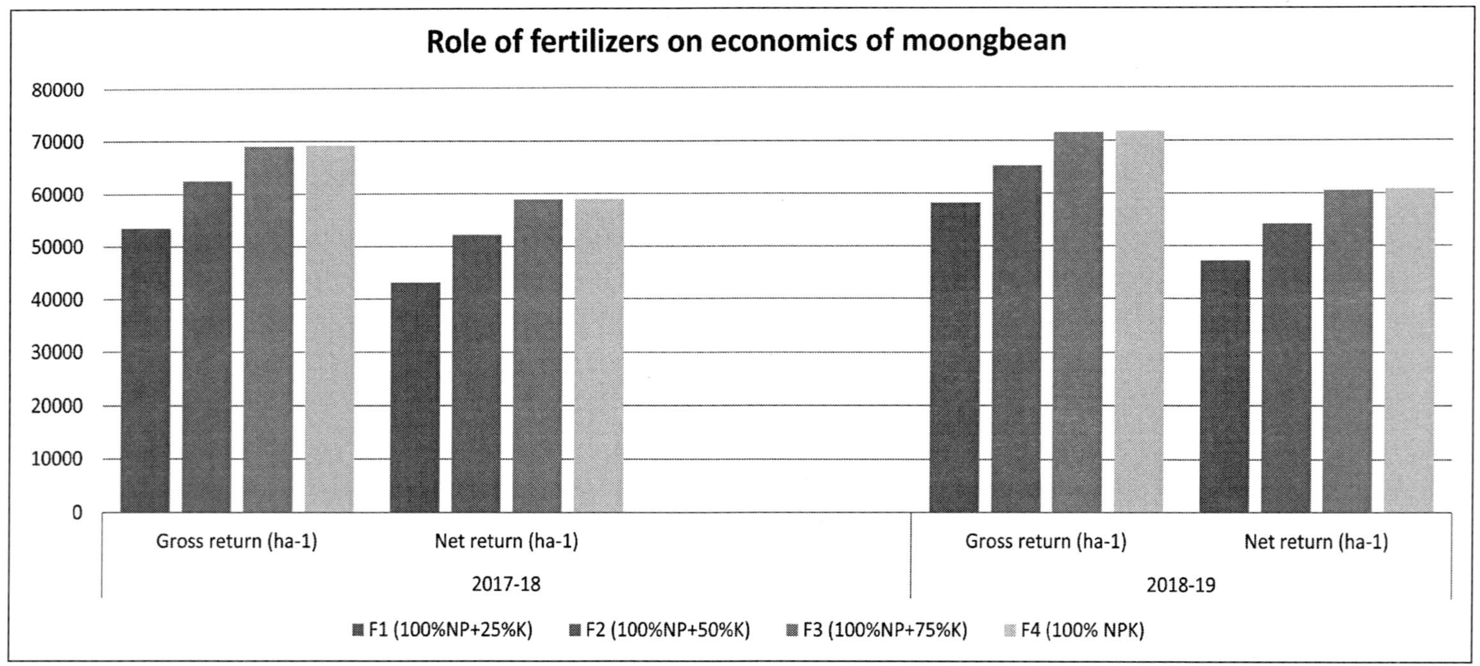

Role of fertilizers on economics of moongbean
80000
70000
60000
50000
40000
30000
20000
10000
0
Gross return (ha-1)
Net return (ha-1)
2017-18
Gross return (ha-1)
Net return (ha-1)
2018-19
F1 (100%NP+25%K)
F2 (100%NP+50%K)
F3 (100%NP+75%K)
F4 (100% NPK)

Fig. 4.13

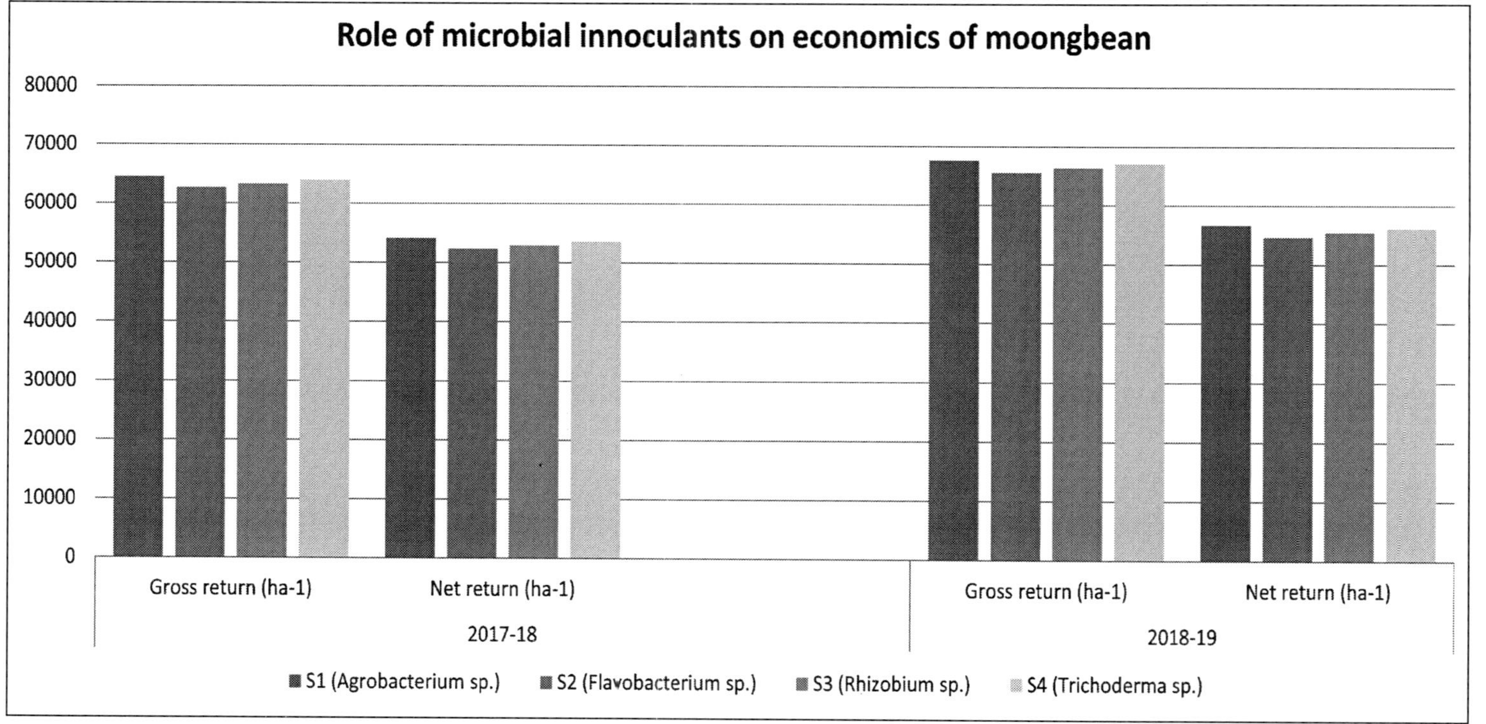
Role of microbial innoculants on economics of moongbean
80000
70000
60000
50000
40000
30000
20000
10000
0
Gross return (ha-1)
Net return (ha-1)
2017-18
Gross return (ha-1)
Net return (ha-1)
2018-19
S1 (Agrobacterium sp.)
S2 (Flavobacterium sp.)
S3 (Rhizobium sp.)
S4 (Trichoderma sp.)

Fig. 4.14

Fertilizer Levels

Perusal of the data indicated significant variation in net return of moong due to different fertility levels applied to baby corn. 100%NP+75%K (F_3) and 100%NPK (F_4) recorded higher net return but remained statistically at par with each other. The response of net return to different fertility levels was in the order of F_4, F_3> F_2> F_1 Further, on an average F_3 was found to produce 32.10% and 12.17% more net return than 100%NP+25%K (F_1) and 100%NP+50%K (F_2) respectively.

Microbial innoculum

It was evident from the data that there was marked variation in net return due to different microbial innoculum. Among all the innoculum *Agrobacterium* sp. (S_1) generated the highest net return which was 3.59% more than *Flavobacterium* sp. (S_2). Like that of other characters the order was S_1> S_4> S_3> S_2.

Interaction

Interaction was not found to be significant in affecting any change in the net return during any of the years of investigation.

Benefit: cost ratio

It was clear from the data (Table 4.36) that benefit: cost ratio of moong was significantly affected by fertility levels and microbial innoculum during both the years.

Fertilizer Levels

The data indicated that increasing fertility levels registered an increased benefit: cost ratio of moong. Application of 100% NP+75%K (F_3) recorded 32.19% and 12.10% more benefit: cost ratio than 100% NP+25%K (F_1) and 100% NP+50%K (F_2) respectively, although F_3 remained at par with 100% NPK (F_4) during both the years.

Microbial innoculum

Perusal of data (Table 4.36) indicated significant effect of microbial innoculum on benefit: cost ratio of moong crop. *Agrobacterium* sp. (S_1) recorded 3.58% higher benefit: cost ratio than *Flavobacterium* sp. (S_2). Overall the B:C ratio due to microbial innoculum was in the order of S_1> S_4> S_3> S_2.

Interaction

Both the variables failed to interact significantly with each other in enhancing the B:C ratio of moong.

Outcomes

The yield of crop is the resultant effect of genotype and the environment interactions. Genotype refers to the character of plant while the important environmental factors comprise soil physio-chemical, biological and microbiological properties along with the climatic parameters like rainfall, temperature, sunshine, evapotranspiration, wind velocity, relative humidity etc. Under defined agro-climatic conditions, exploitation of maximum yield potential depends on agronomic manipulation of micro environment mainly the edaphic factor and growth of the genotype. Thus, agricultural production being consequence of an integrated interaction of soil-water-nutrient-climate continuum requires a wishful and scientific management of this complex system. The productive resources of our country are adversely affected by the use of chemical fertilizers. Excessive use of inorganic fertilizers leads to decrease in the quality of soil and environment (Lynn *et al.*, 2013) which needless to say, calls for immediate attention for improving soil fertility in terms of both quality and quantity. Potassium is known as the quality element for its roles in managing quality of crops (Srinivasarao *et al.* 2000b). In recent years, potassium has become imbalanced in soil because of increased removal, system leakage and demand for rapid plant growth. For addressing this nutrient imbalance and shortages, production of potassic fertiliser is required to be enhanced (Meena *et al.*, 2013). On an average 47.36 lac tons of K is imported annually by our country (FAI, 2018-19) for meeting the internal demand.

Biofertilizers are organic products containing living cells of different types of micro-organism, which have the ability to convert nutritionally important elements from unavailable to available form through biological process (Vessey, 2003). Inoculations with KSB and other useful microbial cultures in the soil mandatorily restore and maintain the effective microbial populations that solubilizes the chemically fixed form of potassium and make other macro and micronutrients available to plants.

Trichoderma asperellum has the ability to promote plant growth through different mechanisms, such as solubilization of phosphates, potassium and minerals like Fe, Mn and Mg that have important role to play in plant growth (Mastouri *et al.*, 2010). *Trichoderma* increases the rate of germination and seedling growth of maize. A number of mechanisms for plant growth promotion by *Trichoderma* have been proposed (Vinale *et al.*, 2008). *Trichoderma* promotes primary root length and root branching in maize by inducing lateral root growth (Lynch, 2013). Combination of Trichoderma inoculum and fertilizers performes better than single application of either fertilizer or inoculum. Wu *et al.* (2005) reported that the application of biofertilizer containing mycorrhizal fungus and three species of bacteria significantly increased the growth of maize.

Maize is a heavy feeder of K and needs ample quantity of K for its better production. It then becomes imperative to apply an optimum amount of K through fertilizer and biofertilizer (KSB and *Trichoderma*) at the sowing time when it is most efficiently and effectively utilized. Several potential benefits of providing K to cereals via biofertilizer like KSB have been suggested by many workers (Zakaria, 2009, Archana *et al.*, 2008).

Realizing and recognizing the importance of all the above mentioned facts, the present investigation entitled *"Eco-friendly Production of Baby Corn and Moongbean"* was undertaken during the winter season of 2017-2018 and 2018-2019 at the Agricultural Research Farm, Institute of Agricultural Sciences, Banaras Hindu University, Varanasi, Uttar Pradesh (India). Depending on the established theories and principles an attempt has been made to discuss and explain the cause and effect of the results obtained in the field experiment.

Effect of Weather Conditions

Every crop requires a set of favourable climatic conditions to achieve proper growth and development for its overall performance. The climatic factors matching to crop phenology during the growing season, do help to exploit genetic potential of the crops. If weather component gets fluctuated from their normal limits, it suppresses the plants and does not allow it to achieve real expression of growth and yield. Hence weather conditions prevailed during the course of present investigation were studied and various parameters (rainfall, temperature, relative humidity, sunshine duration and evaporation) recorded were presented in table 3.2.

The growth, yield attributes and yield were greater during second year (2018-19). A fairly bright sunshine led to better photosynthetic activity of the crop in the second year and this along with other weather conditions caused comparatively more growth and yield of the crop.

Effect of Fertilizer Levels on Growth Parameters of Baby Corn

Nitrogen has numerous functions in the plant and is an essential element of amino acids- the building blocks of proteins and part of nucleic acids, DNA and RNA. It plays an important role in photosynthesis and is essential for enzymatic, biochemical and physiological reactions in plant metabolism. Nitrogen is a structural constituent and essential component of chlorophyll. Thus, greater availability of nitrogen at higher fertilizer doses might have improved protein synthesis and photosynthesis leading thereby to rapid cell division and cell enlargement, which ultimately resulted in vigorous plant growth (Rizwan *et al.*, 2003 and Saleem *et al.*, 2009).

Phosphorus, as a constituent of ADP and ATP, plays a key role in energy transformation. It also helps in assimilation of photosynthates into other metabolites and hence acts as an activity zone for CO_2 assimilation. Moreover, as an integral part of chromosomes, it stimulates cell division and meristematic growth. Thus, adequate supply of phosphorus helps in rapid growth of plant. Phosphorus, as an activator of enzymes, is engaged in protein and carbohydrate metabolism and regulates carbohydrates translocation, synthesis of protein and maintenance of stability (Cordell *et al.*, 2009). As such adequate and balanced supply of P at higher doses to the baby corn crop might have favoured greater availability of this nutrient that ultimately resulted in enhanced growth of the crop (Khan *et al.*, 2010).

Potassium is associated with movement of water, nutrients and carbohydrates in plant tissue (Ashley *et al.*, 2006). If potassium is deficient or not supplied in adequate amount, growth is stunted and yields are reduced. It is involved in the adjustment of plant cellular osmotic pressure and the transportation of compounds in plants. Potassium helps in the building of protein, photosynthesis, corn quality and reduction of diseases. Potassium is supplied to plants by soil minerals, organic materials, and fertilizer. It promotes the activation of enzymes, the utilization of nitrogen (N), syntheses of protein and sugar and boosts plant photosynthesis. Plants can only take K through the soil. Without adequate potassium, the plants will have poorly developed roots, grow slowly, produce small seeds and have lower yields. (Cakmak, 2005, Martineau *et al.*, 2017)

In the present study, fertility levels recorded a positive effect on the initial plant stand. Significant differences in final plant stand were also observed due to different fertility levels with F3 (100%NP+75%K) and F_4 (100% NPK) remained at par with each other produced higher plant stand and it was in the order of F_4, F_3 >F_2>F_1. Greater availability of nutrients at F_3 and F_4 resulted in more number of plants up to the final stage of the crop. Sahoo and Panda (2001) and Sahoo (2011) also reported beneficial effect of balanced nutrition on the plant stand in baby corn. The data (Table 4.1) indicated significant decrease in barren plant/m^2 with increasing fertility levels. Significant reduction in the number of barren plant was found with F_3 and F_4. Enhancement of available nutrients in soil through higher fertility level encourages higher cob setting and consequent reduction in number of barren plants [Panwar and Munda (2006); Thakur *et al.* (1997); Bindhani *et al.* (2008) and Singh, *et al.* (2016a)].

Different growth parameters (plant height, number of green leaves, leaf area, LAI, dry matter production and chlorophyll content) were found to have a marked improvement at almost all the stages of crop growth due to varied levels of fertilizer. Among the fertility levels 100%NP+75%K (F3) and 100% NPK (F4) brought about higher growth of plant during both the years and remained at par with each other. This supports the well-established fact that combined application of nitrogen, phosphorus and potassium in adequate quantity are beneficial for growth and development of the crop (Singh, *et al.*, 2010 and Kumar *et al.*, 2015).

Plant height is a useful index of plant development to give an idea of dry matter production leading to ultimate yield. Higher plant height with F_3 and F_4 might be due to greater availability of nitrogen at higher fertilizer dose. Similar effects of higher rate of fertilizer have also been realized on growth characters of baby corn by several workers (Thakur *et al.*, 1997; Panwar and Munda, 2006; Bindhani *et al.*, 2007; Ibrahim and Hala, 2007; Bindhani *et al.*, 2008 and Kumar and Bohra, 2014).

The number of green leaves per plant (recorded at 20, 40, 60, 80 DAS and at harvest) increased significantly with increasing level of N, P and K at all the stages of growth and the maximum number of green leaves was associated with the higher levels of fertilizer at F_3 and F_4. Higher dose of fertilizer accelerated growth over the lower doses and maintained more number of green leaves (plant^{-1}) along with higher leaf area and leaf area index. This variation was mainly due to higher absorption of nutrients and higher photosynthetic activity and was in conformity with the findings of Panwar and Munda (2006); Ashoka *et al.* (2008); Law-Ogbomo and Law-Ogbomo (2009); Zende *et al.* (2009) and Kumar and Bohra (2014).

At all the growth stages the dry matter production increased significantly with the increasing doses of fertility and was found to be higher with F_3 and F_4. Overall the effect of fertility levels on dry matter production was in the order of F_4, F_3> F_2> F_1 (Table 4.9). Adequate and balanced fertilization promoted the plant growth parameters viz. plant height, number of green leaf, leaf area index and photosynthetic activity which ultimately produced higher dry matter plant-1 (Muthukumar *et al.*, 2005a; Kumar and Ahlawat, 2006; Dadarwal *et al.*, 2009 and Zende *et al.*, 2009).

The combination of 100% NP+75% K (F_3) and Agrobacterium (S_1) recorded higher plant height (141.18 and 142.66 cm) although it was found to be at par with 100%NPK (F_4).

Chlorophyll content (SPAD value) recorded at 20, 40, 60 and 80 DAS increased consistently with the advancement of crop growth but the value decreased at the time of harvest. Chlorophyll content increased significantly with each successive increment in fertility level from 100% NP+25%K (F_1) to 100% NPK (F_4) (Table 4.7) and the higher (SPAD value) was recorded with the application of F_3 and F_4 which remained at par with each other. The higher leaf chlorophyll level is associated with more efficient N removal and better photosynthetic leaf function, especially during late growth stages which leads to a longer "stay-green" period and corresponding higher yield (Byju and Anand, 2009).

Combined effect of fertility levels and microbial strains in increasing the dry matter of plant at 80 DAS was found siginificant during both the years (Table 4.10). Higher dry matter production at 100% NP+75% K (F_3) and *Agrobacterium* sp. (S1) was recorded (167.50 and 170.01 cm) although it remained at par with 100%NPK (F_4).

Effect of microbial innoculum on growth characters of baby corn

Potassium is an established essential mineral nutrient for plants and a major constituent of all living cells. Because of this potassium is retained in soil in larger amounts than other nutrients; but considerable amount of this element is held in unavailable form for plant removal. On the other hand chemical fertilizers exert a very adverse effect on the soil ecosystem which disturbs the environmental sustainability. It is a well known fact that potassium solubilizing bacteria (KSB) solubilizes Kbearing minerals and converts the insoluble K to soluble forms thereby increasing its availability to plant. Among various bacteria- *Agrobacterium* sp., *Flavobacterium* sp., *Rhizobium* sp. (identified by SSAC, BHU) *Paenibacillus* spp., *B. cirulans* (to mention a few) have been found to have the capacity to solubilize K minerals like biotite, feldspar, illite, mica *etc.* KSB are ubiquitous, although their number, diversity and ability of K solubilisation vary according to the soil and climatic condition. KSB produces organic and inorganic acids, acidolysis, polysaccharides, complexolysis etc. and releases K by dissolving silicate minerals. Depending on soil type, 90 to 98% of soil K is mineral which is mostly unavailable to plant (Sparks and Huang, 1985). K in soil solution is the only K which is directly and readily available to plants and microbes in soil, the concentration of which varies from 2 to 5 mg l^{-1} in most normal agricultural soils (Sparks and Huang, 1985) play an important role in it. Against this background, the production and management of biological fertilizers containing KSB can be an effective alternative to chemicals (Etesami *et al.*, 2017).

The growth parameters viz., plant height, number of green leaves, leaf area, LAI, chlorophyll content (SPAD values) and dry matter production were all markedly improved at almost all the stages of growth due to microbial strains. *Agrobacterium* sp. increased these attributes better than other KSB strains and this was followed by *Trichoderma* sp. during both the years of investigation (Table 4.2, 4.4, 4.5, 4.6, 4.7 and 4.9).

Significant effect of microbial strains on plant height was recorded with *Agrobacterium* sp. (S_1). In the interaction effect, combination of both bacterial inoculation and fertility levels consequently resulted in higher availability of nutrients to plant particularly potassium thereby increasing photosynthetic activity and protein synthesis. This caused rapid cell division and cell enlargement which led to greater plant height (Mahajan *et al.*, 2007 and Mehta *et al.*, 2011). It is possible that KSB might have enhanced the availability of soluble K in soil for crop (Lin *et al.*, 2002; Egamberdiyeva and Hoflich, 2003; Basak and Biswas, 2009).

Maximum number of green leaves found with *Agrobacterium* sp. (S1) might be due to more availability of K in soil solution by the application of KSB and higher doses of potassic fertilizers (Supanjani *et al.*, 2006; Bagyalakshmi *et al.*, 2012). The solubilisation by KSB increased the available form of K from unavailable form in soil and enabled the plant to use it more efficiently. These bioinoculants led to changes in crop characteristics resulting in strong stem, higher plant height, more efficient photosynthesis with higher dry matter accumulation and removal of nutrients (Wang *et al.*, 2000; Moritsuka *et al.*, 2004; Basavesha *et al.*, 2016; Iqbal *et al.*, 2012).

Favorable improvement in leaf area (cm^2) and leaf area index of baby corn were recorded with Agrobacterium sp. (S_1) and the maximum leaf area (cm^2) and leaf area index were recorded at 80 DAS. Biofertilizer like KSB and *Trichoderma* is associated with improved soil health which increases availability of nutrient in the rhizospheric zone leading to more assimilation of macro and micronutrients by crop plant from rootzone. The removal of these nutrients facilitates better leaf function, especially during the growth period which leads to an increase in cell elongation and divisions. Higher leaf area (cm^2) and LAI were the resultant effect of all these advantages. Similar findings were also reported by Wang *et al.* (2000) and Moritsuka *et al.* (2004). Kandil *et al.* (2004) reported that inoculation of seeds with bioinoculants resulted in significant increase in the number and total area of leaves. Maurya *et al.* (2004) and Zarei *et al.* (2011) reported that the application of biological fertilizers on plants significantly increased the leaf area index of maize and soybean.

This might be attributed to the significantly superior growth components viz., plant height, leaf area, number of leaves per plant and dry matter production observed under *Agrobacterium* sp. (S_1). Conformity of result of the present investigation was also reported by Archana *et al.* (2008); Sangeeth *et al.* (2012) Bagyalakshmi *et al.* (2012).

KSB and *Trichoderma* depicted higher leaf chlorophyll content which is associated with better leaf photosynthesis (Kumar *et al.*, 2014; Maurya *et al.*, 2015). K influences the total chlorophyll and carotenoid contents of the leaves which may also directly or indirectly improve crop yield through increased photosynthesis. Similar kind of result were reported by Jayaganesh *et al.* (2011). Bagyalakshmi *et al.* (2012) have reported that application of indigenous KSB formulation with various doses of potassic fertilizers with N & P enhanced green leaf yield and productivity in tea. The increase in yield might be due to the solubilization of nutrients in the soil through organic acids produced by KSB.

Meena *et al.* (2018) reported that the application of potassium solubilizing bacteria improved biological activity and absorption of nutrients responsible for the increase of leaf area and LAI. Khaliq *et al.* (2006) and Bulgarelli *et al.* (2013) observed an increase in chlorophyll content of leaves following inoculation by microbial strain, probably due to more nitrogen content in vegetative tissues. The results are comparable with Kim *et al.* (2003). Higher available K due to the solubilization by inoculated KSB might have led to more removal from soil (Hu *et al.*, 2006). Higher rates of K allowed efficient use of more nitrogen, which resulted in better early vegetative growth. Borie *et al.* (2002) reported that fertilizers with *Trichoderma* sp. increased plant performance (growth attributes) and mineral acquisition.

Agrobacterium sp. produced the highest dry matter of baby corn followed by *Trichoderma* sp. The dry matter yield was in the order of S_1> S_4> S_3> S_2. *Trichoderma* sp. have been found to stimulate plant growth through the production of plant-growthpromoting (PGP) compounds (Ousley *et al.* 1994; Contreras-Cornejo *et al.* 2009; Vinale *et al.* 2009). Growth stimulation was evidenced by increases in biomass productivity, stress resistance, and increased nutrient absorption (Hoyos-Carvajal *et al.* 2009).

Effect of fertilizer levels on yield and yield attributes of baby corn

Yield attributes of baby corn viz. length of baby corn, weight of baby corn (with and without husk), girth of baby corn, number of baby corn plant^{-1} and baby corn (with husk): baby corn (without husk) ratio were markedly affected by the fertility levels (Table 4.11).

100%NP+75%K (F_3) and 100% NPK (F_4) correspondingly increased the baby corn length and girth (without husk) and they remained statistically at par with each other. On an average F_3 recorded 36.86% increase over F_1 (100%NP+25%K) and 30.61% increase over F_2 (100%NP+50%K) in corn yield. Overall the effect of fertility levels on baby corn yield (without husk) was in the order of F_4, F_3> F_2> F_1.

High fertility levels caused greater photosynthetic accumulation which might have enhanced length and girth of baby corn. Similar results were also noted in baby corn by Sahoo and Panda (1997); Bindhani *et al.* (2008) and Golada *et al.* (2013).

Enhanced levels of fertilizer had favorable effect on number of baby corn plant^{-1}. Higher number of baby corn plant^{-1} was recorded under the F_3 and F_4 levels of fertilizer. Higher number of baby corn plant^{-1} is consistently associated with the plant growth parameters viz., plant height, number of leaf plant^{-1}, leaf area index and dry matter production (Saha and Mondal, 2006). The results were in conformity with the findings of Zende *et al.* (2009); Singh, *et al.* (2010); Aravinth *et al.* (2011) and Lone *et al.* (2013).

An increase in baby corn weight for every unit increase in the level of fertilizers upto 100% NPK was observed. Higher baby corn (with and without husk) weight was recorded with F_3 and F_4 where it remained at par with each other. This improvement in yield attributes was the result of higher nutrient removal, enhanced source sink ratio and improved vegetative growth in terms of leaf area index and dry matter production. Higher fertility levels ensured enhanced supply of photosynthates for formation of baby corn, its length, girth and weight (with and without husk) in the present study. These findings were in close agreement with those reported by Sahoo and Mahapatra (2007); Panwar (2008); Singh, *et al.* (2010) and Sobhana *et al.* (2012).

Increase in fertility levels correspondingly increased the number of cobs ha^{-1} at individual harvests. Higher number of cobs ha^{-1} was noted with F_3 and F_4 at all the pluckings and these were found to be significantly superior to other treatments. The highest number of cobs was harvested at 3rd plucking after which there was a progressive decline in the number of harvested baby corns.

It was evident from the data (Table 4.13) that higher fertility levels F_3 and F_4 registered higher baby corn (with and without husk) yield. Higher leaf area intercepted more radiation and resulted in more dry matter production and ultimately increased yield. Higher cob weight and yield of crop were the resultant effect of more efficient dry matter partitioning with crop (Ramachandrappa *et al.*, 2004; Sahoo and Mahapatra, 2005, 2007 and Dadarwal *et al.*, 2009).

Similarly higher stover yield was obtained with the application of F_3 and F_4 level of fertility during both the years. Higher growth parameters under these treatments led to higher stover yield [Sahoo and Mahapatra (2005); Saha and Mondal (2006) and Singh *et al.* (2010)].

Functional Relationship between Fertility Levels and yield

Functional relationship between fertility levels and baby corn yield was found to be linear in nature. The computed r values (Fig. 5.1 and

Fig. 5.2) of 0.98 and 0.99 during 2017-18 and 2018-19 respectively indicated that 96% (1st year) and 98% (2nd year) of the variation in the mean yield could be explained by the linear regression equation estimated.

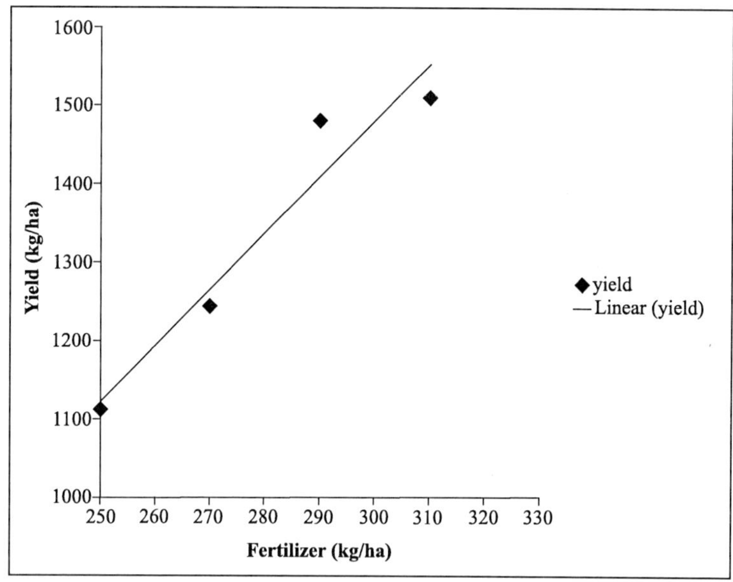

Fig. 5.1: Functional relationship of fertilizer vs yield (2017-18) in baby corn yield (q/ha) (without husk)

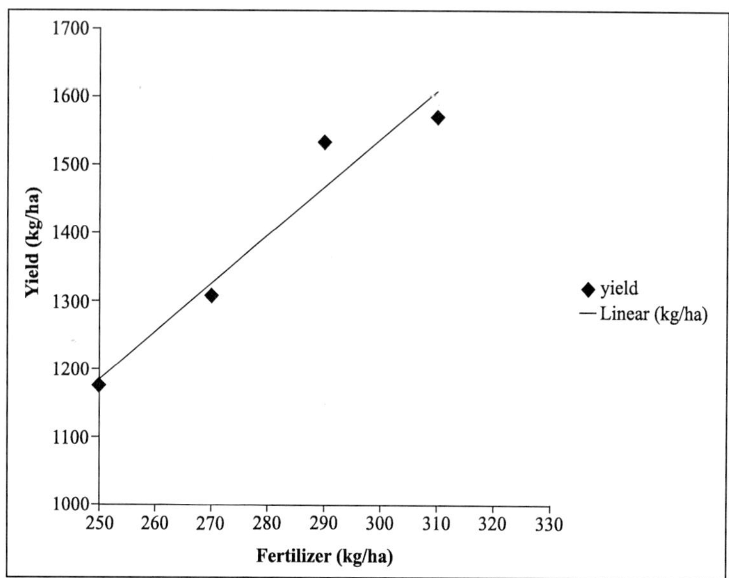

Fig. 5.2: Functional relationship of fertilizer vs yield (2018-19) in baby corn yield (q/ha) (without husk)

Significant interactions observed between fertility levels and microbial strains increased the baby corn yield. 100%NP+75%K (F_3) and *Agrobacterium* sp. (S1) recorded higher baby corn yield (16.25 and 16.29 q/ha) but remained at par with 100%NPK (F_4) and exhibited distinct superiority over other combinations.

Effect of microbial strains on yield and yield attributes of baby corn

Next to N and P, potassium (K) is the most important plant nutrient which plays a key role in the growth, metabolism and development of plants. Among other things K is required to activate over 80 different enzymes responsible for plant and animal processes such as energy metabolism, starch synthesis, nitrate reduction, photosynthesis and sugar degradation (Almeida *et al.*, 2015, Hussain *et al.*, 2016 and Yang *et al.*, 2015).

It is a well-known fact that microbial soil community can influence soil fertility through soil processes like mineralization, storage, release etc. (Parmar and Sindhu, 2013). Some beneficial soil microorganisms can solubilize the insoluble K to soluble forms of K through various mechanisms. Among these microorganisms, K solubilizing bacteria (KSB) when applied as seed inoculum can promote the plant growth and yield by releasing K from inorganic and insoluble pools of total soil K through solubilisation (Archana *et al.*, 2013, Gundala *et al.*, 2013; Saha *et al.*, 2016 and Zhang *et al.*, 2013). This shows that KSB can provide an alternative technology to make K available to plants. Thus, identification of efficient bacterial strains can quickly conserve the existing resources and mitigate environmental pollution caused by heavy application of synthetic K- fertilizers (Etesami *et al.*, 2017).

Biofertilizers influenced significantly baby corn length and girth. *Agrobacterium* sp. (S1) recorded significantly higher baby corn (without husk) length and girth followed by *Trichoderma* sp. (Table 4.11). This might be due to the improvement in growth parameters which resulted in significant increase in yield attributes of baby corn [Singh *et al.* (2009a); and Ahmad *et al.* (2012)]. Biofertilizers brought about significant variation in baby corn and stover yields with *Agrobacterium* sp. (S_1) exhibiting the maximum yield. This might be attributed to the fact that biofertilizers mobilized the fixed form of nutrients and increased the ability of the plant to extract more nutrient from the soil and thereby increasing its use efficiency. Conformity of result of the present investigation was also reported by Archana *et al.* (2008); Sangeeth *et al.* (2012); Bagyalakshmi *et al.* (2012).

A close examination of the data further revealed that *Agrobacterium* sp. (S1) brought about significant variation in number of baby corn plant^{-1} (Table 4.11). Maximum number of cobs plant^{-1} and weight of baby corn (with and without husk) were obtained from this strain (S_1). KSB ensured more nutrients availability for better plant growth, higher photosynthetic rate and accumulation of more assimilates with a corresponding effect on yield and yield attributes. Baldi *et al.* (2010); Singh *et al.* (2009a) and Zhang and Kong (2014) also observed an increased microbial activity in root zone due to KSB bio fertilizer application. Higher number of cobs ha-1 was harvested with Agrobacterium sp. (S1) at all the individual plucking while the highest was noticed at 3 rd plucking (Table 4.11). Overall the yields obtained from different microbial strains were in the order of $S_1 > S_4 > S_3 > S_2$.

Stover yield is closely associated with the supply of nutrients such as N, P and K where biofertilizers provide higher availability of nutrients to the plant by increasing organic nitrogen, organic matter, microbial activities and enzymatic activities (Lynn *et al.*, 2013), which in turn improve the plant growth and yield.

Sheng *et al.* (2002) reported that KSB namely *Bacillus mucilaginosus* is able to solubilize inorganic source of K like muriate of potash and sulphate by means of production of organic acids. The plants which received higher level of K produced higher yield in all the years (Natesan *et al.*, 1984).

A critical analysis of the data showed an improvement in baby corn (without husk) length and girth with *Agrobacterium* sp. (S_1) followed by *Trichoderma* sp. (S_4) (Table 4.11). The elevated stature of yield attributes might be due to more efficient translocation of metabolites to the sink. It might also be due to the production of amino acids, vitamins and growth promoting substance like IAA and gibberelic acid by microorganisms which resulted in enhanced nutrient removal, translocation and synthesis of photosynthates leading to increased plant growth characters and economically profitable yield (Singh and Dhar, 2011; Ponmurugan and Gopi, 2006 and Suke *et al.*, 2011). Increasing number of baby corn plant^{-1} might be due to its good source-sink relationship which improved the plant yield and yield attributes (Gad, 2011). These results were in line with the findings of Cakmak (2005); Han and Lee (2005); Grzebisz *et al.* (2010).

Strains brought about significant variation in baby corn (with and without husk) yield (Table 4.13) and the critical examination of data showed that *Agrobacterium* sp. (S_1) followed by *Trichoderma*. Effect of phosphorus sources, levels and biofertilizers on yield attributes, yield and economics of moongbean (*Phaseolus radiata* L.). (S_4) increased baby corn (with and without husk) yield. Biofertilizer enhanced the nutrient availability in soil which led to higher removal of nutrients by plant. The results of the present investigation were in close conformity with the observations of Park *et al.* (2003); Ebrahimpour *et al.* (2011); Sugumaran and Janarthanam (2007).

Trichoderma sp. has very often resulted in higher growth of plant and improved yield of several crops. Haque *et al.* (2010) studied the effects of *Trichoderma* enriched biofertilizer on mustard (*Brassica campestris*) under field condition and Mokhtar *et al.* (2013) found an increased seed yield per plant with *Trichoderma* enriched biofertilizer. Zhang *et al.* (2012) showed that *Trichoderma* sp. (T-E5) enhanced the production of IAA and plant colonization ability in cucumber and finally enhanced the yield.

Effect of fertility levels on quality of baby corn

There was significant enhancement in quality attributes *viz.* protein, carbohydrate, starch and sugar content in baby corn (Table 4.16). The quality attributes increased significantly with an increase in fertility levels upto 100%NP+75%K (F_3) and 100% NPK (F_4) which remained statistically at par with each other. The response of quality attributes in baby corn to different fertility levels was in the order of F_4, F_3 > F_2 > F_1. Nitrogen often plays a great role in the synthesis of protein by enhancing the amino acid formation (Mengel *et al.*, 2001), while phosphorus is the constituent of enzyme nitrogenase, which converts NO^{-3} into protein (Gill *et al.*, 2009) and potassium is responsible for the protein and starch synthesis alongwith osmoregulation. When plants are deficient in K, proteins are not synthesized despite an abundance of available N (Hedge *et al.*, 1999). The enzyme nitrate reductase catalyzes the formation of proteins and is responsible for its activation and synthesis. It was therefore, quite obvious that higher availability of N and P would result in enhanced carbohydrate in plant which on conversion would produce more protein in the presence of nitrogenase enzymes. Potassium on the other hand promotes photosynthetic activity, flow of assimilates, translocation and storage of assimilates in plant system (Cakmak *et al.*, 1994). Consequently, NPK due to their involvement in physico-chemical reactions in plant enhanced carbohydrate, sugar, starch and protein contents in plant parts. The conformity of this result was also recorded by Rasheed *et al.* (2004); Zende *et al.* (2009) and Durga *et al.* (2012).

Effect of microbial strains on quality parameters

Data pertaining to quality attributes of baby corn viz. protein, carbohydrate, sugar and starch was significantly influenced by microbial strains. *Agrobacterium* sp. (S_1) recorded the highest protein content in baby corn followed by *Trichoderma* sp. (S_4). Jabbar *et al.* (2009) and Archana *et al.* (2012) also reported an increase in quality parameters with an increase in the availability of nutrients for maize.

Agrobacterium sp. (S_1) proved itself highly efficient in translocation of N for enrichment of the cob and stover. Mirzaei *et al.* (2010) also reported different sugar, starch and carbohydrate contents in sweet corn quality due to biofertilisers.

Effect of fertility levels on nutrient content and their removal by baby corn and stover

Data clearly revealed that 100%NP+75%K (F_3) and 100% NPK (F_4) remaining at par with each other registered higher N, P and K content and removal by baby corn and stover and they remained significantly superior to other levels (Table 4.17, 4.18, 4.19). The response of different fertility levels to N, P and K content and removal was in the order of F_4, F_3> F_2> F_1. This was mainly due to higher availability as well as better absorption of these nutrients from soil (Singh, *et al.*, 2009). Ashoka *et al.* (2009) and Das *et al.* (2011) also reported that the nutrient content and their removal were improved by an increase in the levels of fertilizer.

The content of N and P was more in baby corn than in stover while K content was found to be higher in stover than baby corn. This was because of the fact that only a limited amount of K was translocated to baby corn while greater amount remained accumulated in stover (Kumar and Bohra, 2013).

Fertility levels F_3 and F_4 produced more healthy and vigorous plants as it was witnessed in the form of more height, active leaf and leaf area index and dry matter production. Such healthy and vigorous plants showed higher concentration of N, P, K and their subsequent removal.

Effect of microbial strains on nutrients content and removal by baby corn and stover

An examination of the data further revealed that the nutrient (N, P and K) content and their removal by baby corn (Table 4.17, 4.18, 4.19) varied markedly with microbial strains. *Agrobacterium* sp. (S_1) exhibited higher nutrient content in baby corn during both the years. The effect of microbial strains on nutrients content and their removal by plant were also recorded by Sheng (2005); Govaerts *et al.* (2007); Rudresh *et al.* (2005), Han and Lee (2005) and Sheng and He (2006), Kowalska (2011). Mohammadi *et al.* (2010) applied T. harzianum in combination with other biofertilizers and observed significant increase in N, P, K, Fe and Mg content in leaves and grains of chick pea. Improvements in removal of nutrients and growth due to application of *Trichoderma* were also noticed in sugarcane which improved root growth, water-holding capacity of plants and nutrient removal (i.e., N, P and K) (Srivastava *et al.* 2006; Yadav *et al.* 2008; Shukla *et al.* 2008).

Effect of fertility levels on soil microbial population and microbial biomass carbon

Greater number of colonies (Table 4.20, 4.21 and 4.22) was observed at 100%NP+75%K (F3) and 100%NPK (F4) where they remained at par with each other. Fertility level of 100%NP+75%K (F3) on the basis of average of two year data exhibited 18.49%, 9.43% and 22.26% more bacterial, actinomycetes and fungal colonies than 100%NP+25%K (F1) at 60 DAS. Nakhro and Dkhar (2010) and Liu, *et al.* (2008) reported increase in microbial counts in response to fertilization.

Similar trend was observed with soil microbial biomass carbon (Table 4.23) where F_3 and F_4 found at par with each other and superior to other treatments. The biomass carbon at F_3 was 17.86% higher than the F_1 on average of two years data. Higher biomass carbon was observed at 60 DAS of crop growth and was in the order F_4, F_3> F_2> F_1.

Geisseler and Scow (2014) observed an increase in soil microbial biomass carbon with an increase in fertilization of agricultural soil. High SMBC due to balanced fertilization promotes soil microbial development. Fertilizers influence microbial biomass, its activities and diversity in different ways (Zhang *et al.*, 2005, Liu *et al.*, 2008). Fertilization directly or indirectly cause changes in the soil's physical, chemical, biological and microbiological properties (Wei *et al.*, 2008).

Effect of microbial strains on soil microbial population and microbial biomass carbon

Data revealed that maximum bacterial, actinomycetes and fungal colonies was observed with *Agrobacterium* sp. (S1) at 60 DAS followed by *Trichoderma* sp. (S4). Chishi (2010) studied the effect of potash solubilizing bacteria on maize and revealed higher microbial population with KSB than control. Over all the effect was found in the order of $S_1 > S_4 > S_3 > S_2$. Hridya *et al.* (2014) found that the microbial inoculations significantly increased microbial biomass carbon in soil. *Trichoderma* colonizes the roots through hyphal growth favouring more microbial colonies in soil (Dandurand and Khudsen, 1993).

Effect of fertility levels on economics of baby corn

Economics in terms of cost of cultivation, gross returns, net returns and benefit: cost ratio (Table 4.24) revealed that increasing fertility levels considerably enhanced cost of cultivation, gross and net returns and benefit: cost ratio. Higher values were recorded with the 100%NP+75%K (F3) and 100% NPK (F4) but they remained statistically at par with each other. These enhancements in cost of cultivation were due to increase in quantity of inputs, their application and total cost. Higher yield of baby corn with increasing fertility levels enhanced the returns and benefit: cost ratio. These results were in close proximity with Sahoo and Mahapatra (2005); Singh, *et al.* (2010) and Kumar and Bohra (2013) who reported an increase in the returns and B:C ratio of baby corn with increasing fertility levels. On an average F3 registered 56.68% and 37.63% more net returns than 100%NP+25%K (F1) and 100%NP+50%K (F_2).

Interaction effect between 100%NP+75%K (F_3) and *Agrobacterium* sp. (S_1) had higher net return and was significantly superior to other treatments. The response of the crop in its net return to different fertility levels was in the order of F_4, $F_3 > F_2 > F_1$.

Effect of microbial strains on economics of baby corn

Perusal of data (Table 4.24) indicated variation in gross return, net return and benefit: cost ratio due to different microbial strains during both the years of experimentation. *Agrobacterium* sp. (S_1) showed highest gross return, net return and benefit: cost ratio followed by *Trichoderma* sp. (S_4). Singh *et al.* (2010); Basak and Biswas (2012); Zhang *et al.* (2013) and Zhang and Kong (2014) reported an increase in the yield, reduction in the cost of cultivation and increase in net return by the applications of biofertilisers while economic gain of *Trichoderma* sp. was observed by Purushottam *et al.* (2014). Overall the yield obtained from different microbial strains was in the order of $S_1 > S_4 > S_3 > S_2$.

Effect of fertility levels on soil health after harvesting of baby corn

It was evident from the data (Table 4.28) that soil pH and electrical conductivity (EC) and OC of soil could not differ significantly but F_3 and F_4 recorded higher available N, P and K in soil and they remained at par with each other. The increase in available nutrient N, P and K might be due to an increased level of fertilizers added to the soil. Similar results were reported by Verma *et al.* (2005) and Banerjee *et al.* (2006).

Effect of microbial strains on soil health after harvesting of baby corn

Agrobacterium sp. (S1) left maximum available N, P and K in soil after harvest of baby corn.

Application of K-solubilizing bacteria increases the amount of available K in the soil and promotes K uptake by plant maize (Abou-el-Seoud and Abdel-Megeed, 2012). Garcia *et al.* (2004) also showed that inoculation with KSB improved K availability in soils by producing organic acids and other chemicals. Prajapati *et al.* (2013) suggested that the plant growth promotion was related to K solubilization plus release of organic acids by KSB strains. The other possible hypotheses/mechanisms of mobilization of mineral K are the formation of biofilm on the rhizospheric mineral surfaces by certain potassium solubilising bacteria (KSB) (Balogh-Brunstad *et al.* 2008). The availability of N, P and K in rhizosphere soil was found to be higher in the Trichoderma-enriched bio-organic fertilizer treatment (Cai *et al.* 2015). The colonization of plant roots by Trichoderma asperellum was reported to have enhanced the availability of P and K to plants (Yedidia *et al.* 2001).

Residual effect of fertility levels on yield and yield attribute of moong

It was evident from the data (Table 4.31) that higher fertility levels to the previous crop produced higher moong yield (grain and stover) and yield attributes viz., no. of pods plant^{-1}, no. of seeds pod^{-1} and 1000-grain weight. 100%NP+75%K (F_3) and 100% NPK (F_4) recorded higher moong yield (grain and stover) and its attributes viz., grain weight per ear, number of grains per plant and 1000-grain weight and they remained significantly superior to other treatments. This might be due to the effect of residue which provided adequate groundcover and contributed effectively in the improvement of soil chemical, physical, biological and microbiological properties. Mubarak *et al.* (2003a) and Almaz *et al.* (2017) reported an increase in moong yields with increasing level of fertilizer. Yadav (2011) and Yadav *et al.* (2011) reported increase in moong yields due to combination of fertilizer and biofertiliser. F_3 fertility level recorded 24.72% and 9.44% more yield than F_1 and F_2 respectively. Overall the effect of fertility levels on moong yield was in the order of F_4, F_3> F_2> F_1.

Residual effect of microbial strains on yield and yield attributes of moong

Biofertilisers recorded significantly higher grain and stover yields during both the years. Residual effect creates mulching of soil surface with different organic materials by improving soil biological activities, retain soil moisture for longer time and helps to control weeds (Singh *et al.*, 2015; Gajera *et al.*, 2014). *Agrobacterium* sp. (S_1) recorded 3.04%, 1.86% and 0.74% increase over S_2 (*Flavobacterium* sp.), S_3 (Rhizobium sp.) and S_4 (*Trichoderma* sp.) in grain yield respectively. Overall the yield obtained from different microbial strains was in the order of S_1> S_4> S_3> S_2.

Residual effect of fertility levels on nutrient content and their removal by moong

It was evident from the data (Table 4.32, 4.33 and 4.34) that residual fertility levels resulted in significant variation in N, P and K contents (%) in grain and straw of moong. Higher value was recorded with residual F_3 and F_4 but they remained at par with each other. Similarly residual fertility levels recorded significant variation in N, P and K removal by grain and straw of moong (kg ha^{-1}) and higher values were found with residual F_3 and F_4. High nutrient content in grain and straw and its removal by F_3 might be associated with the effect of crop residues in soil properties viz., physical, chemical and biological properties. Anyanzwa *et al.* (2010) noticed that the crop residues had an additive effect on crop production, soil organic carbon and soil total nitrogen. Similar effect of crop residue in nutrient content and removal was also reported by Singh and Sharma (2000); Ghuman and Sur (2001); Mubarak *et al.* (2002) and Malhi and Lemke (2007).

Residual effect of microbial strains on nutrient content and removal by moong

The N, P and K content in moong grain and straw as well as their removal was highest with *Agrobacterium* sp. but it could not reach the level of significance. Use of crop residues retained in soil improves soil aggregation and stability and increases C and N from the soil microbial biomass (Baque *et al.*, 2006; Prasad *et al.*, 2010).

Residual effect of fertility levels on soil health after moong

Crop residue is very important for maintaining the nutrient recycling thereby increasing fertility, productivity and controlling weed. Different amount of baby corn biomass that was incorporated into the soil of each plot after harvesting also added nutrients to the soil and enriched its health. Of course it took some time for total decomposition after which only the nutrients became available to the plant. However its effect was reflected in the performance of baby corn and moong of the subsequent year. The variation in residual nutrient content of the soil is well known due to differential absorption of nutrients by the plants. Nutrient profiles depend on balance between influx and replenishment of ions and degree of the soil nutrient depletion, which is related to rate and amount of nutrients released from soil solid phase to soil solution (Anyanzwa *et al.*, 2010). Plants can mobilize large quantities of nutrients from soil solution apart from microbial nutrient. Data (Table 4.35) on available N, P and K in soil after harvesting of moong recorded significant difference due to various fertility levels. F_3 and F_4 recorded higher available N, P and K in soil. The increase in available nutrient in soil is generally attributed to the fact that crop residue incorporation increases the availability of nutrient in soil through decomposition of the residues which release nutrients to the soil with positive effect on soil physical, chemical, biological and microbiological properties (Du Preez *et al.*, 2001; Raghvendra *et al.*, 2017 and Anyanzwa *et al.*, 2010; Kumar and Dhar, 2010)

Residual effect of microbial strains on soil health after moong

Biofertilizer has a positive role in influencing available N, P and K in soil. Application of biofertilizer with crop residues can be considered as an alternative practice that improves soil health and yield over time (Davari *et al.* (2012); Bhardwaj *et al.* (2014).

Residual effect of fertility levels on economics of moong

Perusal of the data indicated significant enhancement in economics of moong viz. gross returns, net returns and benefit: cost ratio of baby corn and moong by fertility levels (Table 4.36). Data revealed an increase in sequence economics with increment in fertility levels. F_3 (100%NP+75%K) and F_4 (100% NPK) remaining at par with each other registered higher gross return, net return, and benefit: cost ratio. The increase in cost of cultivation was due to increase in quantity of inputs and their total cost. Jain and Dhama (2005) and Kumawat (2013) reported an increase in the economics of moong with increase in fertility levels and residue application. The response of sequence economics to different fertility levels was in the order of F_4, $F_3 > F_2 > F_1$.

Residual effect of microbial strains on economics of moong

An analysis of the data revealed marked variation in sequence economics viz. gross returns, net returns and benefit: cost ratio of baby corn and moong due to various strains. *Agrobacterium* sp. registered higher gross return, net return, benefit cost ratio and it was followed by *Trichoderma* sp. Overall the microbial strains on sequence economics was in the order of $S_1 > S_4 > S_3 > S_2$.

Conclusion

Maize (*Zea mays* L.) is the third most important cereal crop in India after rice and wheat. It accounts for 9 per cent of total food grain production in the country. Karnataka, Rajasthan, Andhra Pradesh, Maharashtra and Uttar Pradesh are the major producing states contributing 60 per cent of area and 70 per cent of maize production in India. Baby corn is unfertilized maize ear which is harvested within two to three days of silk emergence of the cob. The plant enters into the reproductive phase within 45-55 days of sowing and ends its life-cycle by 75-90 days. Being a delicious vegetable available throughout the year it is preferred by almost all the groups of society. Because of its nutritive value and popularity income and employment both can be enhanced through production of baby corn. The importance of nutrient (N, P and K) in maize becomes more relevant when it is grown as baby corn in which demand becomes extreme because of high plant density and very short duration.

Most of the farmers use nitrogen and phosphorus only without potassic fertilizer due to unawareness which leads to the problem of K-deficiency. Moreover K fertilizer is also costly as compared to other chemical fertilizers as India is totally dependent on other countries for its import. Therefore, an efficient potassium solubilizing bacteria (KSB) as biofertilizer should be used as an alternative of chemical fertilizer. Applied KSB strain solubilizes the fixed K and makes the unavailable K available in the soils through different mechanisms like acidolysis, chelation, exchange reactions, complexolysis and production of organic acids. This available K can be easily taken up by the plant for its growth and development (Meena *et al.*, 2014).

Trichoderma asperellum is a fungus found in many regions of the world. *Trichoderma* have the ability to promote plant growth through different mechanisms like solubilization of phosphates, potassium and minerals such as Fe, Mn and Mg that have important role in plant growth (Mastouri *et al.*, 2010). In addition to this, *Trichoderma* increases the rate of germination of maize and its seedling growth. A number of mechanisms for plant growth promotion by *Trichoderma* have been proposed (Harman *et al.*, 2006) which includes promotion of primary root length and root branching in maize by inducing lateral root growth (Bjorkman, 2006). Cumulative effects of all these factors led to improved function of NPK involved in many physico-chemical reactions which enhanced carbohydrate, sugars, starch, protein and ultimately yield (Fahong *et al.*, 2004) of the crop.

Moong or moongbean (*Vigna radiata* (L.) is one of the popular short duration grain legumes and occupies third place after chickpea and pigeonpea and provides the best solution to alleviate protein-calorie malnutrition. It is an important source of dietary protein (21-25%), carbodydrate (60%), minerals and vitamins for mankind and its stover is used as feed in India for domestic cattle. Moreover it improves and sustains soil productivity through biological nitrogen fixation and addition of large amount of organic matter to soil. Crop residue management is another key consideration for optimizing fertility in conservation agriculture systems. Incorporation of crop residues improves soil health and fertility of soil and reduces nutrient losses (Shafi *et al.*, 2007).

Keeping this in view the following book entitled *"Eco-friendly Production of Baby Corn and Moongbean"* was conducted with the objectives given below:

Objectives

(i) To find out the effect of KSB and *Trichoderma* on yield and quality of baby corn.

(ii) To find out their effect on K availability in soil.

(iii) To find out its residual effect on moongbean.

(iv) To work out the economics of different treatments.

Experimental details

The trial was carried out during rabi seasons of 2017-18 and 2018-19 at the Agricultural Research Farm, Banaras Hindu University, Varanasi (India). The geographical location of the site was 25°21′21.6″N latitude and 82°52′37.7″E longitude and at an altitude of 76 meters from mean sea level in the northern gangetic alluvial plains. During baby corn growing period temperature ranged from 14.5 to 35.5°C, while succeeding moong underwent comparatively warmer temperature ranging from 33.9 to 42.8°C. The experimental site was fairly uniform in topography and well drained in nature.

The soil was sandy clay loam in texture having pH (7.39), electrical conductivity (0.31dS/m at 25 °C) and moderate fertility with 0.41% organic carbon, 194.67 kg/ha available N, 18.85 kg/ha available P and 199.88 kg/ha available K. The field trial consisting of 4 fertility levels 100%NP+25%K (F_1), 100%NP+50%K (F_2), 100%NP+75%K (F_3) and 100% NPK (F_4) and 4 microbial strains including 3 strains of potassium solubilizing bacteria (*Agrobacterium tumefaciens, Flavobacterium anhuiense* and *Rhizobium pusense*) and 1 fungal strain (*Trichoderma asperellum*) making 16 treatment combinations was laid out in a split plot design with 4 replications by keeping fertility levels in the main plot and microbial strains in the sub plots. The recommended dose of NPK fertilizer (RDF) was 150, 80 and 80 of N, P_2O_5 and K_2O/ha. Nutrients (N, P and K) were applied as per treatment through Urea, DAP and MOP respectively. Half of the recommended dose of nitrogen and full doses of P and K were applied as basal and rest two (one fourth) of nitrogen was top dressed through urea at knee high and tassel emergence stages respectively. Intercultural operations were carried out as per requirement of crop. Baby corn (unfertilized maize ear) was harvested at 2-3 days of silk emergence stage and marketed as fresh corn (without husk). After harvesting of the baby corn the whole plant stover cut at ground level was spread over respective plots in small pieces for incorporation with the soil.

Moong was planted in the same lay out without any addition of fertilizer to study the residual effect of the first crop.

Results

Growth attributes

During both the years of study, application of 100% NP+75% K (F_3) and 100% NPK (F_4) which remained statistically at par with each other recorded higher plant height, number of green leaves plant^{-1}, leaf area, leaf area index, fresh weight and dry matter production of growth attributes at all the stages during both the years.

Agrobacterium sp. (S_1) registered the highest plant height, number of green leaves plant^{-1} leaf area, leaf area index, fresh weight and dry matter production followed by *Trichoderma* sp. (S_4).

The combination between fertility levels and microbial strains interacted significantly in enhancing plant height and dry matter production. 100% NP+75% K (F_3) and *Agrobacterium* sp. (S_1) produced significantly higher plant height and dry matter production than other strains but remained at par with 100% NPK (F_4) at 80 DAS among all the combinations.

Baby corn yield

Fertility levels exhibited marked improvement in the yield and yield attributes of baby corn *i.e.* baby corn (with and without husk) and stover yields, baby corn (length and girth), baby corn (with and without husk) weight, number of cobs plant^{-1} and baby corn (with husk) and baby corn (without husk) ratio. Among the fertility levels application of 100%NP+75%K (F_3) and 100%NPK (F_4) exhibited higher values but remained statistically at par with each other. On an average F_3 recorded 36.86% increase over F_1

(100%NP+25%K) and 30.61% increase over F_2 (100%NP+50%K) in corn yield. Overall the effect of fertility levels on baby corn yield (without husk) was in the order of F_4, F_3> F_2> F_1.

Microbial strains had also a significant effect on yield and yield attributes. *Agrobacterium* sp. (S_1) recorded 12.97%, 10.55% and 5.72% increase over S_2 (*Flavobacterium* sp.), S_3 (*Rhizobium* sp.) and S_4 (*Trichoderma* sp.) respectively in baby corn yield. Overall the yields obtained from different microbial strains were in the order of S_1> S_4> S_3> S_2.

Fertility levels and microbial strains interacted significantly in enhancing the baby corn yield (with and without husk). 100%NP+75%K (F_3) with *Agrobacterium* sp. (S_1) recorded higher baby corn yield (16.25 and 16.29 q/ha) but remained at par with 100%NPK (F_4) and exhibited distinct superiority over other combinations.

Nutrient content and removal by baby corn

The nutrient content and removal of N, P and K varied significantly with respect to different fertility levels. 100%NP+75%K (F_3) and 100% NPK (F_4) – remaining statistically at par with each other showed higher content and removal than other treatments. F_3 recorded 44.92%, 22.91% and 24.24% more N removal than F_1 by corn, stover and total; 52.83%, 43.11% and 43.89% more P removal than F_1 by baby corn, stover and total; and 45.63%, 27.38% and 27.91% more K removal than F_1 by baby corn, stover and total and it was in the order of F_4, F_3> F_2> F_1.

Agrobacterium sp. (S_1) followed by *Trichoderma* sp. (S_4) registered higher nutrient content and removal of N, P and K by baby corn, stover and consequent total than S_2 and S_3 during both the years of experimentation.

Microbial population and SMBC

Greater number of colonies was observed at 100%NP+75%K (F_3) and 100%NPK (F_4) levels but they remained statistically at par with each other. They exhibited more bacterial, actinomycetes and fungal colonies cfu/g in soil than 100%NP+25%K (F_1) and 100%NP+50%K (F_2).

Agrobacterium sp. (S_1) registered the highest bacterial, actinomycetes and fungal colonies followed by *Trichoderma* sp. (S_4) during both the years of experimentation.

Quality parameters

100%NP+75%K (F_3) and 100% NPK (F_4) resulted in higher protein, carbohydrate, sugar and starch contents while 100%NP+25%K (F_1) produced the least.

Protein content increased markedly with *Agrobacterium* sp. (S_1) followed by *Trichoderma* sp. (S_4). *Agrobacterium* sp. also registered the highest carbohydrate, sugar and starch content among all the strains and finally it was found to be in the order of S_1> S_4> S_3> S_2 during both the years of experimentation.

Economics of baby corn

Gross return, net return and benefit cost ratio were calculated to find out the profitability of treatments. F_3 recorded a gross return of (₹234143.71 and ₹ 241119.01), net return of (₹ 172203.63 and ₹ 178128.93) and benefit: cost ratio of (₹ 2.78 and ₹ 2.83) but remained statistically at par with F_4. The economics due to fertility levels was in the order F_4, F_3> F_2> F_1 during both the years.

Higher gross return (₹ 218276.29 and ₹ 227209.50), net return (₹ 156641.40 and ₹ 164524.61) and benefit cost ratio (₹ 2.54 and ₹ 2.62) was recorded with *Agrobacterium* sp. (S_1) followed by *Trichoderma* sp. (S_4) and it was found to be in the order S_1>S_4>S_3>S_2 during both the years.

The interaction between fertility levels and microbial strains (Table 4.26) registered significant effect in respect of net return and B:C ratio. 100%NP+75%K (F_3) and *Agrobacterium* sp. (S_1) registered the net return of (₹ 191383.98 and ₹ 192178.42) and B:C ratio of (3.09 and 3.05) and remained at par with 100%NPK (F_4) during both the years of experimentation.

Soil status after harvesting of baby corn

After harvesting of baby corn, plots treated with different fertility levels showed significant variation in residual nutrient status of soil. Available nitrogen, phosphorus and potassium (kg/ha) in soil were influenced by different fertility levels and microbial strains. 100%NP+75%K (F_3) and 100% NPK (F_4) registered higher available nutrients (N, P and K) in soil. On an average F_3 recorded 10.93% and 8.06% % more available N, 25.68% and 19.49% more available phosphorus and 17.70% and 8.13% more available K than 100% NP+25%K (F_1) and 100% NP+50%K (F_2) respectively in soil during both the years.

Among the microbial strains *Agrobacterium* sp. (S_1) recorded 10.89% % more N, 23.43% more P and 15.58% more available K than *Flavobacterium* sp. (S_2) in soil and this was followed by *Trichoderma* sp. (S_4).

Moong yield

Residual fertility levels caused significant variation in moong (grain and stover) yields and yield attributes *i.e.* number of grains per plant, 1000 grain weight (g) and grain weight per pod (g). The higher grain yield was recorded with residual fertilizer 100%NP+75%K (F_3) and 100%NPK (F_4) which remained statistically at par with each other but significantly superior to other treatments. F_3 recorded 24.72% more yield than F_1 (100%NP+25%K) and 9.44% more yield than F_2 (100%NP+50%K) on an average of two years. Overall the effect of fertility levels on moong yield was in the order of F_4, F_3> F_2> F_1. Similar trend was recorded in case of stover yield also where F_3 (100%NP+75%K) fertility level registered 39.39% increase over F_1 (100%NP+25%K) and 9.88% increase over F_2. F_3 and F_4 remained statistically at par with each other.

Agrobacterium sp. (S_1) recorded 3.04% increase over S_2 (*Flavobacterium* sp.), 1.86% increase over S_3 (*Rhizobium* sp.) and 0.74% increase over S_4 (*Trichoderma* sp.) in grain yield and 2.69% increase over S_2 (*Flavobacterium* sp.), 1.73% increase over S_3 (*Rhizobium* sp.) and 0.91% increase over S_4 (*Trichoderma* sp.) in stover yield.

Soil status after harvesting of moong

Residual fertility levels failed to bring about any significant variation in soil pH, electrical conductivity (EC) and OC but had a significant effect on available N, P and K in soil. Higher values were recorded with 100%NP+75%K (F_3) and 100% of NPK (F_4) which remained at par with each other. On an average F_3 recorded 16.75% and 11.77% more available N, 31.68% and 18.60% more available phosphorus and 7.72% and 4.85% more available K than 100% NP+25%K (F_1) and 100% NP+50%K (F_2) respectively in soil during 1st and 2nd year respectively.

Agrobacterium sp. (S_1) recorded the highest available nitrogen, phosphorus and potassium (kg/ha) content in soil after harvesting of moong followed by *Trichoderma* sp. (S_4).

Nutrient content and removal by moong and stover

Higher N, P and K content in grain and stover was recorded with residual 100%NP+75%K (F_3) and 100% of NPK (F_4) which remained at par with each other but significantly superior to other treatments during both the years. Overall it was in the order of F_4, F_3> F_2> F_1. Similar trend was recorded in case of removal of N, P and K by moong and stover both and consequent total removal.

Like that of nutrient content, removal of N and P were not significantly influenced by microbial strains in any of the years. However, in case of K, its removal by moong and stover and consequent total removal were significantly affected by the microbial strains. *Agrobacterium* sp. (S_1) resulted in maximum increase in K content, removal and total removal from the soil by the crop. Again the overall effect was in the order of S_1>S_4>S_3>S_2 respectively.

Economics of moong

Like other parameters 100%NP+75%K (F_3) and 100% of NPK (F_4) which remained statistically at par with each other recorded significantly higher gross return, net return and benefit:cost ratio of moong during both the years.

Agrobacterium sp. (S_1) registered significantly higher gross return, net return and benefit:cost ratio followed by *Trichoderma* sp. (S_4) and it was found to be in the order of S_1> S_4> S_3> S_2.

Conclusion

Based on above findings, following conclusion can be drawn:

- 100%NP+75%K (F_3) and 100% NPK (F_4) remaining at par with each other registered higher plant height, dry matter production, yield attributing characters, yield of baby corn and stover, nutrient content and removal (N, P and K) of baby corn and stover. Same effect was observed in protein, carbohydrate, sugar and starch content in baby corn and available nutrients (N, P and K) in the soil.

- Application of 100%NP+75%K (F_3) and 100% NPK (F_4) registered higher microbial population *viz.* bacterial, actinomycetes and fungal colonies (cfu/g) in soil and soil microbial biomass carbon (µg C g^{-1} soil).
- In case of economics of baby corn and sequence economics of both crops (baby corn+moong), 100%NP+75%K (F_3) and 100% NPK (F_4) remaining at par with each other registered higher gross return, net return and B: C ratio of baby corn.
- The residual effect of 100%NP+75%K (F_3) and 100% NPK (F_4) also showed the same trend and showed higher values on yield attributing characters of moong, its grain and stover yields, nutrients content (N, P and K) and their removal by moong and residual available nutrients (N, P and K) in soil.
- *Agrobacterium* sp. (S_1) was most effective in positively influencing growth parameters, yield attributing characters, yields, nutrient contents and their removal, protein, carbohydrate, sugar and starch content of baby corn followed by *Trichoderma* sp. (S_4).
- *Agrobacterium* sp. (S_1) recorded significantly higher bacterial, actinomycetes and fungal colonies (cfu/g) in soil and soil microbial biomass carbon (µg C g^{-1} soil) followed by *Trichoderma* sp. (S_4).
- Among different strains *Agrobacterium* sp. (S_1) recorded higher yield attributes, yield and economics (gross return, net return and B: C ratio) of baby corn. This was followed by *Trichoderma* sp. (S_4).
- Even though F_4 (100% NPK) exhibited a little better result in respect of the performance of both baby corn and moong than F_3 (100%NP+75%K) but it could not reach the level of significance in any of the years. F_3 was therefore considered to be better option because of 25% saving in potassic fertilizer of the recommended dose.

Recommendation

On the basis of the above finding, 100%NP+75%K (F_3) in combination with potassium solubilizing bacteria- *Agrobacterium* sp. can be recommended for better soil health and higher growth, yield and profit of baby corn and moong on residual fertility.

References

Abdel–Rahaman, M.A. and Merwad. 2016. Efficiency of K-sulphate and K-feldspar Combined with Silicate Dissolving Bacteria on Yield and Nutrient Uptake by Maize Plants. *Egyptian Journal of Soil Sciences* 56(2): 249-259.

Abou El Seoud, I.I.A., Elham, A.B. and El Shimaa, A.E. 2009. Response of Two Sugar Beet Varieties to Chicken Manure and Phosphorine Application. *Alexandria Science Exchange Journal* 30(4): 433-444.

Abou-el-Seoud, I.I. and Abdel-Mageed, A. 2012. Impact of Rock Materials and Bio-fertilization on P and K availability for Maize (*Zea maize*) under Calcareous Soil Conditions. *Saudi Journal of Biological Sciences* 19: 55-63.

Ahmad, M., Zahir, Z.A., Asghar, H.N. and Arshad, M. 2012. The Combined Application of Rhizobial Strains and Plant Growth Promoting Rhizobacteria Improves Growth and Productivity of Mung Bean (*Vigna radiata* L.) under Salt-stressed Conditions. *Annals of Microbiology* 62: 1321-1330.

Almaz, M.G., Halim, R.A., Yusoff, M.M. and Wahid, S.A. 2017. Effect of Incorporation of Crop Residue and Inorganic Fertilizer on yield and Grain Quality of Maize. *Indian Journal of Agriculture Research* 51(6): 574-579.

Almeida, H.J., Pancelli, M.A., Prado, R.M., Cavalcante, V.S., Cruz, F.J.R. 2015. Effect of Potassium on Nutritional Status and Productivity of Peanuts in Succession with Sugarcane. *Journal of Soil Science and Plant Nutrition* 15(1): 1-10.

Amgain, L.P., Shrma, A.R, Das, T.K. and Behera, U.K. 2013. Effect of Residue Management on Productivity and Economics of Pearlmillet based Cropping System under Zero till Condition. *Indian Journal of Agronomy* 58(3): 298-302.

Anna, A. and Francisco, R. 2012. *Potassium in Plants.* John Wiley & Sons Ltd, Chichester.

Anonymous, 2016-17, Annual Review, Fertilizer Statistics, Fertilizer Association of India, New Delhi.

Anonymous. 2015. Healthy Soil for Sustaining Food & Human Security, *News Letter* 18(2).

Anu Lavanya, G. and Ganapathy, M. 2011. Effect of DAP, NAA and Residual Effect of Inorganic Fertilizers and Organic Manures on Growth and yield of Greengram in Rice based Cropping Sequence. *Journal of Agricultural Technology* 7(3): 599-604.

Anu Lavanya, G. and Ganapathy, M. 2011. Effect of DAP, NAA and Residual Effect of Inorganic Fertilizers and Organic Manures on Growth and yield of Greengram in Rice based Cropping Sequence. *Journal of Agricultural Technology* 7(3): 599-604.

Anwar, F., Latif, S., Przybylski, R., Sultana, B. and Ashraf, M. 2007. Chemical Composition and Antioxidant Activity of Seeds of different Cultivars of Mung Bean. *Journal of Clinical Investigation* 117(9): 2486-2495.

Anyanzwa, H., Okalebo, J., Othieno, C., Bationo, A., Waswa, B. and Kihara, J. 2010. Effects of Conservation Tillage, Crop Residue and Cropping Systems on Changes in Soil Organic matter and Maize–legume Production: A Case Study in Teso District. *Nutrient Cycling in Agroecosystems* 88(1): 39-47.

Aravinth, V., Kuppuswamy, G. and and Ganapathy, M. 2011. Growth and yield of Baby Corn (*Zea mays*) as Influenced by Intercropping, Planting Geometry and Nutrient Management. *Indian Journal of Agricultural Sciences* 81(9): 875-877.

Archana, D.S., Nandish, M.S., Savalagi, V. and Alagawadi, A. 2013. Characterization of Potassium Solubilizing Bacteria (KSB) from Rhizosphere Soil. *Bioinfolet* 10: 248-257.

Archana, D.S., Nandish, M.S., Savalagi, V.P. and Alagawadi, A.R. 2012. Screening of Potassium Solubilizing Bacteria (KSB) for Plant Growth Promotional Activity. *Bioinfolet* 9: 627-630.

Archana, D.S., Savalgi, V.P. and Alagawadi, A.R. 2008. Effect of Potassium Solubilizing Bacteria on Growth and yield of Maize. *Soil Biological and Ecology* 28(1- 2): 9-18.

Archana, D.S., Savalgi, V.P. and Alagawadi, A.R. 2008. Effect of Potassium Solubilizing Bacteria on Growth and yield of Maize. *Soil Biology and Ecology* 28: 9-18.

Ashley, M.K., Grant, M, and Grabov, A. 2006. Plant Responses to Potassium Deficiencies: A Role for Potassium Transport Proteins. *Journal of Experimental Botany* 57(2): 425-436.

Ashoka, P., Anand, S. and Smitha, R. 2009. Effect of Macro and Micronutrients with Organics on Growth, Quality, yield and Economics of Baby Corn (*Zea mays*L.) in Tungabhadra Command Area. *Crop Research* 37(1/3): 15-18.

Ashoka, P., Mudalagiriyappa, B.T., Pujari, P., Hugar, P.S. and Desai, B.K. 2008. Effect of Micronutrients with or without Organic Manures on Yield of Baby Corn (*Zea mays* L. – Chickpea (*Cicer artietinum* L.) Sequence. *Karnataka Journal of Agriculture Sciences* 21(4): 485-487.

Ashraf, M., M. Mueen-Ud-Din and N. H. Warraich. 2003. Production Efficiency of Mungbean (*Vigna radiata* L.) as affected by Seed Inoculation and NPK Application. *International Journal of Agricultural Biology* 5(2): 179-180.

Ashraf, M., Mueen-Ud-Din, M. and Warraich, N.H. 2003. Production Efficiency of Mungbean (*Vigna radiata* L) as affected by Seed Inoculation and NPK Application. *International Journal of Agricultural Biology* 5(2): 179-180.

Badr, M.A. 2006. Efficiency of K-feldspar Combined with Organic Materials and Silicate Dissolving Bacteria on Tomato yield. *Journal of Applied Science and Research* 2(12): 1191-1198.

Badr, M.A., Shafei, A.M. and Sharaf, S.H. and El-Deen. 2006. The Dissolution of K and Phosphorus Bearing Minerals by Silicate Dissolving Bacteria and their Effect on Sorghum Growth. *Research Journal of Agriculture and Biological Sciences* 2: 5-11.

Bagyalakshmi, B., Ponmurugan, P. and Marimuthu, S. 2012. Influence of Potassium Solubilizing Bacteria on Crop Productivity and Quality of Tea (*Camellia sinensis*). *African Journal of Agricultural Research* 7: 4250-4259.

Bahadur, I., Maurya, B.R., Meena, V.S., Saha, M., Kumar, A. and Aeron, A. 2017. Mineral Release Dynamics of Tricalcium Phosphate and Waste Muscovite by Mineral-Solubilizing Rhizobacteria Isolated from Indo-Gangetic Plain of India, *Geomicrobiology Journal* 34(5): 454-466.

Bahadur, I., Maurya, B.R., Kumar, A., Meena, V.S. and Raghuwanshi, R. 2016. Towards the Soil Sustainability and Potassium-solubilizing Microorganisms. New Delhi: Springer, p. 255-266.

Bai, Y., Wang, L., Lu, Y., Zhou, L. and Cheng, M. 2015. Effects of Long-term Full Straw return on yield and Potassium Response in Wheat-maize Rotation. *Journal of Integrative Agriculture* 14(12): 2467-2476.

Bal, U. and Altintas, S. 2006. A Positive Side Effect from Trichoderma Harzianum, the Biological Control Agent: Increased yield in Vegetable Crops. *Journal of Environmental Protection and Ecology* 7: 383-387.

Baldi, E., Toselli, M., Eissenstat, D.M. and Marangon, B. 2010. Organic Fertilization Leads to Increased Peach Root Production and Lifespan. *Tree Physiology* 30: 1373-1382.

Balogh-Brunstad, Z., Keller, C.K., Gill, R.A., Bormann, B.T. and Li, C.Y. 2008. The Effect of Bacteria and Fungi on Chemical Weathering and Chemical Denudation Fluxes in Pine Growth Experiments. *Biogeochemistry* 88(2): 153-167.

Bandick, A.K. and Dick, R.P. 1999. Field Management Effects on Soil Enzyme Activities. *Soil Biology and Biochemistry* 31: 1471-1479.

Banerjee, M., Rai, R.K., Maiti, D. and Dhas., Mahua S. 2006, Impact of Chemical Fertilizers and Bio-fertilizers on yield and Fertility Build-up of Soil under Maize (Zea mays) – Wheat (Triticum aestivum) Cropping System *Indian Journal of Agricultural Science* 76(12): 753-755.

Baque, M.A., Karim, M.A., Hamid, A. and Tetsushi, H. 2006. Effects of Fertilizer Potassium on Growth, yield and Nutrient uptake of Wheat (*Triticum aestivum*) under Water Stress Conditions. *South Pacific Studies* 27(1): 25-35.

Basak, B. and Biswas, D. 2012 Modification of Waste mica for Alternative Source of Potassium: Evaluation of Potassium release in Soil from Waste Mica Treated with Potassium Solubilizing Bacteria (KSB). *LAMBERT Academic Publishing*, Germany, pp. 25-141.

Basak, B.B. and Biswas, D.R. 209. Influence of Potassium Solubilizing Microorganism (*Bacillus mucilaginosus*) and Waste mica on Potassium uptake Dynamics by Sudan Grass (*Sorghum vulgare* Pers.) Grown under Two Alfisols. *Plant Soil* 317: 235-255.

Basavesha, K.N., Savalgi, V.P., Sreenivasa, M.N. and Manjunatha, H. 2016. Impact of Bacteria Solubilizing both Potassium and Phosphorus on Growth and yield of Maize (*Zea mays* L.). *Research in Environment and Life Sciences* 9(4): 464-465.

Beary, T.P., Boopathy, R. and Templet P. 2002. Accelerated Decomposition of Sugarcane Crop Residue using a Fungal Bacterial Consortium. *International Journal of Biodeterioration and Biodegradation* 50: 41-46.

Beg, M.A. and Singh, J.K. 2009. Effect of bio Fertilizers and Fertility Level on Growth, yield and Nutrient Removal of Green Gram (*Vigna radiata* L.) under Kashmir Conditions. *Indian Journal of Agricultural Sciences* 79(5): 388-390.

Bhardwaj D., Ansari M.W., Sahoo R.K., Tuteja N. 2014. Biofertilizers Function as Key Player in Sustainable Agriculture by Improving Soil Fertility, Plant Tolerance and Crop Productivity. *Microbial Cell Factories* 13: 66.

Bhuiyan, M.A.H. and Mian, M.H. 2007. Effect of Bradyrhizobium Inoculation on Nodulation, Biomass Production and Yield of Mungbean. *Bangladesh J Microbiol* 24(2): 95-99.

Bindhani, A., Barik, K., Garnayak, L. and Mahapatra, P. 2008. Productivity and Nitrogen-use Efficiency of Baby Corn (*Zea mays*) at different Levels and Timing of Nitrogen Application under Rainfed Conditions. *Indian Journal of Agricultural Sciences* 78(7): 629-631.

Bindhani, A., Barik, K.C., Garnayak, F.M. and Mahapatra, P.L. 2007. Productivity and Nitrogen use Efficiency of Baby Corn (Zea mays L.) at different Level and Time of Nitrogen Application under Rainfed Condition. *Indian Journal of Agricultural Sciences*, 78: 629-631.

Bindhani., Anita., Barik, K.C., Garnayak, L.M. and Mahapatra, P.K. 2008. Productivity and Nitrogen-use Efficiency of Baby Corn (*Zea mays* L.) at Different Levels and Timing of Nitrogen Application under Rainfed Conditions. *Indian Journal of Agricultural Sciences* 78(7): 629-631.

Bjorkman. 2004. Effect of Trichoderma Colonization on Auxin-mediated Regulation of Root Elongation. *Plant Growth Regulation* 43: 89-92.

Black, C.A., Evans, D.D. and Dinauer, R.C. 1965. *Methods of Soil Analysis*, American Society of Agronomy Madison, WI, Vol. 9.

Black, C.A., Evans, D.D. and Dinauer, R.C. 1965. *Methods of Soil Analysis*, American Society of Agronomy Madison, WI, (Vol. 9).

Blanco-Canqui, H. and Lal, R. 2006. Impact of Long-term Wheat Straw Management on Soil Hydraulic Properties under no-tillage. *Soil Science Society of America Journal* 71: 1166-1173.

Blevins, R.L. and Frye, W.W. 1993. Conservation Tillage: An Ecological Approach to Soil Management. *Advances in Agronomy* 41: 33-78.

Borie, A.K., Sharma, M.L. and Singh, S.P. 2002. Bio-degradation of Crop Residues by Trichoderma Species vis-a-vis Nutrient Quality of the Prepared Compost. *Sugar Technology* 3(7): 154-160.

Borie, A.K., Sharma, M.L. and Singh, S.P. 2002. Bio-degradation of Crop Residues by Trichoderma Species vis-a-vis Nutrient Quality of the Prepared Compost. *Sugar Technology* 3(7): 154-160.

Bouyoucos, G.J. 1962. Hydrometer method Improved for making Particle Size Analyses of Soils. *Agronomy Journal* 54(5): 464-465.

Briggs, L.J. and. Shantz, H.L. 1912. The Wilting Coefficient and its Indirect Determination. *Botanical Gazette* 53(1): 20-37.

Bulgarelli, D., Schlaeppi, K., Spaepen, S., Ver Loren van Themaat, E. and SchulzeLefert, P. (2013) Structure and Functions of the Bacterial Microbiota of Plants. *Annul Review of Plant Biology* 64: 807-838.

Buresh, R.J. and De Datta. S.K. 1991. Nitrogen Dynamics and Management in Rice~ Legume Cropping Systems. *Advances in Agronomy* 45: 1-59.

Byju, G. and Anand, M.H. 2009. Differential Response of Short-and Long-duration Cassava Cultivars to Applied Mineral Nitrogen. *Journal of Plant Nutrition and Soil Science* 172: 572-576.

Cai, F., Chen, W., Wei, Z., Pangm G,, Li, R., Ran, W. and Shen, Q. 2015. Colonization of Trichoderma Harzianum Strain SQR-T037 on Tomato Roots and its Relationship to Growth, Nutrient Availability and Soil Microflora. *Plant and Soil* 388: 337-350.

Cakmak, I. 2005. The Role of Potassium in Alleviating Detrimental Effects of Abiotic Stresses in Plants. *Journal of Plant Nutrition and Soil Science* 168: 521-530.

Cakmak, I., Hengeler, C. and Marschner, H. 1994. Partitioning of Shoot and Root Dry matter and Carbohydrates in Bean Plants Suffering from Phosphorus, Potassium and Magnesium Deficiency. *Journal of Experimental Botany* 45(9): 1245-1250.

Chandra, R. 2011. Effect of Summer Crops and their Residue Management on yield of Succeeding Wheat and Soil Properties. *Journal of the Indian Society of Soil Science* 59(1): 37 42.

Chishi, K.Y. 2010. Studies on Dual Inoculation of Potassium Solubilizing Bacteria and Phosphorus Solubilizing Bacteria on Growth and yield of Maize (*Zea mays* L.). M.Sc.(Agri.) Theses. Agricultural Microbiology UAS, Dharwad. India.

Chu, H., Lin, X., Fujii, T., Morimoto, S., Yagi, K., Hu, J. and Zhang, J., 2007. Soil Microbial Biomass, Dehydrogenase Activity, Bacterial Community Structure in Response to Long Term Fertilizer Management. *Soil Biology and Biochemistry* 39(11): 2971-2976.

Clarson, D. 2004. Potash Biofertilizer for Ecofriendly Agriculture. Agro-clinic and Research Centre, Poovanthuruthu, Kottayam (Kerala), India, pp. 98-110.

Contreras-Cornejo, H., Macias-Rodriguez, L., CortesPenagos, C. and Lopez-Bucio, J. 2009. Trichoderma virens, a Plant Beneficial Fungus, Enhances Biomass Production and Promotes Lateral Root Growth through an Auxin-dependent Mechanism in Arabidopsis. *Plant Physiology* 149: 1579-1592.

Cordell, D., Drangert, J.O. and White, S. 2009. The Story of Phosphorus: Global Food Security and Food for thought. *Global Environmental Change* 2009; 19: 292-305.

Cropstaticsmaize2019.www.farmer.gov.in/ M_cropstaticsmaize.aspx+&cd=19&hl=en&ct=clnk&gl=in.

Dadarwal, R.S., Jain, N.K. and Singh, D. 2009. Integrated Nutrient Management in Baby Corn (*Zea mays*). *Indian Journal of Agricultural Sciences* 79(12): 1023-1025.

Dadarwal, R.S.; Jain, N.K. and Singh, D. 2009. Integrated Nutrient Management in Baby Corn (Zea mays). *Indian Journal of Agricultural Science* 79: 1023-1025.

Dadarwal, R.S., Jain, N.K. and Singh, D. 2009. Integrated Nutrient Management in Baby Corn (*Zea mays*). *Indian Journal of Agriculture Sciences* 79(12): 1023-1025.

Dadarwal, R.S., Jain, N.K. and Singh, D. 2009. Integrated Nutrient Management in Baby Corn (*Zea mays*). *Indian Journal of Agricultural Sciences* 79(12): 1023-1025.

Dandurand, L. and Khudsen, G. 1993. Influence of Pseudomonas Fluorescens on Hyphal Growth and Biocontrol Activity of *Trichoderma harzianum* in the Spermosphere and Rhizosphere of Pea. *Phytopathology* 83: 265-270.

Das, A., Patel, D.P., Munda, G.C. and Ghosh, P.K. 2011. Effect of Organic and Inorganic Sources of Nutrients on yield, Nutrient uptake and Soil Fertility of Maize (*Zea mays*)—mustard (Brassica campestris) Cropping System. *Indian Journal of Agriculture Sciences* 80.

Das, P.K., Sanrangi, D., Jena, M.K. and Mohanthy, S. 2002. Response of Greengram (*Vigna radiata* L.) to Integrated Application of Vermicompost and Chemical Fertilizer in Acid Lateritic Soil. *Indian Agriculture* 46(2): 79-81.

Das, S.K. and Varma A. 2011. Role of Enzymes in Maintaining Soil Health. pp. 25-42.

Davari, M., Sharma, S.N. and Mirzakhani, M. 2012. Residual Influence of Organic Materials, Crop Residues, and Biofertilizers on Performance of Succeeding Mung Bean in an Organic Rice-based Cropping System. *International Journal of Recycling of Organic Waste in Agriculture* 14(1): 2-9.

Dekker, R.F.H. and Richards, G.N. 1971. Determination of Starch in Plant Material. *Journal of Science and Food Agriculture* 22(9): 441-444.

Deshmukh, S.B., Raundal, P.U. and Kunjir, N.T. Effect of Foliar Spray of Nutrients on Growth, yield and Quality of Summer Greengram (*Vigna radiata* (L), *Bioinfolet* 10(3B): 1060-1064.

Dong, W., Hu, C., Chen, S. and Zhang Y. 2009. Tillage and Residue Management Effects on Soil Carbon and CO2 Emission in Wheat – Corn Double-cropping System. *Nutrient Cycling in Agroecosystems* 83: 27-37.

Du Preez, C.C., Steyn, J.T. and Kotze, E. Long-term Effects of Wheat Residue Management on some Fertility Indicators of a Semi-arid Plinthosol. *Soil and Tillage Research* 63(1-2): 25-33.

Dubois, M., Gilles, K.A., Hamilton, J.K., Rebers, P.T. and Smith, F. 1956. Colorimetric method for Determination of Sugars and related Substances. *Analytical Chemistry* 28(3): 350-356.

Durai R Singh, K. Vairavan and M. Ramasamy 2002. Integrated Phosphorus Management in Green Gram. *Madras Journal of Agriculture* 89(1-3): 149-150.

Durga, K.K., Varma, V.S., Sreelatha, D. and Reddy, V. 2012. Influence of Planting methods, Spacing and Fertilization on yield and Quality of Sweet Corn. *Maize Journal* 4000: 121-123.

Ebrahimpour, F., Eidizadeh, K.H. and Damghani, A.M. 2011. Sustainable Nutrient Management in Maize with Integrated Application of Biological and Chemical Fertilizers. *International Journal of Agricultural Sciences* 1: 423-426.

Egamberdiyeva, D. and Hoflich, G. 2003. Influence of Growth Promoting Bacteria on the Growth of Wheat at different Soils and Temperatures. *Soil Biology and Biochemistry* 35: 973-978.

Epstein, E. and Bloom, A.J. 2005. *Mineral Nutrition of Plants: Principles and Perspectives*. 2nd Edition, Sinauer Associates, Inc., Sunderland.

Etesami, H. Emami, S. and Alikhani, H.A. 2017. Potassium Solubilizing Bacteria (KSB): Mechanisms, Promotion of Plant Growth, and Future Prospects - *Journal of Soil Science and Plant Nutrition* 17(4): 897-911.

FAI, 2018-19. https://krishijagran.com/list-of-association/fertilizer-association-of-india/

Freeman, S., Minz, D., Kolesnik, I., Barbul, O., Zreibil, A.M. Maymon, Y. Nitzani, B. Kirshner, D. Rav-David, A. Bilu, A. Dag, S. Shafir, and Y. Elad. 2004. Trichoderma Biocontrol of Colletotrichum Acutatum and Botrytis Cinerea, and Survival in Strawberry. *European Journal of Plant Pathology* 110: 361-370.

Gad, W.M. 2011. Physiological Studies on *Foeniculum vulgare* Mill and *Anethum graveolens*L. M.Sc. Thesis, Faculty of Agriculture, Kafr El-Sheikh, Tanta University, Egypt. p. 214.

Gadde, B., Bonnet, S., Menke, C. and Garivait, S. 2009. Air Pollutant Emissions from Rice Straw open Field Burning in India, Thailand and the Philippines. *Environmental Pollution* 157: 1554-1558.

Gaind, S. and Nain, L. 2011. Soil Health in Response to Bio-augmented Paddy Straw Compost. *World Journal of Agricultural Sciences* 4: 480-488.

Gajera, R.J., Khafi, H.R., Raj, A.D., Yadav, V., Lad, A.N. 2014. Effect of Phosphorus and Bio-fertilizers on Growth yield and Economics of Summer Green Gram [*Vigna radiata* (L.) Wilczek]. *Agriculture Update* 9(1): 98-102.

Garcia, L., Probanza, A., Ramos, B., Barriuso, J., Gutierrez Manero, F.J. 2004. Effects of Inoculation with Plant Growth Promoting Rhizobacteria (PGPR) and Sinorhizobium Fredii on Biological Nitrogen Fixation, Nodulation and Growth of *Glycine max*. *Plant Soil* 267: 143-153.

Geisseler, D. and Scow, K.M. 2014. Longterm Effects of Minereal Fertilizers on Soil Microorganisms- A Review. *Soil Biology and Biochemistry* 75: 54-63.

Ghuman, B. and Sur, H. Tillage and Residue Management Effects on Soil Properties and yields of Rainfed Maize and Wheat in a Subhumid Subtropical Climate. *Soil and Tillage Research* 58(1): 1-10.

Gilberto J., Roberto M.B., Mario, R.M., Belmont, M., Monroy, R., Augusto, J., Ramón, S., Gabriela, S.J. Effect of Trichoderma asperellum Applications and Mineral Fertilization on Growth Promotion and the content of Phenolic Compounds and Flavonoids in Onions. *Scientia Horticulturae*. 195(2015) 8-16.

Gill, M.S., Sarkar, A., Ahlawat, I.P.S. and Gangaiah, B. 2009. *Plant-water-nutrient Relationship in Crop Production*. New Delhi: *Indian Society of Agronomy*.

Girgis, M.G.Z., Khalil, H.M.A. and Sharaf, M.S. 2008. Invitro Evaluation of Rock Phosphate and Potassium Solubilizing Potential of some Bacillus strains. *Australian Journal of Basic and Applied Sciences* 2(1): 68-81.

Giri S. and Pati B.R. 2004. A Comparative Study on Phyllosphere Nitrogen Fixation by Newly Isolated Corynebacterium sp. & Flavobacterium sp. and their Potentialities as Biofertilizer. *Acta Microbiolagica Immunologica Hungarica* 51(1-2): 47-56.

Golada, S.L., Sharma, G.L. and Jain, H. 2013. Performance of Baby Corn (zea mays l.) as Influenced by Spacing, Nitrogen Fertilization and Plant Growth Regulators under sub Humid Condition in Rajasthan, India. *African Journal of Agricultural Research* 8(12): 1100-1107.

Gomez, K.A. and Gomez, A.A. 1984. *Statistical Procedures for Agricultural Research*: John Wiley & Sons, Inc.

Gorade, V.N., Chavan, L.S., Gagtap, D.N and Koleka, A.B. 2014. Response of Greengram (*Vigna radiata* L.) Varieties to Integrated Nutrient Management in Summer Season. *Agricultural Science Digest* 34(1): 36-40.

Govaerts, B., Sayre, K.D., Lichter, K., Dendooven, L. and Deckers, J. 2007. Influence of Permanent Bed Planting and Residue Management on Physical and Chemical Soil Quality in Rain Fed Maize/Wheat Systems. *Plant and Soil* 291: 39-54.

Grzebisz, W., Barlog, P., Szczepaniak, W. and Potarzycki, J. 2010. Effect of Potassium Fertilizing System on Dynamics of Dry matter Accumulation by Maize. *Fertilizers and Fertilization* 40: 57-69.

Gundala, P.B., Chinthala, P. and Sreenivasulu, B. 2013. A New Facultative Alkaliphilic, Potassium Solubilizing, *Bacillus* spp. SVUNM9 isolated from Mica Cores of Nellore District, Andhra Pradesh, India. *Journal of Microbiology and Biotechnology* 2(1): 1-7.

Han, H.S. and Lee, K.D. 2005. Phosphate and Potassium Solubilizing Bacteria Effect on Mineral uptake, Soil Availability and Growth of Eggplant. *Research Journal of Agriculture and Biological Science* 1: 176-180.

Han, H.S. and Lee, K.D. 2005. Phosphate and Potassium Solubilizing Bacteria Effect on Mineral Uptake, Soil Availability and Growth of Eggplant. *Research Journal of Agriculture and Biological Sciences* 1(2): 176-180.

Han, H.S., Supanjani, E. and Lee, K.D. 2006. Effect of co-inoculation with Phosphate and Potassium Solubilizing Bacteria on Mineral uptake and Growth of Pepper and Cucumber. *Plant Soil Environment* 52(3): 130-136.

Haque, M.M., Haque, A.M., Ilias, G.N.M. and Molla, H.A. 2010. Trichoderma-enriched Biofertilizer: A Prospective Substitute of Inorganic Fertilizer for Mustard (Brassica campestris) Production. *Agriculturists* 8(2): 66-73.

Harman GE. Overview of Mechanisms and uses of *Trichoderma spp. Phytopathology*. 2006; 96(2): 190-194.

Harman, G.E., Howell, C.R., Viterbo, A., Chet, I. and Lorito, M. 2004. Trichoderma species – Opportunistic, Avirulent Plant Symbionts. *Nature Review and Microbiology* 2: 43-56.

Hedge, J. and Hofreiter, B. 1962. Methods of Estimating Starch and Carbohydrates. *Carbohydrate Chemistry* 17: 163-201.

Hegde, D.M., Dwived, B.S. and Sudhakara, S.N. 1999. Biofertilizers for Cereal Production in India–areview. *Indian Journal of Agriculture Sciences* 69: 73-83.

Hossain, M.S., Karim, M.F,. Biswas, P.K., Kawochar, M.A. and Islam, M.S. 2011. Effect of Rhizobium Inoculation and Chemical Fertilization on the yield and yield Components of Moongbean. *Journal of Experimental Biosciences* 2(1): 69-74.

Hoyos-Carvajal, L., Orduz, S. and Bissett, J. 2009. Growth Stimulation in Bean (Phaseolus vulgaris L.) by Trichoderma. *Biological Control* 51(3): 409-416.

Hridya, A.C., Byju, G. and Misra, R.S. 2014. Effects of Microbial Inoculations on Soil Chemical, Biochemical and Microbial Biomass Carbon of Cassava (Manihot esculenta Crantz) Growing Vertisols. *Archives of Agronomy and Soil Science* 60(2): 239-249.

Hu, X.F., Chen, J. and Guo, J. F. 2006. Two Phosphate and Potassium Solubilizing Bacterial isolated from Tiannu Mountain, Zhijiang, China. *World Journal of Microbiology and Biotehchnology* 22: 983-990.

Humphries, E. 1956. Mineral Components and Ash Analysis *Modern methods of Plant Analysis/moderne Methoden der pflanzenanalyse*, Springer 468-502.

Hussain, M.B., Zahir, Z.A., Asghar, H.N. and Mahmood, S. 2014. Scrutinizing rhizobia to Rescue Maize Growth under Reduced Water Conditions, *Soil Science Society of America Journal* 78: 538-545.

Hussain, M.S., Karim, M.F., Biswas, P.K., Kawochar, M.A. and Islam, M.S. 2011. Effect of *rhizobium* Inoculation and Fertilization on the yield and yield Components of Mungbean, *Journal of Experimental Biosciences* 2(1): 45-51.

Hussain, Z, Khattak, R, Irshad, M., Mahmood, Q. 2016. Effect of Saline Irrigation Water on the Leachability of Salts, Growth and Chemical Composition of Wheat (*Triticum aestivum* L.) in Saline-sodic Soil Supplemented with Phosphorus and Potassium. *Journal of Soil Science and Plant Nutrition* 16(3): 604-620.

ICAR NEWS, 2008. Microbial Consortium for Rapid Bio-conversion of Agro-waste using Organic inputs. In: Innovations for Improving Efficiency, Equity and Environment. Proceedings of the 4th World Congress on Conservation Agriculture, February, 4-7, 2009 New Delhi India pp. 71-79.

Ilyas, N. and Bano, A. 2010. Azospirillum Strains isolated from Roots and Rhizosphere Soil of Wheat (*Triticum aestivum* L.) Grown under different Soil Moisture Conditions. *Biology and Fertility of Soils* 46(4): 393-406.

Iqbal, M.A., Khalid, M., Shahzad, S.M., Ahmad, M., Soleman, N. and Akhtar, N. 2012. Integrated use of Rhizobium leguminosarum, Plant Growth Promoting Rhizobacteria and Enriched Compost for Improving Growth, Nodulation and yield of Lentil (*Lens culinaris* Medik.). *Chilean Journal Agricultural Research* 72: 104-110.

Jabbar, A., Aziz, T., Bhatti, I.H., Virk, Z.A., Khan, M.M. and Wasi, D. 2009. Effect of Potassium Application on yield and Protein content of Late sown Wheat (*Triticum aestivum*) under Field. *Soil and Environment* 28(2): 193-196.

Jackson, M. 1958. Soil Chemical Analysis: Prentice Hall, Englewood Cliffs, NJ. Soil Chemical Analysis. Prentice Hall, Englewood Cliffs, NJ.

Jackson, M. 1973. Soil Chemical Analysis Prentice Hall of India Ltd., New Delhi.

Jain, N.K. and Dhama, A.K. 2005. Residual Effect of Phosphorus and Zinc on yield, Nutrient Content and uptake and Economics of Pearlmillet (*Pennisetum glaucum*)-wheat (*Triticum aestivum*) Cropping System. *Indian Journal of Agricultural Science* 75(5): 281-284.

Jat, R.L. 1996. Studies on Weed Management and Fertilizer Levels of Intercrop with and without Inoculation in Maize + Soybean Intercropping System. Ph.D. Thesis, RAU, Udaipur.

Jayaganesh, S., Venkatesan, S. and Senthurpandian, V.K. 2011. Impact of Sources and doses of Potassic Fertilizer on Biochemical Constituents and Quality Parameter of Black Tea. *Food Chemistry* 90: 535-539.

Kachroo, D. and Dixit, A.K. 2005. Residue-management Practices using Fly Ash and Various Crop Residues for Productivity of Rice (*Oryza sativa*)–wheat (*Triticum aestivum*) Cropping System under Limited Moisture Conditions. *Indian Journal of Agronomy* 50(4): 249-252.

Kandeler, E., Tscherko, D. and Spiegel, H. 1999. Long Term Monitoring of Microbial Biomass, N Mineralization and Enzyme Activities of a Chernozem under different Tillage Management. *Biology and Fertility of Soils* 28: 343-351.

Kandil, A., Badawi, M.A., El-Mursy, S.A. and Abdou, U.M.A. 2004. Effect of Planting Dates, Nitrogen Levels and Biofertilization Treatments on Growth Attributes of Suger Beet (*Beta vulgaris* L.). *Journal of King Faisal University* 5(2): 227-236.

Kanso, A.L., Essam, S.A. and Zeinat. A.N. 1999. Biodegradation and Utilization of Bagasse with Trichoderma reesie. *Polymer Degradation and Stability* 63: 273-278.

Katkar, R.N., Sonune, B.A. and Kadu, P.R. 2011. Long-term Effect of Fertilization on Soil Chemical and Biological Characteristics and Productivity under Sorghum (*Sorghum bicolor*)-Wheat (*Triticum aestivum*) System in Vertisol. *Indian Journal of Agricultural Sciences* 81(8): 734-742.

Kaur, G. and Reddy, M.S. 2015. Effects of Phosphate-solubilizing Bacteria, Rock Phosphate and Chemical Fertilizers on Maize-wheat Cropping Cycle and Economics. *Pedosphere* 25: 428-437.

Kawtra, A. and Sahagal, S. 2007. Value added Product of Maize. Report of the National Conference on Doubling Maize Production. IFFCO Foundation. New Delhi, pp. 76-85.

Khaliq, A., Abbasi, M.K. and Hussain, T. 2006. Effects of Integrated use of Organic and Inorganic Nutrient Sources with Effective Microorganisms (EM) on Seed Cotton yield in Pakistan. *Bioresource Technology* 97(8): 967-972.

Khan, M.B., Muhammad Iqbal Lone, Rehmat Ullah, Shuaib Kaleem and Muhammad Ahmed (2010). Effect of different Phosphatic Fertilizers on Growth Attributes of Wheat (*Triticum aestivum* L.). *Journal of American Science* 6(12): 1256-1262.

Khudsen, D., Peterson, G.A. and Prov, P.F. 1992. Lithium, Sodium and Potassium. In: Page A.L. (Ed.) Methods of Soil Analysis Part (2) Agronomy Monograph 9, 2nd Edn. ASA and SSSA Madison, WI.

Kim, T., Jung, W., Lee, B., Yoneyama, T., Kim, H., Kim, K., 2003, P Effects on N Uptake and Remobilization during Regrowth of Italian Ryegrass (*Lolium mutiflorum*). *Environment and Experimental Botany* 50: 233-242.

Kowalska, J. 2011. Effects of *Trichoderma asperellum* [T1] On *Botrytis cinerea* [Pers.: FR.], Growth and yield of Organic Strawberry. *Acta Scientiarum Polonorum Hortorum Cultus* 10(4): 107-114.

Kumar and Bohra. 2014. Effect of NPKS and Zn Application on Growth, yield, Economics and Quality of Baby Corn. *Indian Journal of Agronomy* 60(9): 1193-1206.

Kumar, A. and Dhar, S. 2010. Evaluation of Organic and Inorganic Sources of Nutrients in Maize (*Zea mays*) and their Residual Effect on Wheat (*Triticum aestivum*) under different Fertility Levels. *Indian Journal of Agricultural Science* 80(5): 364-371.

Kumar, A., Bahadur, I., Maurya, B.R., Raghuwanshi, R., Meena, V.S., Singh, D.K. and Dixit, J. 2015. Does a Plant Growth-promoting Rhizobacteria enhance Agricultural Sustainability? *Journal of Pure and Applied Microbiology* 9(1): 715-724.

Kumar, A., Maurya, B.R. and Raghuwanshi, R. 2014. Isolation and Characterization of PGPR and their Effect on Growth, yield and Nutrient Content in Wheat (Triticum aestivum L.). *Biocatalysis and Agricultural Biotechnology* 3: 121-128.

Kumar, R. and Bohra, J.S. 2013. Effect of NPKS and Zn Application on Growth, yield, Economics and Quality of Baby Corn. *Archives of Agronomy and Soil Science* 60(9): 1193-1206.

Kumar, R., Bohra, J.S., Singh, A.K. and Kumawat, N. 2015. Productivity, Profitability and Nutrient-use Efficiency of Baby Corn (*Zea mays*) as Influenced of Varying Fertility Levels. *Indian Journal of Agronomy*, 60(3): 285-290.

Kumar, S., Singh, R., Saquib, M., Singh, D.and Kumar, A. 2014. Effect of different Combinations of Vermicompost, Biofertiliser and Chemical Fertiliser on Growth, Productivity and Profitability in Chickpea. *Plant Archives* 14(1): 267-270.

Kumar, V. and Ahlawat, I. 2006. Effect of Biofertilizer and Nitrogen on Wheat (T*riticum aestivum*) and their after Effects on Succeeding Maize (*Zea mays*) in Wheat-maize Cropping System. *Indian Journal of Agricultural Sciences* 76(8): 465-468.

Kumawat, A., Pareek, B.L. and Yadav, R.S. 2010. Response of Green Gram (*Vigna radiata*) to Biofertilizers under Different Fertility Levels. *Indian Journal of Agricultural Sciences* 80: 65-57.

Kumawat, P.K., Tiwari, R.C., Golada, S.L., Godara, A.S., Garhwal, R.S. and Choudhary, R. 2013. Effect of Phosphorus Sources, Levels and Biofertilizers on yield Attributes, yield and Economics of Greengram (*Phaseolus radiata* L.). *Legume Research* 36: 70-73.

Kumawat, P.K., Tiwari, R.C., Golada, S.L., Godara, A.S., Garhwal, R.S. and Choudhary, R. 2013. Effect of Phosphorus Sources, Levels and Biofertilizers on yield Attributes, yield and Economics of Greengram (*Phaseolus radiata* L.). *Legume Research* 36: 70-73.

Kumhar, K.C., Babu, A., Bordoloi, M. and Ali, A. 2014. Evaluation of Culture Media for Biomass Production of Trichoderma viride (KBN 24) and their Production Economics. *American Journal of Agriculture and Forestry* 2(6): 317-320.

Kumpawat, B.S. 2010. Integrated Nutrient Management in Blackgram (*Vigna mungo*) and its Residual Effect on Succeeding Mustard (*Brassica juncea*) Crop, *Indian Journal of Agricultural Sciences* 80(1): 76-79.

Law-Ogbomo, K. and Law-Ogbomo, J.E. 2009. The Performance of Zea mays as Influenced by NPK fertilizer Application. *Notulae Scientia Biologicae* 1(1): 59-62.

Lentz, R.D. and Bjorneberg, D.L. 2003. Polyacrylamide and Straw Residue Effects on Irrigation Furrow Erosion and Infiltration. *Journal of Soil and Water Conservation* 58: 312-319.

Lin, Q.M., Rao, Z.H., Sun, Y.X., Yao, J. and Xing L.J. 2002. Identification and Practical Application of Silicate-dissolving Bacteria. *Agricultural Science in China* 1: 81-85.

Liu, A., Hamel, C., Spedding, T., Zhang, T.Q., Mongeau, R., Lamarre, G.R. and Tremblay, G. 2008. Soil Microbial Carbon and Phosphorus as Influenced by Phosphorus Fertilization and Tillage in a Maize-soybean Rotation in South-western Quebec. *Canadian Journal of Soil Science* 88: 21-30.

Lone, A.A., Allai, B. and Nehvi, F. 2013. Growth, yield and Economics of Baby Corn (*Zea mays*L.) as Influenced by Integrated Nutrient Management (INM) Practices. *African Journal of Agricultural Research* 8(36): 4537-4540.

Luo, P., Han, X., Wang, Y., Han, M., Shi, H., Liu, N., and Bai, H. (2015). Influence of Long-term Fertilization on Soil Microbial Biomass, Dehydrogenase Activity, and Bacterial and Fungal Community Structure in a Brown Soil of Northeast China. *Annals of Microbiology* 65(1), 533-542.

Lynch, J.M. and Harper, S.H.T. 1985. The Microbial upgrading of Straw for Agricultural use. *Philosophical Transactions of the Royal Society of London* B 310: 221-226.

Lynch, J.P. 2013. Steep, Cheap and Deep: An Ideotype to Optimize Water and N Acquisition by Maize Root Systems. *Annals of Botany* 112: 347-357.

Lynn, T.M., Win, H.S., Kyaw, E.P., Latt, Z.K. and Yu, S.S. 2013. Characterization of Phosphate Solubilizing and Potassium Decomposing Strains and Study on their Effects on Tomato Cultivation. *International Journal of Innovation and Applied Studies* 3: 959-966.

Lynn, T.M., Win, H.S., Kyaw, E.P., Latt, Z.K., Yu, S.S. 2013. Characterization of Phosphate Solubilizing and Potassium Decomposing Strains and Study on their Effects on Tomato Cultivation. *International Journal of Innovation and Applied Studies* 3: 959-966.

Machado, R.V., Andrade F.V., Passos, R.R., Ribeiro R., Mendonça E. and Mesquita L.F. 2016. Characterization of Ornamental Rock Residue and Potassium Liberation *Via* Organic Acid Application. *Revista Brasileira de Ciência do Solo* 40: 1-13.

Mahajan, G., Sharda, R., Kumar, A. and Singh, K. 2007. Effect of Plastic Mulch on Economizing Irrigation Water and Weed Control in Baby Corn Sown by different methods. *African Journal of Agricultural Research* 2(1): 19-26.

Mahmoud, H., El Komy., A.A. Saleh, A. Eranthodi and Molan. Y.Y. 2015. Characterization of Novel Trichoderma asperellum isolates to Select Effective Biocontrol Agents against Tomato Fusarium Wilt. *Plant Pathology Journal* 31: 50-60.

Malhi, S. and Lemke, R. 2007. Tillage, Crop Residue and N Fertilizer Effects on Crop yield, Nutrient uptake, Soil Quality and Nitrous Oxide Gas Emissions in a Second 4-yr Rotation Cycle. *Soil and Tillage Research* 96(1): 269-283.

Manivannan, V.K., Thanunathan, V., Imayavaramban and Ramanathan, N. 2002. Effect of Foliar Application of NPK and Chelated Micronutrients on Rice-fallow Urdbean, *Legume Research* 25(4): 270-272.

Manivannan, V.K., Thanunathan, V., Imayavaramban and Ramanathan, N. 2002. Effect of Foliar Application of NPK and Chelated Micronutrients on Rice-fallow Urdbean, *Legume Research* 25(4): 270-272.

Maqsood, M., Shehzad, M.A., Wahid, A. and Ahm, A. 2013. Improving Drought Tolerance in Maize (Zea mays) with Potassium Application in Furrow Irrigation Systems. *International Journal of Agriculture & Biology*. 15(2): 1193-1198.

Marimuthu, S., Subbian, P., Ramamoorthy, V. and Samiyappan R. 2002. Synergistic Effect of Combined Application of Azospirillum and *Pseudomonas fluorescens* with Inorganic Fertilizers on Root Rot Incidence and yield of Cotton. Zeit. Pflanzenkrankheiten. *Pflanzenschutz* 109(6): 569-577.

Marinori, S., Mascinadaro, G., Ceccanti, B. and Grego, S. 2000. Influence of Organic and Mineral Fertilizers on Soil Biological and Physical Properties. *Bioresource Technology* 72: 9-17.

Martin, J.P. 1950. Use of Acid Rose Bengal and Streptomycin in the Plate method for Estimating Soil Fungi. *Soil Science* 69: 215.

Martineau, E., Domec, J.C. and Bosc, A. 2017. The Effects of Potassium Nutrition on Water use in Field-grown Maize (*Zea mays* L.). *Environmental and Experimental Botany* 134: 62-71.

Mastouri, F., Bjorkman, T. and Harman, G. E. (2010). Seed Treatment with Trichoderma Harzianum Alleviates Biotic, Abiotic, and Physiological Stresses in Germinating Seeds and Seedlings. *Phytopathology* 100(2): 1213-1221.

Mathew, M.M. and Hameed, S.M.S. 2003. Effect of Microbial Inoculants and Phosphorus Levels on yield Attributes, yield and Quality Characters of Vegetable Cowpea (Vigna unguiculata subsp. sesquipedalis (L.) Verdcourt) in an oxisol. Sou. *Indian Horticulture* 51(1/6): 186-190.

Maurya, B.R., Kumar, A., Raghuwanshi, R., Bahadur, I. and Meena, V.S. 2015. Effect of Phosphate Solubilizing Isolates on Growth, yield and Phosphate Acquisition by Rice and Wheat Crops. *African Journal of Microbiology Research* 9(9): XX.

Maurya, B.R., Meena, V.S. and Meena, O.P. 2014. Influence of inceptisol and Alfisol's Potassium Solubilizing Bacteria (KSB) Isolates on Release of K from Waste mica. *Journal of Soil Sciences Vegetos* 140: 33-39.

Maurya, K.L., Sharma, H.P., Tripathi, H.P. and Singh, S. 2004. Effect of Fertility Levels of Nitrogen and Sulphur on Growth, yield and Quality of Winter Maize. *Haryana Journal of Agronomy* 20: 80-81.

Meena, H.N., Rana, K.S., Ashok Kumar, Pooniya, V., Shukla, L. and Biswas, D.R. 2018. Productivity of Wheat as Influenced by Crop Residue and Potassium Management in Maize (Zea mays L.) - Wheat (Triticum aestivum L.) - Mungbean Cropping System. *International Journal of Current Microbiology and Applied Science* 7(2): 1775-1785.

Meena, V.S., Maurya, B.R. and Bahadur, I. 2014a. Potassium Solubilization by Bacterial Strain in Waste mica. *Bangladesh Journal of Botany* 43(2): 235-237.

Meena, V.S., Maurya, B.R. and Verma, J.P. 2014b. Does a Rhizospheric Microorganism enhance K+ availability in Agricultural Soils? *Microbiological Research* 169: 337-347.

Meena,O.P., Maurya B.R. and Meena, V.S. Influence of K-solubilising Bacteria on Release of Potassium from Waste mica. *Agriculture for Sustainable Development* 1(1): 53-56.

Mehta, S., Bedi, S. and Vashist, K.K. 2011. Performance of Winter Maize (*Zea mays*) Hybrid to Planting methods and Nitrogen Levels. *The Indian Journal of Agricultural Sciences* 81(1).

Mengel, K. and Kirkby, E.A., Kosegarten, H. and Appel, T. 2001. *Principles of Plant Nutrition* (5 ed.). New Delhi India: Springer.

Mia, M.A.B and Shamsuddin, Z.H. 2010. Rhizobium as a Crop Enhancer and Biofertilizer for Increased Cereal Production. *African Journal of Biotechnology* 9(37): 6001-6009.

Mikajlo, I., Záhora, J., Dvoøáèková, H., Hynšt, J. and Elbl, J. 2015. Effect of Plant Growth Promoting Bacteria Inoculation, Addition of Biochar, and Mineral N Fertilization on Mycorrhizal Colonization. World Academy of Science, Engineering and Technology. *International Journal of Agricultural and Biosystems Engineering* 9(12): 55-58.

Mikhailouskaya, N. and Tcherhysh, A. 2005. K Mobilizing Bacteria and their Effect on Wheat yield. *Latvian Journal of Agronomy* 8: 154-157.

Mikhailouskaya, N. and Tcherhysh, A., 2005, K-mobilizing Bacteria and their Effect on Wheat yield. *Latvian Journal of Agronomy* 8: 154-157.

Mikled, C., Jiraporncharoen, S. and Potikanond, N. 1994. Fermented Slurry as Fertilizer for the Production of Forage Crops. Final Report, thai-german Biogas Application Programme. *Fertilizer Research* 8: 297-306.

Miles, A.A., Misra, S.S. and Irwin, J.O. 1938. "The Estimation of the Bactericidal Power of the Blood". *The Journal of Hygiene* 38(6): 732-749.

Mirzaei, A., Vazan, S. and Naseri, R. 2010. Response of yield Components of Safflower (*Carthamus tinctorius* L.) to Seed Incolution with *Azotobacter* and *Azosprilium* and different Nitrogen Levels under Dry Land Condition. *World Applied Science Journal* 11(10): 1287-1291.

Mishra, A., Prasad, K., and Rai, G. 2010. Effect of Bio-fertilizer Inoculations on Growth and yield of Dwarf Field Pea (*Pisum sativum* L.) in Conjunction with different doses of Chemical Fertilizers. *Journal of Agronomy* 9(4): 163-168.

Mishra, S.K. 2003. Effect of Rhizobium Inoculation, Nitrogen and Phosphorus on Root Nodulation and Nutrient uptake in Cowpea (Vigna sinensis). *Annals of Agricultural Research* 24: 139-141.

MNRE, 2009. Ministry of New and Renewable Energy Resources, Government of India.

Mohammad Akrami, Mohsen Sabzi, Farhad Baghbani Mehmandar and Ehsan Khodadadi. 2012. Effect of Seed Treatment with Trichoderma Harzianum and Trichoderma asperellum species for Controlling Fusarium rot of Common Bean. *Annals of Biological Research* 3(5): 2187-2189.

Mohammadi, K., Ghalavand, A. and Aghaalikhani, M. 2010. Study the Efficacies of Green Manure Application as Chickpea Pre Plant. *World Academic Science Engineering Technology* 4: 10-20.

Mohanty, T.R., Roul, P.K., Maity, S.K. and Nayak. A. 2015. Productivity and Profitability of Greengram (*Vigna radiata* l.) as Influenced by Rice Crop Establishment and Nutrient Management Practices in Rice-greengram Cropping System. *Journal Crop and Weed* 11(1): 92-97.

Mokhtar, M.A.K., Abdel-Kareem, F., El-Mougy, N.S. and El-Mohamady, R.S. 2013. Integration between Compost, Trichoderma Harzianum and Essential Oils for Controlling Peanut Crown Rot under Field Conditions. *Journal of Mycology* 1-7.

Mondal, M.M.A., Malek, M.A., Sattar, M.A., Puteh A.B., Rafii, M.Y. and Ismail M.R. 2013. Response of Biofertilizer and Urea on Growth and yield in Mungbean. *Legume Research* 36(5): 448-452.

Moritsuka, N., Yanai, J. and Kosaki, T. 2004. Possible Processes Releasing Nonexchangeable Potassium from the Rhizosphere of Maize. *Plant and Soil* 258: 261-268.

Mubarak, A., Rosenani, A., Anuar, A. and Siti Zauyah, D. 2002. Effect of Incorporation of Crop Residues on a Maize–groundnut Sequence in the Humid Tropics. I. Yield and Nutrient uptake. *Journal of Plant Nutrition* 26(9): 1841-1858.

Mubarak, A.R., Rosenani, A.B., Zauyah, S.D., Anuar, A.R. 2003a. Effect of Incorporation of Crop Residues on a Maize – Groundnut Sequence in the Humid Tropics. I: Yield and Nutrient uptake. *Journal of Plant and Nutrition* 26: 1841-1858.

Muthukumar, V.B., Velayudham, K. and Thavaprakaash, N. 2005a. Growth and yield of Baby Corn (*Zea mays* L.) as Influenced by Plant Growth Regulators and different Time of Nitrogen Application. *Research Journal of Agriculture and Biological Sciences* 1(4): 303-307.

Nakhro, N. and Dkhar, M.S. 2010. Impact of Organic and Inorganic Fertilizers on Microbial Populations and Biomass Carbon in Paddy Field Soil. *Journal of Agronomy* 9: 102-110.

Natesan, S., Subrahmanya Bhat, S. and Ranganathan, V. 1984. Agronomic and Cultural Factors Interacting with Potassium Manuring in Tea. In: Proc. 5thAnnu. Symp. Plantation Crops, Kasaragod, (India). PLACROSYM Standing Committee. *Indian Society of Plantation Crops.* Kasaragod Kerala India.

Nayak, B., 2001. Uptake of Potash by different Plants with the use of Potash Mobilizing Bacteria (*Frateuria aurantia*). Thesis, OUAT, Bhubaneswar.

Nazir, H., Hassan, B., Habib, R., Chand, L., Ali, A. and Hussain. A. 2011. Response of Bio-fertilizers on Growth and yield Attributes of Blackgram. *International Journal of Current Research* 2(1): 148-150.

Nazir, H.B., Hassan, R., Habib, L., Chand, A., Ali and Hussain, A. 2011. Response of Bio-fertilizers on Growth and yield Attributes of Blackgram, *International Journal of Current Research* 2(1): 148-150.

Neupane, M.P., Singh, R.K., Kumar, R. and Kumari, A. 2012. Response of Baby Corn (*Zea mays* L.) to Nitrogen sources and Row Spacing. *Environment and Ecology* 29: 1176-1179.

Nishanth and Biswas. 2008. Kinetics of Phosphorus and Potassium release from Rock Phosphate and Waste mica Enriched Compost and their Effect on yield and Nutrient uptake by Wheat (*Triticum aestivum*). *Bioresource Technology.* 99(9): 3342-3353.

Nyoki, D. and Ndakidemi, P.A. 2016. Intercropping System, Rhizobia Inoculation, Phosphorus and Potassium Fertilization: A Strategy of Soil Replenishment for Improved Crop Yield. *International Journal of Current Microbiological and Applied Sciences* 5(10): 504-522.

Ogireddy, S.D. & Paul, S. & Sarkar, D. & Rajput, R. & Singh, S. & Parihar, M. & Parewa, H. & Pal, S. & Singh, H. & Rakshit, A. 2019. Trichoderma: A Part of Possible answer towards Crop Residue Disposal. *Journal of Applied and Natural Science.* 11. 516-523.

Ogunmwonyi, I.N., Igbinosa, O.E., Aiyegoro, O.A. and Odjadjare, E.E. 2008. Microbial analysis of different Top Soil Samples of selected site in Obafemi Awolowo University, *Nigeria Scientific Research* 3(3): 120-124.

Olsen, S.R., Cole, C., Watanabe, F.S. and Dean, L. 1954. Estimation of Available Phosphorus in Soils by Extraction with Sodium Bicarbonate, US Department of Agriculture Washington, DC (Vol. 939).

Ousley, M.A., Lynch, J.M. and Whipps, J.M. 1994. Potential of Trichoderma spp. as Consistent Plant Growth Stimulators. *Biology and Fertility of Soils* 17: 85-90.

Padma, S.D. and Sukumar, J. 2015. Response of Mulberry to Inoculation of Potash mobilizing Bacterial isolation and other Bio-inoculants. *Global Journal of Bioscience and Biotechnology* 4(1): 50-53.

Palaniappan, SP. *et al.* 1990 In: Proc. International Symposium on National Resources Management for Sustainable Agriculture, 6-10 February, 1990, New Delhi. p. 220.

Pandey, A.K., Gaind, S., Ali, A. and Nain, L. 2009. Effect of Bio-augmentation and Nitrogen Supplementation on Composting of Paddy Straw. *Biodegradation* 20: 293-306.

Pandey, A.K., Mani, V.P., Ved Prakash, Singh, R.D. and Gupta, H.S. 2002. Effect of Varieties and Plant Densities on yield, yield Attributes and Economics of Baby Corn (*Zea mays*). *Indian Journal of Agronomy* 47(2): 221-226.

Panwar, A. 2008. Effect of Integrated Nutrient Management in Maize (*Zea mays*)-mustard (*Brassica compestris* var toria) Cropping system in mid Hills Altitude. *Indian Journal of Agricultural Science* 78(1): 27-31.

Panwar, A.S. and Munda, G.C. 2006. Response of Baby corn (*Zea mays* L.) to Nitrogen and Land Configuration in Mid Hills of Meghalaya. *Indian Journal of Agricultural Sciences* 76(5): 293-296.

Park, M., Singvilay, D., Seok, Y., Chung, J., Ahn, K. and Sat, 2003. Effect of Phosphate Solubilizing Fungi on P uptake and Growth of Tobacco with Rock Phosphate Application in Soil. *Korean Journal of Soil Science and Fertile* 36: 233-238.

Pathak, H., Aggarwal, P.K. and Singh, S.D. 2009. Climate change Impact, Adaptation and Mitigation in Agriculture: Methodology for Assessment and Applications. Indian Agricultural Research Institute, New Delhi, p 302.

Piper, C.S. 1966. Soil and Plant Analysis. *International Science Publisher inc.,* New York.

Ponmurugan, P. and Gopi, C. 2006. In vitro Production of Growth Regulators and Phosphate Activity by Phosphate Solubilizing Bacteria. *African Journal of Biotechnology* 5: 348-350.

Powell, J.M. and Unger, P.W. 1997. Alternatives to Crop Residues for Soil Amendment. In: Renard, C. (ed.), Crop Residues in Sustainable mixed crop/Livestock Farming Systems. pp 215-240.

Prajapati, K. 2016. Impact of Potassium Solubilizing Bacteria on Growth and Yield of Mungbean Vigna radiata. *Indian Journal of Applied Research,* 6(2): 390-392.

Prajapati, K., Sharma, M.C. and Modi, H.A. 2013. Growth Promoting Effect of Potassium Solubilizing Microorganisms on Okra (*Abelmoscus esculentus*). *International Journal of Research in Agriculture Science* (IJRAS) 1: 181-188.

Prajapati, S.K. 2014. Effect of Integrated Nutrient Management on Growth, yield, Quality and Economics of Summer Green Gram [*Vigna radiata (L.) Wilczek*], M.Sc. (Ag.) Thesis, J.N.K.V.V., Jabalpur, pp. 89.

Pramanik P., Goswami A.J., Ghosh S. and Kalita, C. (2019). An Indigenous Strain of Potassium Solubilizing Bacteria *Bacillus pseudomycoides* Enhanced Potassium uptake in Tea Plants by Increasing Potassium Availability in the mica Waste Treated Soil of North East India. *Journal of Applied Microbiology*.126 (1) 215-222.

Prasad, R. 2005. Rice-wheat Cropping System. *Advances in Agronomy* 86: 255-339.

Prasad, R.K., Kumar, V., Prasad, B. and Singh, A.P. 2010. Long-term Effect of Crop Residues and Zinc Fertilizer on Crop yield, Nutrient uptake and Fertility build-up under Rice-wheat Cropping System in Calciorthents. *Indian Society of Soil Science* 58(2): 205-211.

Priyanka Parmar and Sindhu, S.S. 2013. Potassium Solubilization by Rhizosphere Bacteria: Influence of Nutritional and Environmental Conditions. *Journal of Microbiology Research* 3(1): 25-31.

Purbey, S.K. and Sen, N.L. 2005. Effect of Bio-inoculants and Bio-regulators on Productivity and Quality of Fenugreek (*Trigonella foenum-graecum*). *Indian Journal Agriculture Sciences* 75(9): 608-611.

Purushottam, K.S., Warnalakshmi, P.R., Saabale, L. and Ninawe, A.S. 2014. On - Farm Demonstrations of Trichoderma Harzianum in Pulse Crops under Rainfed Conditions of Bundelkhand - A Case Study *International Journal of Current Microbiology and Applied Sciences* 3(11): 471-478.

Raghavendra, M., Singh, Y.V., Das, T.K. and Meena, M.C. 2017. Effect of Crop Residue and Potassium Management Practices on Productivity and Economics of Conservation Agriculture based Maize (*Zea mays*)-wheat (*Triticum aestivum*) Cropping System. *Indian Journal of Agricultural Sciences* 87: 854-861.

Raj, S.A. 2004. Solubilization on a Silicate and Concurrent release of Phosphorus and Potassium in Rice Ecosystem. Biofertilizer Technology for Rice Based Cropping System, pp. 372-378.

Ramachandrappa, B., Nanjappa, H. and Shivakumar, H. 2004. Yield and Quality of Baby Corn (*Zea mays* L.) as Influenced by Spacing and Fertilization Levels. *Acta Agronomica Hungarica* 52(3): 237-243.

Ramachandrappa, B.K., Nanjappa, H.V. and Shivakumar, H.K. 2009. Yield and Quality of Baby corn (*Zea mays* L.) as Influenced by Spacing and Fertilizer Levels. *Acta Agronomica-Hungarica* 52(3): 237-241.

Ramarethinam, S. and Chandra, K. 2005. Studies on the Effect of Potash Solubilizing/mobilizing Bacteria *Frateuria aurantia* on Brinjal Growth and yield. *Pestology* 11: 35-39.

Ramarethinam, S. and Chandra, K. 2006. Studies on the Effect of Potash Solubilizing Bacteria Frateuria aurantia (Symbion-K- Liquid Formulation) on Brinjal (Solanum melongena L) Growth and yield. *Pestology* 11: 35-39.

Rasheed, M., Kalid, J. and Hussain, M. 2004. Biological Response of Maize (*Zea mays* L.) to Variable Grades of Phosphorus and Planting Geometry. *International Journal of Agricultural Biology* 6(3): 462-464.

Reddy, K.N. 2001. Effects of Cereal and Legume Cover Crop Residues on Weeds, Yield, and Net Return in Soybean (Glycine max). *Weed Technology* 15(4): 660-668.

Rizwan, M., Maqsood, M., Rafiq, M., Saeed, M. and Ali, Z. 2003. Maize (*Zea mays* L.) response to Split Application on Nitrogen. *International Journal of Agriculture and Biology* 5(1): 19-21.

Romheld, V. and Kirkby, E.A. 2010. Research on Potassium in Agriculture: Needs and Prospects Plant Relationship between Soil Potassium forms and Mineralogy. *Soil Science Society American Journal* 52(1): 1023-1028.

Rudresh, D.L., Shivaprakash, M.K. and Prasad, R.D. 2005. Tricalcium Phosphate Solubilizing Abilities of Trichoderma spp. in relation to P uptake and Growth and yield Parameters of Chickpea (*Cicer arietinum* L.). *Canadian Journal of Microbiology* 51(3): 217-222.

Rudreshaopa, T.S. and Halikatti, S.I. 2002. Response of Greengram to Nitrogen, Phosphorus Levels in Paddy Fallow. *Karnataka Journal of Research* 15(1): 89-92.

Saha, M. and Mondal, S. 2006. Influence of Integrated Plant Nutrient Supply on Growth, Productivity and Quality of Baby Corn (*Zea mays*) in Indo-gangetic Plains. *Indian Journal of Agronomy* 51(3): 202-205.

Saha, M., Maurya, B.R., Meena, V.S., Bahadur, I., Kumar, A. 2016. Identification and Characterization of Potassium Solubilizing Bacteria (KSB) from Indo-Gangetic Plains of India. *Biocatalysis and Agriculture Biotechnology* 7: 202-209.

Saha, Madhumonti, Maurya, Bihari Ram, Meena, Vijay Singh, Bahadur, Indra and Kumar, Ashok. 2016. Identification and Characterization of Potassium Solubilizing Bacteria (KSB) from Indo-Gangetic Plains of India. *Biocatalysis and Agricultural Biotechnology* 7: 202-209.

Sahoo, S. and Panda, M. 1997. Fertilizer Requirement of Babycorn (*Zea mays* L.) in Wet and Winter Seasons. *The Indian Journal of Agricultural Sciences* 67(9).

Sahoo, S.C. and Mahapatra, P.K. 2005. Response of Sweet corn (*Zea mays* L.) to Fertility Levels under on-farm Situation. *Indian Journal of Agricultural Sciences* 75(9): 603-604.

Sahoo, S.C. and Mahapatra, P.K. 2007. Response of Sweet Corn to Plant Population and Fertility Levels during Rabi. *Indian Journal of Agricultural Sciences* 77(11): 779-781.

Sahoo, S.C. 2011. Yield and Economics of Baby Corn (*Zea mays* L.) as affected by Varieties and Levels of Nitrogen. *Range Management and Agroforestry* 32(2): 135-137.

Sahoo, S.C. and Panda, M. 2001. Effect of Phosphorus and Detasseling on Yield of Baby Corn. *Indian Journal of Agricultural Sciences* 71: 21-22.

Saini, V.K., Bhandari, S.C., Sharma, S.K. and Tarafdar, J.C. 2005. Assessment of Microbial Biomass under Integrated Nutrient Management in Soybean-winter Maize Cropping Sequence. *Journal of the Indian Society of Soil Science* 53(3): 346-351.

Saleem, M.F., Randhawa, M.S., Hussain, S., Wahid, M.A. and Anjum, S.A. 2009. Nitrogen Management Studies in Autumn Planted Maize (Zea mays L.) Hybrids. *Journal of Animal and Plant Sciences* 19(3): 140-143.

Sangeeth, K.P., Bhai, R.S. and Srinivasan, V. 2012. *Paenibacillus glucanolyticus*, a Promising Potassium Solubilizing Bacterium isolated from Black Pepper (*Piper nigrum* L.) Rhizosphere. *Journal of Spice Aromatic Crops* 21: 118-124.

Sardana, V., Singh, S. and Sheoran, P. 2006. Efficacy and Economics of Weed Management Practices in Blackgram (*Vigna mungo* L.) under Rainfed Conditions. *Indian Journal of Weed Sciences* 38(1&2): 77-80.

Sarikhani, M.R. Oustan, S., Ebrahimi M. and Aliasgharzad, N. 2018. Isolation and Identification of Potassium releasing Bacteria in Soil and Assessment of their Ability to release Potassium for Plants, *World Journal of Microbiology and Biotechnology*, 69 (6): 1078-1086.

Sarma, B.K., Singh, D.P., Mehta, S., Singh, H.B., Singh, U.P. 2002. Plant Growth-promoting Rhizobacteria-elicited Alterations in Phenolic Profile of Chickpea (*Cicer arietinum*) infected by Sclerotium rolfsii. *Journal of Phytopathology* 150; 277-282.

Sarsan, S. 2016. Effect of Phosphate Solubilising Bacteria Bacillus PSB24 on Growth of Tomato Plants. *International Journal of Current Microbiological and Applied Sciences* 5(7): 311-320.

Savaliya, N.V., Mathukia, R.K., Solanki, J.N. and Barsiya, R.A. 2017. Response of Wheat (*Triticum aestivum*) to Phosphate and Potash Solubilizing Bacteria on Calcareous Clayey Soil. *International Journal of Pure and Applied Biosciences* 5(6): 247-251.

Seerat, N. and Bharose, R. 2004. Effect of Bio-fertilizers on the Enrichment of Soil Fertility with Special Reference to Soil Phosphorus Status and its effect on yield of Green Gram (*Vigna radiata* L.), *New Agriculturist,* 15(1/2): 129-131.

Sengupta, S.K., Dwivedi, Y.C. and Kushwah, S.S. 2002. Response of Tomato (*Lycopersicon esculentum* Mill.) to Bioinoculants at different Levels of Nitrogen. *Vegetable Sciences* 29(2): 186-188.

Sharma, B.L. 2012. Bio-degradation of Crop Residues by Trichoderma Species vis-a-vis Nutrient Quality of the Prepared Compost. Sujeet Pratap Singh, Mukut Lal Sharma. *Sugar Technology* 14(2): 174-180.

Sharma, R.C. and Banik, P. 2014. *Arbuscular mycorrhiza,* Azospirillum and Chemical Fertilizer Application to Baby Corn (*Zea mays* L.). Effects on Productivity, Nutrients use Efficiency, Economic Feasibility and Soil Fertility, *Journal of Plant Nutrition* 37(2): 209-223.

Sheikhalipour, P., Bolandndnazar, S.A., Panahandeh, J. 2016. Influence of KSB, PSB and NFB on Fruit Quality and Potassium contents in Tomato. *International Journal of Advanced Biological and Biomedical Research* 4(2): 170-178.

Sheng, X.F, He, L.Y. 2006. Solubilization of Potassium bearing Minerals by a Wild Type Strain of *Bacillus edaphicus* and its Mutants and Increased Potassium uptake by Wheat. *Canadian Journal of Microbiology* 52: 66-72.

Sheng, X.F. 2005, Growth Promotion and increased Potassium uptake of Cotton and Rape by a Potassium releasing Strain of bacillus edaphicus. *Soil Biology and Biochemistry* 37(1): 1918-1922.

Sheng, X.F. 2006. Growth Promotion and Increased Potassium uptake of Cotton and Rape Seed by a Potassium releasing Strain of *Bacillus edaphicus. Soil Biology and Biochemistry* 37(1): 1918-1922.

Sheng, X.F. and He, L.Y. 2006. Solubilization of Potassium bearing Minerals by a Wild Type Strain of Bacillus edaphicus and its Mutants and increased Potassium uptake by Wheat. *Canadian Journal of Microbiology* 52(1): 66-72.

Sheng, X.F. and He, L.Y. 2006. Solubilization of Potassium-bearing Minerals by a Wildtype Strain of *Bacillus edaphicus* and its Mutants and Increased Potassium uptake by Wheat. *Canadian Journal of Microbiology* 52: 66-69.

Sheng, X.F. and Huang, W.Y. 2002. Mechanism of Potassium release from Feldspar affected by the Strain NBT of Silicate bacterium. *Acta Pedologica Sinica* 39: 863-871.

Sheng, X.F. and Huang, W.Y. 2002. Mechanism of Potassium release from Feldspar affected by the Strain NBT of Silicate Bacterium. *Acta Pedologica Sinica* 39: 863-871.

Sheng, X.F. and Huang, W.Y. 2002. Study on the Conditions of Potassium release by Strain NBT of Silicate Bacteria. *Scientia Agricultura Sinica* 35(6): 673-677.

Sheng, X.F., He, L.Y. and Huang, W. 2002. The Conditions of releasing Potassium by a Silicate Dissolving Bacterial Strain NBT. *Agricultural Sciences in China* 1: 662-666.

Sheng, X.F., Xia, J.J. and Cheng, J. 2003. Mutagenesis of the *Bacillus edaphicus* Strain NBT and its Effect on Growth of Chilli and Cotton. *Agricultural Sciences in China* 32: 258-265.

Sheng, X.F., Xia, J.J. and Cheng, J. 2003. Mutagenesis of the *Bacillus edaphicus* Strain NBT and its Effect on Growth of Chilli and Cotton. *Agricultural Sciences in China* 32: 258-265.

Shoresh, M. and Harman, G.E. 2008. The Molecular basis of Shoot responses of Maize Seedlings to *Trichoderma harzianum* T22 Inoculation of the Root: A Proteomic Approach. *Plant Physiology* 100(11): 2147-2163.

Shukla, S.K., Yadav, R.L., Suman, A. and Singh, P.N. 2008. Improving Rhizospheric Environment and Sugarcane Ratoon yield through Bioagents Amended Farm yard Manure in udic ustochrept Soil. *Soil Tillage Research* 99: 158-168.

Shumin, L. and Fan. W. 2011. Nitrogen uptake Facilitation in Soybean/ Maize Intercropping System inoculated with Rhizobium and Arbuscular Mycorrhizal Fungi. *Journal of Plant Nutrition and Fertilizer* 17(1): 110-116.

Singh, M.K., Singh, R.N., Singh, S.P., Yadav, M.K. and Singh, V.K. 2010. Integrated Nutrient Management for Higher yield, Quality and Profitability of Baby Corn (*Zea mays*). *Indian Journal of Agronomy* 55: 100-104.

Singh, B.N., Singh, A., Singh, G.S. and Dwivedi, P. 2015. Potential Role of Trichoderma asperellum T42 Strain in Growth of Pea Plant for Sustainable Agriculture. *Journal of Pure and Applied Microbiology* 9(2): 1069-1074.

Singh, G., Kumar, D. and Sharma P. 2015. Effect of Organics, Biofertilizers and Crop Residue Application on Soil Microbial Activity in Rice – Wheat and Rice-wheat Mungbean Cropping systems in the Indo-Gangetic Plains. *Cogent Geoscience* 1(1): 1085-96.

Singh, G., Marwaha, T.S. and Kumar, D. 2009a. Effect of Resource-conserving Techniques on Soil Microbiological Parameters under long-term Maize (Zea mays)–wheat (Triticum aestivum) Crop rotation. *Indian Journal of Agricultural Sciences* 79(2): 94-100.

Singh, G., Marwaha, T.S. and Kumar, D. 2009a. Effect of Resource-conserving Techniques on Soil Microbiological Parameters under long-term Maize (*Zea mays*) - Wheat (*Triticum aestivum*) Crop Rotation. *Indian Journal of Agricultural Sciences* 79(2): 94-100.

Singh, G., Singh, N. and Kaur, R. 2016a. Effect of Integrated Nutrient Management on yield and Quality Parameters of Baby Corn (*Zea mays* L.). *International Journal of Applied Pure Science Agriculture* 2: 161-166.

Singh, M. and Sharma, S.N. 2000. Effect of Wheat Residue Management Practices and Nitrogen rates on Productivity and Nutrient uptake of Rice (*Oryza sativa*)-wheat (*Triticum aestivum*) Cropping System. *Indian Journal of Agricultural Science,* 70(12): 835-839.

Singh, M.K., Singh, R.N., Singh, S.P., Yadav, M.K. and Singh, V.K. 2010. Integrated Nutrient Management for Higher yield, Quality and Profitability of Baby Corn (*Zea mays* L.). *Indian Journal of Agronomy* 55(2): 100-104.

Singh, M., Singh, R.N. and Singh, S. 2009. Effect of Integrated Nutrient Management on Growth, yield and yield Attributes of Baby Corn (*Zea mays* L.). *Vegetable Science,* 36(1): 77-79.

Singh, R.P., Gupta, S.C. and Yadav, A.S. 2008. Effect of Levels and Sources of Phosphorus and PSB on Growth and yield of Blackgram (*Vigna mungo* L.) *Legume Research* 31(2): 139-141.

Singh, Raghvendra, Singh, Prabhat, Singh, Vipul and Yadav, R.A. 2018. Effect of Phosphorus and PSB on yield Attributes, Quality and Economics of Summer Greengram (*Vigna radiata* L.). *Journal of Pharmacognosy and Phytochemistry* 7(2): 404-408.

Singh, V., Upadhyaya, R.S., Sarma B.K., Singh, H.B. 2016. *Trichoderma asperellum* spore dose depended Modulation of Plant Growth in Vegetable Crops. *Microbiological Research* 193: 74-86.

Singh, Y.V. and Dhar, D.W. 2011. Changes in Soil Organic Carbon and Microbial Population under Organically Managed Rice (*Oryza sativa*) - Wheat (*Triticum aestivum*)- Green Gram (*Vigna radiata*) Cropping System. *Indian Journal of Agricultural Sciences* 81(4): 363-365.

Sirinivasa Perumal, A.P. and Sundari, A. 2004. Response of Rice Fallow Blackgram cv. ADT 5 to the Application of DAP and Phosphobacteria, *Legume Research* 27(1): 73-74.

Smith, J.L. and Paul, E.A. 1990. The Significance of Soil Microbial Biomass Estimation. *Publication of Soil Biology and Soil Biochemistry* 6: 357-396.

Sobhana, V., Kumar, A., Idnani, L. and Singh, I. 2012. Plant Population and Nutrient Requirement for Baby Corn Hybrids (*Zea mays* L.). *Indian Journal of Agronomy* 57(3): 294-296.

Soltani. A.A. 2010. Plant Growth Promoting Characteristics in Some Flavobacterium spp. Isolated from Soils of Iran. *Journal of Agricultural Science* 2(4): 106-115.

Sparks, D.L. and Huang, P.M. 1985. Physical Chemistry of Soil Potassium. p. 201-276. In R.D. Munson (ed.) Potassium in Agriculture. *American Society of Agronomy,* Madison, WI.

Srinivasa Rao, Ch., Rupa, T.R., Subba Rao, A. and Bansal, S.K. 2000b. Potassium Fixation Characteristics of major Benchmark Soils of India. *Journal of the Indian Society of Soil Science* 48: 220-228.

Srinivasarao, C., Rupa, T.R., Subbarao, A., Ramesh, G. and Bansal, S.K. 2006. Release Kinetics of Non-exchangeable Potassium by different Extractants from Soils of varying Mineralogy and Depth. *Soil Science and Plant Analysis* 37(3/4): 473-491.

Srinivasarao, Ch., Subba Rao, A. Rao, K.V., Venkateswarlu, B. and Singh, A.K. 2010. Categorization of Districts based on Nonexchangeable Potassium: Implications in Efficient K Fertility Management in Indian Agriculture. *Indian Journal of Fertilizers* 6(7): 1-15.

Srinivasrao, 2010. Rationalizing Potassium Fertilizer Recommendations in Indian Agriculture. XIV Sukumar Basu Memorial Lecture, Indian Agricultural Research Institute, New Delhi, Feb 13th, 2010.

Srivastava, S.N., Singh, V. and Awasthi, S.K. 2006. Trichoderma induced Improvement in Growth, yield and Quality of Sugarcane. *Sugar Technology*. 8: 166-169.

Styriakova, I., Styriak, I., Galko, I., Hradil, D. and Bezdicka, P. 2003. The release of Iron bearing Minerals and Dissolution of feldspar by Heterotrophic Bacteria of Bacillus species. *Ceramic Silicaty* 47(1): 20-26.

Subba Rao, N.S. 1999. Soil Microbiology IVth Edition of Soil Microorganism and Plant Growth pp. 390-391.

Subbiah, B. and Asija, G. 1956. A Rapid Procedure for the Estimation of Available Nitrogen in Soils. *Current Science* 25(8): 259-260.

Subramani, M. and Solaimalai, A. 2000. Influence of Plant Populations and methods of Nutrient Application on Growth and yield of Blackgram, *Legume Research* 23(3): 197-198.

Sugumaran, P. and Janarthanam, B., 2007. Solubilization of Potassium Containing Minerals by Bacteria and their Effect on Plant Growth. *World Journal of Agriculture Sciences* 3(3): 350-355.

Suke, S.N., Deotale, R.D., Priyanka, Hiradeve, Mitali, Deogirkar and Sorte, S.N. 2011. Effect of Nutrients and Biofertilizers of Chemical and Biochemical Parameters of Maize (*Zea mays* L.). *Journal of Soils and Crops* 21(1): 107-112.

Supanjani, Han, H.S., Jung, S.J. and Lee, K.D. 2006. Rock Phosphate Potassium and Rock Solubilizing Bacteria as Alternative Sustainable Fertilizers. *Agronomy for Sustainable Development* 26: 233-240.

Thakur, A.K. and Panwar, J.D. 1995. Effect of Rhizobium VAM Intercactions on Growth and yield of Mungbean (*Vigna radiata* L.) under Field Conditions. *Indian Journal of Plant Pathology* 38: 62-65.

Thakur, D.R., Prakash, O.M., Kharwara, P.C. and Bhalla, S.K. 1997. Effect of Nitrogen and Plant spacing on Growth, Development and yield of Baby Corn. *Indian Journal of Agronomy* 42(3): 479-483.

Vadgave, S.M. 2010. Studies on Integrated Nutrient Management on Seed yield, Quality and Storability in Green Gram [*Vigna radiata (L.) Wilczek*], M.Sc. (Ag.) Thesis, University of Agricultural Sciences, Dharwad, pp. 86.

Vance, E.D., Brookes, P.C. and Jenkinson, D.S. 1987. An Extraction method for measuring Soil Microbial Biomass C. *Soil Biol Biochem* 19: 703-707.

Verma, A.K., Harika, A.S., Singh, P.K., Kaur, K. and Yadav, A. 2012. International Conference on Sustainable Agriculture for Food and Livelihood Security (701-702), Punjab Agricultural University, Ludhiana.

Verma., A., Nepalia, V. and Kanthalia, P.C. 2005. Effect of Continuous Cropping and Fertilization on Crop yields and Nutrient Status of Typic Haplustep. *Journal of Indian Society of Soil Science* 53(3): 365-368.

Vessey, K.J. 2003. Plant Growth Promoting Rhizobacteria as Biofertilizers. *Plant and Soil* 25: 557-586.

Vijila K. and Jebaraj S. 2008. Studies on the Improvement of Rhizobium-green Gram [*Vigna radiata* (L.) Wilczek] Symbiosis in Low Nutrient, Acid Stress Soil. *Legume Research* 31(2): 126-129.

Vikram, A., Alagawadi A.R. Hamzehzarghani H.P., Krishnaraj, U. Efficacy of Phosphate Solubilizing Bacteria on the Yield and Phosphorus Uptake of Green Gram (*Vigna radiata* (L.) Wilczek). *Research Journal of Microbiology* 3: 62-72.

Vinale, F., Flemattoi, G., Sivasith, A.K., Lorito, M., Marra, R. and Skelton, B.W. 2009. Harzianic Acid, an Antifungal and Plant Growth Promoting Metabolite from *Trichoderma harzianum*. *Journal of Natural Products* 72: 2032-2035.

Vinale, F., Sivasithamparam, K., Ghisalberti, E.L., Marra, R., Barbetti, M.J., Li, H., Woo, S. L. and Lorito, M. 2008. A Novel Role for Trichoderma Secondary Metabolites in the Interactions with Plants. *Physiological and Molecular Plant Pathology* 72, 80-86.

Wafaa, Seddik M.A. and Mona, A. Osman. 2015. Impact of Feldspar Acidulation on Potassium Dissolution and Pea Production. *International Journal of Chemtech Research* 8(11): 01-10.

Wang, J.G., Zhang, F.S., Zhang, X.L., Cao, Y.P. 2000. Release of Potassium from K-bearing Minerals: Effect of Plant Roots under P deficiency. *Nutrient Cycling in Agroecosystem* 56: 45-52.

Wei, D., Yang, Q., Zhang, J.Z., Wang, S., Chen, X.L., Zhang, X.L. and Li, W.Q. 2008. Bacterial Community Structure and Diversity in a Black Soil as affected by long-term Fertilization. *Pedosphere* 18: 582-592.

Wollum, A.G. 1982. Cultural methods for Soil Microorganisms. In: Methods of Soil Analysis, Part II, Chemical and Microbiological properties. American Society of Agronomy, 781-802.

Wu, S.C, Cao, Z.H., Li, Z.G., Cheung, K.C. and Wong, M.H. 2005. Effects of Biofertilizer Containing N-fixer, P and K Solubilizers and AM Fungi on Maize Growth: A Greenhouse Trial. *Geoderma* 125: 155-166.

Yadav, B.K. 2011. Improvement of Mungbean Growth and Productivity by Phosphate Dissolving Fungi Aspergillus Niger Seed Inoculation. *Legume Research* 34: 217-221.

Yadav, R.L., Singh, V., Srivastav, S.N., Lal, R.J., Sangeeta, S., Awasthi, S.K. and Joshi, B.B. 2008. Use of Trichoderma Harzianum for the Control of Red Rot Disease of Sugarcane. *Sugar Technology* 26: 28-33.

Yadav, S.K., Dave, A., Sarkar, A., Singh, H.B. and Sarma B.K. 2013. *Co-inoculated Biopriming with Trichoderma, Pseudomonas and Rhizobium Improves Crop Growth in Cicer arietinum and Phaseolus vulgaris. International Journal of Agriculture, Environment & Biotechnology* 6(2): 255-259.

Yang, J., Zhao, W., Hu, W., Wang, Y., Chen, B., Zhou, Z. 2015. Indicators of Cotton (*Gossypium hirsutum* L.) Cultivar Screening for Low Potassium Tolerance in Seeding Stage and its Relationship with yield and Quality. *Cotton Science* 26: 301-309.

Yang, Y, Wang, N, Guo, X, Zhang, Y and Ye, B. 2017. Comparative analysis of Bacterial Community Structure in the Rhizosphere of Maize by High-throughput Pyrosequencing. *Plos one* 12(5): e0178425.

Yedidia, I., Srivastava, A.K., Kapulnik, Y. and Chet, I. 2001. Effects of Trichoderma Harzianum on Microelement Concentrations and Increased Growth of Cucumber Plants. *Plant and Soil* 2(3): 235-242.

Zakaria, A.A.B. 2009. Growth Optimization of Potassium Solubilizing Bacteria Isolated from Biofertilizer. Malaysia Pahang: Bachelor of Chemical Bibliography xxii Engineering (Biotechnology), Faculty of Chemical, Natural Resources Engineering University pp. 40.

Zarei, I., Khah, E.M., Mohammadi, G. and Petropoulos, S. 2011. Assessment of Growth and yield Components following the Application of different Biological Fertilizers on Soybean (*Glycine max* L.) Cultivation. Aust *Journal of Crop Science* 5(13): 1776-1782.

Zende, N.B., Pinjari, S.S., Suryawanshi, J.S. and Bhonodve, T.S. 2009. Effect of Nutrient Management on Growth, yield, Quality, Economics and Nutrient Partitioning of Sweet Corn. *Bioinfolet* 6(1): 16-21.

Zhang, A., Zhao, G., Gao, T., Wang, W., Li, J., Zhang, S., Zhu, B. 2013. Solubilization of Insoluble Potassium and Phosphate by Paenibacillus kribensis CX-7: A Soil Microorganism with Biological Control Potential. *African Journal of Microbiological Research* 7: 41-47.

Zhang, C. and Kong, F. 2014. Isolation and Identification of Potassium-solubilizing Bacteria from Tobacco Rhizospheric Soil and their Effect on Tobacco Plants. *Applied Soil Ecology* 82: 18-25.

Zhang, F., Yuan, J., Yang, X., Cui, Y., Chen, L., Ran, W. and Shen, Q. 2012. Putative Trichoderma Harzianum Mutant Promotes Cucumber Growth by Enhanced Production of Indole Acetic Acid and Plant Colonization. *Plant and Soil* 12: 1519-6.

Zhang, Y.D., Sun, Z.H. and Shen, Y.X. 2005. Effect of Fertilization on Soil Microorganism of Deteriorated Grassland in Dry-Hot Valley Region of Jinsha River, *Journal of Soil Water Conservation* 19(2): 88.

Zhao, F., Zhang, Y. and Zhang, J. 2014. Involvement of *Trichoderma asperellum* Strain T6 in Regulating Iron Acquisition in Plants *Journal of Basic Microbiology* 54: S115-S124.

Index

L

M

❑ ❑ ❑ ❑ ❑